Western Lands, Western Voices

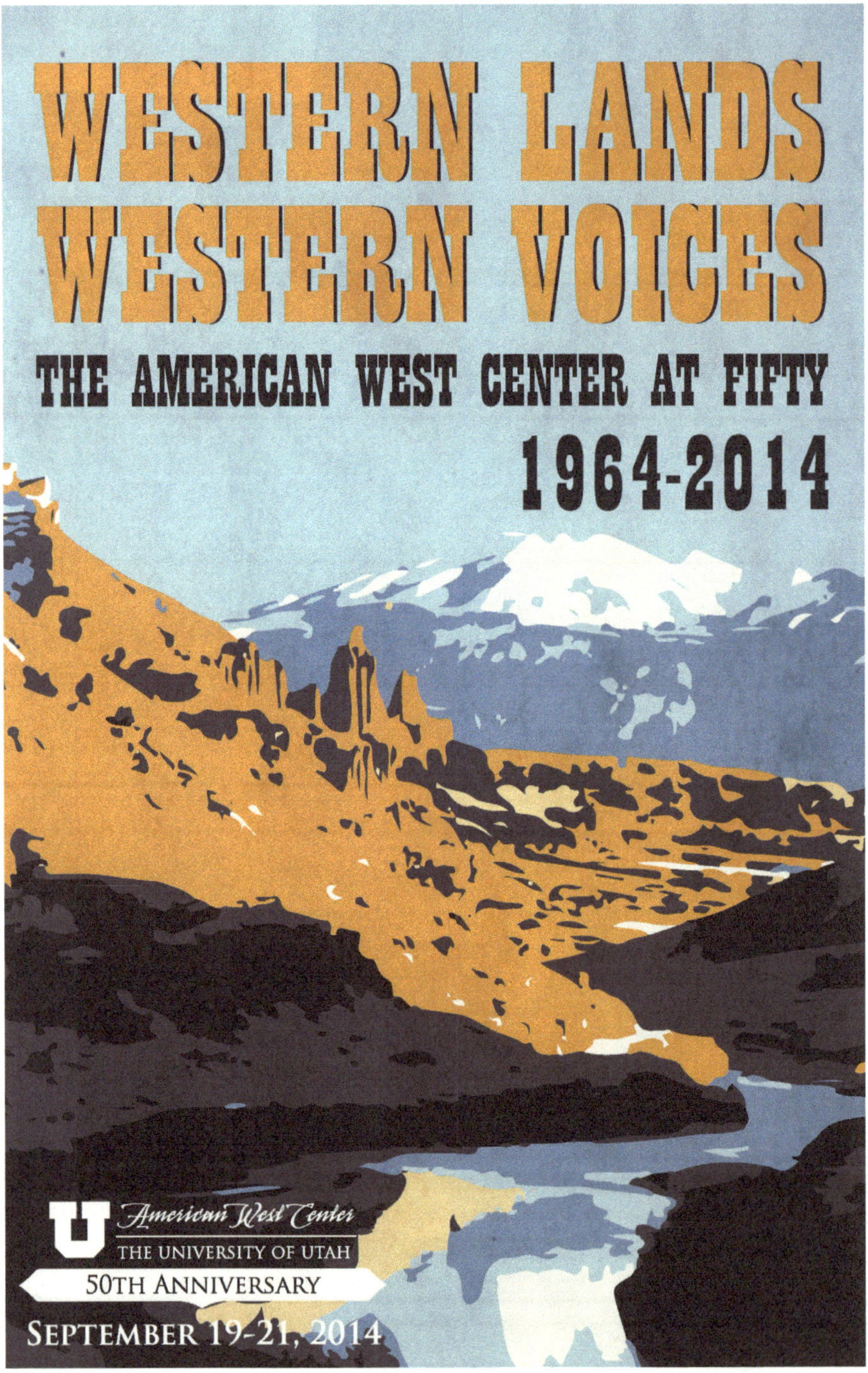
WESTERN LANDS
WESTERN VOICES
THE AMERICAN WEST CENTER AT FIFTY
1964-2014
American West Center
THE UNIVERSITY OF UTAH
50TH ANNIVERSARY
SEPTEMBER 19-21, 2014

Western Lands, Western Voices

ESSAYS ON PUBLIC HISTORY IN THE AMERICAN WEST

EDITED BY GREGORY E. SMOAK

THE UNIVERSITY OF UTAH PRESS
Salt Lake City

The Defiance House Man colophon is a registered trademark of The University of Utah Press. It is based on a four-foot-tall Ancient Puebloan pictograph (late PIII) near Glen Canyon, Utah.

Library of Congress Cataloging-in-Publication Data

Names: Smoak, Gregory E., 1962– editor. | Thompson, Gregory C. (Gregory Coyne), 1943- writer of foreword.
Title: Western lands, western voices : essays on public history in the American West / edited by Gregory E. Smoak.
Description: Salt Lake City : University of Utah Press, [2021] | Includes bibliographical references and index. | Summary: "This collection of essays explores the meanings and uses of contemporary public history in the American West"—Provided by publisher.
Identifiers: LCCN 2021007612 (print) | LCCN 2021007613 (ebook) | ISBN 9781647690342 (paperback) | ISBN 9781647690366 (cloth) | ISBN 9781647690359 (ebook)
Subjects: LCSH: University of Utah. American West Center—History. | Public history—West (U.S.)—History. | Public lands—West (U.S.)—Management. | Public historians—West (U.S.)
Classification: LCC D16.163 .W47 2021 (print) | LCC D16.163 (ebook) | DDC 978—dc23
LC record available at https://lccn.loc.gov/2021007612
LC ebook record available at https://lccn.loc.gov/2021007613

Errata and further information on this and other titles available online at UofUpress.com

Printed and bound in the United States of America.

Frontispiece. Poster for the American West Center at Fifty symposium. Courtesy of the American West Center.

For
Floyd A. O'Neil
and
Louise Pubols

Contents

Foreword ix
Gregory C. Thompson

Editor's Acknowledgments xi

Introduction: Putting History to Work in the American West 1
Gregory E. Smoak

1. Posing the Question: What Makes Public History Public? 13
Richard White

2. Taking a Public Turn: Public History as Public Service in the American West 23
Leisl Carr Childers

3. Rothman's West: The Education of a Western Public Intellectual 41
Michael Childers

4. Mythic Spaces, Real Places: Thoughts on Administrative History in the Western National Parks 57
Leighton M. Quarles

5. Prospecting the Past: How Public History and Tourism Remade Lake City, Colorado 71
Mette Flynt

6. Finding and Building Community on the Manito Trail 85
Trisha Venisa-Alicia Martínez and Vanessa Fonseca-Chávez

7. "Working on the Dark Side": Public Land Management and Tribal Relations 101
Yvette Towersap Tuell

8. The Adjudication of Three Tribes' Water Rights 114
E. Richard Hart

9. "This Is Our Home; This Is Our Land": Memory, Visual Sovereignty, and Museum Exhibition on the Klamath River Basin 126
Brittani R. Orona

10. Placemaking in Public: Building a Native American Studies Program on the Indigenous Columbia Plateau 141
Laurie Arnold

11. Scholarship, the Public, and the Challenge of Local History 155
Jedediah Rogers

12. Building Bridges 170
Stephen Aron and Virginia Scharff

Notes 185

Contributors 213

Index 219

Foreword: A Legacy of Publicly Engaged Scholarship

Fifty years and counting! Fifty years is a very long time for a regional studies center embedded in the humanities, social sciences, and education to survive. But survive the American West Center has, with tremendous energy and creativity. For more than half a century now, the Center has served the diverse peoples of Utah and the American West and in the process contributed to the development of public history and public humanities practice. When the center hosted the "Western Lands, Western Voices: The American West Center at Fifty" symposium to mark its golden anniversary, community members and scholars from across the nation noted and celebrated the importance of publicly engaged scholarship. While the contributions to this volume range far beyond the Center and the symposium, they reflect the same spirit that has always been at the heart of the Center's work.

Community-engaged scholarship is the American West Center's greatest legacy. In December 1966, the University of Utah, along with six other universities, received personal grants from tobacco heiress Doris Duke to document the history of American Indian peoples in their own voices. The then two-year-old Western History Center was designated to administer and conduct the project. The Doris Duke American Indian Oral History Project was launched in January 1967 with C. Gregory Crampton as director and Floyd A. O'Neil heading field operations. The five-year project changed the Center's course and set the foundations for its future mission and programing. The Doris Duke project began long-term collaborations between Center staff and tribal members and leaders. Together, they used oral history practices as a medium for developing primary archival resources for writing tribal histories, as well as for use by American tribal administrators and attorneys for legal and cultural purposes.

These same methods, combining oral history with substantial research in the nation's major archives, helped the Center's leadership, primarily Dr. O'Neil, take what was learned in the course of the Duke project and apply it to work with many other peoples and communities whose histories had largely been ignored or forgotten. In addition to over two dozen American Indian tribes, the Center has worked with Latino, Asian-American, Pacific Islander, and Eastern and Western European immigrant communities to tell their histories and develop teaching materials for K–12 schools, colleges, and universities. The Center has also been part of a broader initiative to document the stories of United States military veterans in World War II, and the Korean, Vietnam, Afghan, and Iraq Wars.

Importantly, the Center joined forces with the Special Collections Department of the University of Utah's Marriott Library to build archives and oral history collections relating to the history of the University, documenting Utah's ski history, mountaineering and river-running histories, as well as the Library's Medical, Engineering, and Science archives. Virtually all Center projects have been placed in Special Collections in an effort to provide full access for the researching public. Hundreds of researchers each year have their own work enhanced by the Center's documentation efforts.

Finally, no assessment of the American West Center's legacy would be complete without recognition of the training it provided for hundreds of undergraduate and graduate students as public historians capable of stepping into agencies across the nation as administrators and research specialists. Students had their career goals changed and lives reshaped by their involvement with the Center and its staff. They have worked as consultants, curators, editors, administrators, teachers, professors, and even diplomats. In this regard, I am proud to say that my own career began at the American West Center over fifty years ago!

Gregory C. Thompson
Associate Dean for Special Collections
J. Willard Marriott Library
University of Utah

Editor's Acknowledgments

My heartfelt thanks to the contributors to this volume. Public historians are a generous and collaborative bunch, and I am indebted to you all for your thoughtfulness, dedication, and patience. The concept for this volume began in discussions with University of Utah Press editor and American West Center alum John Alley. Tom Krause stepped in upon John's retirement to see the project through. Thanks to the two anonymous reviewers who provided valuable feedback on individual essays and the shape of the collection as a whole.

The "Western Lands, Western Voices" symposium, which served as the inspiration for this collection was made possible by the generosity of nearly two dozen sponsors, as well as the hard work of the American West Center's staff. Cassandra L. Clark, Leighton Quarles, and Michelle Turner did much of the heavy lifting. A very special thanks is due Robert Newman, who as dean of the University of Utah's College of Humanities stepped in at a critical moment to ensure the American West Center's survival. Robert remained a stalwart supporter throughout his tenure as dean and the symposium could not have happened without his enthusiastic support.

The American West Center is truly a multigenerational community of scholars whose reach extends far beyond the University of Utah campus. Floyd O'Neil was the lynchpin, but his successors as center director—Patricia Albers, Dan McCool, and Matt Basso—all worked to sustain that community. I have been associated with the center now for over three decades and have had the good fortune to work with colleagues, community partners, and friends including Sharon Austin, Will Bagley, Alicia Barber, Laura Bayer, Meg Brady, Larry Cesspooch, Beth Clement, Forest Cuch, Gino Defa, Janet Ellingson, Winston Erickson, Jared Farmer,

Richard Hart, Eric Hinderaker, David Rich Lewis, Becky Lloyd, Jennifer Lowry, Kathryn MacKay, Vicky Newman, Phil Notarianni, Shauna O'Neil, Darren Parry, Jennifer Robinson, Jay Taylor, Yvette Tuell, Megan Van Frank, and Brad Westwood. It is impossible to calculate the importance of Greg Thompson's work in keeping the center vibrant and viable. Michelle Judd has been an invaluable partner in managing the center.

I am continually inspired by the dedicated and talented graduate students who have worked with me at the American West Center. They include Erin Adam, Lisa Barr, Suzanne Catherine, Ami Chopine, Cassandra Clark, Jenel Cope, Chris Dunsmore, John Flynn, Tim Glenn, Ben Kiser, Scott Morris, Leighton Quarles, Travis Ross, Amanda Scheuerman, Michael Shamo, Patrick Thompson, Megan Weiss, and Chelsey Zamir. And always I am thankful for Ginger Smoak's love and support.

Finally, this volume is dedicated to two public historians who made the West a better place. You will learn more about Floyd O'Neil's long life and lasting influence in the pages that follow. Louise Pubols's career was far shorter, but her impact was great. In her work at the Autry Museum of the American West and then the Oakland Museum of California, Louise created award-winning exhibits that taught and inspired public audiences. At the same time, she authored the prize-winning *The Father of All: The de la Guerra Family, Power, and Patriarchy in Mexican California*. And, in her long battle against cancer, she inspired her friends with the way she chose to fully live life.

Introduction

Putting History to Work in the American West

GREGORY E. SMOAK

Over three days in September 2014, eighty scholars and practitioners gathered in Salt Lake City to mark the fiftieth anniversary of the University of Utah's American West Center. If the Center's birthday provided ample reason for celebration, the greater object of the symposium titled "Western Lands, Western Voices" was to explore the power and promise of publicly engaged scholarship in the American West.[1] The participants were a diverse lot representing fifty-five universities, colleges, museums, research centers, historical and cultural organizations, municipalities, community groups, and Native Nations. They included historians, poets, curators, artists, writers, community activists, archivists, editors, historic preservation officers, tribal government and cultural officials, and even one small-town mayor. Some had ties to the American West Center stretching back decades. Many others only learned of the Center's rich history at the symposium. What united them all was a shared commitment to publicly engaged and applied scholarship.

The presentations and conversations that took place that weekend in Salt Lake City inspired this eponymous volume. I say "inspired" because this is not a conference proceedings per se. In fact, the essays here focus on several important facets of a regional public history practice rather than on a larger set of issues regarding Western regionalism that would necessarily encompass the breadth of the humanities and social sciences. They are essays about ways of *doing* public history in the American West. Moreover, while most of the contributors here took part in the symposium, others were recruited specifically for this volume to better capture the breadth and diversity of public history work in the American West. With that said, the collection is not a comprehensive survey of all the ways that public history is done in the American West, nor of all the communities that its practice engages.

Readers will also learn about the Center's history in several of the essays, but recounting its past is not the chief purpose of the volume. Institutions like the American West Center are but one nexus of public history practice. The contributors here include tribal government officials, state and federal historians, independent scholars and historical consultants, as well as university faculty. They address issues including community history and public interpretation, tribal sovereignty, mythic popular visions of the American West, the practical application of history to land-management issues, and the relationship between the academy and public history practice. And so, my goal for this introduction is to provide a brief history of the American West Center and its legacies and to set the context for our discussion of a regional public history practice in the West.

My perspective on public history has been formed by over thirty years of association with the American West Center. The Center is a truly special place, the oldest regional studies center in the United States, and it helped shape the practice of public history in the American West. Today, the Center's mission is threefold: researching and interpreting the history and cultures of the American West in collaboration with community partners and clients; providing enlightening and accessible programing for public audiences; and training the next generation of publicly engaged humanities scholars.

Regional studies centers were not a familiar part of the academic landscape in 1964 when C. Gregory Crampton and A. Russell Mortensen founded the Western History Center within the University of Utah's history department.[2] Their initial purpose in creating the Center was to edit and publish *American West* magazine in partnership with the Western History Association. That cooperative venture proved short lived, as might have the Center if not for the substantial grant that tobacco heiress Doris Duke made to the University of Utah (and six other universities) to fund the collection of American Indian oral histories in 1967.

The Duke oral history project transformed the Center in three crucial ways. First, it oriented the Center toward direct engagement with Native communities. Beyond collecting oral histories, the Center's staff would

Floyd O'Neil in 2018.

subsequently document tribal land and water claims and treaty rights, help build tribal archives, produce curricular materials for K–12 schools, and coauthor over two dozen tribal histories. While never the singular focus of its work, projects for and with Western tribes remain at the core of the Center's existence to the present day.

Secondly, the Center became a leader in the field of oral history. Following on the heels of the Duke project, a diverse range of oral history initiatives recorded and preserved the stories of Utah's ethnic communities (Latinx, African, Japanese, Greek, and Italian Americans), veterans, outdoor recreation, the University of Utah, polio survivors, and Great Salt Lake, to name but a few. In addition to dedicated oral history projects, the methodology has also been essential for many of the Center's other projects, especially those with Native peoples focused on developing curriculum or documenting traditional land and water use.

Finally, it was through the Duke oral histories that Floyd A. O'Neil, who more than any other individual shaped its culture and achievements, came to the American West Center.

Floyd was born in Utah's Uinta Basin on July 14, 1927, and spent his early childhood on the Uintah and Ouray Reservation. Ute children were his schoolmates and earliest friends. Throughout the course of his life, he maintained these friendships, many of which became intergenerational. And although he did not know it at the time, Floyd's childhood and the enduring ties to Ute people it engendered became the basis for his life's work. The O'Neil family moved to Price in Carbon County when Floyd was in his early teens. While his father and brothers went to work in the coal mines, Floyd suffered from health issues, including a life-threatening heart condition and juvenile arthritis. Ironically, these maladies contributed to a long life. They kept him out of the mines, where he tragically lost one of his brothers, and disqualified him for military service. (Shortly before his passing in April 2018, Floyd joked, "How many ninety-year-old coal miners do you know?!") Instead, he set his sights on a life in education. After taking his BA from the University of Utah in 1957, he taught high school in Price and then Salt Lake City. By the mid-1960s, his passion for history pulled him back to the University and graduate study. It was then, due to his life-long association with Ute people and his knowledge of Native history, that Floyd was recruited to work on the Duke oral history project.

First as a graduate student, and then as assistant director and director, Floyd managed a series of successful projects that established the American West Center's reputation in Utah and throughout the West. In these projects, Floyd pioneered an innovative approach that began to address the legacies of academic colonialism in Native communities. Working directly with tribal members as authors, he and other Center scholars essentially mobilized the resources of a research university to help Native peoples tell their own histories. And while he was met with resistance in the university administration, he insisted that the tribes would hold the copyright to their published histories rather than the Center or the university.

Of course, Floyd did not do this alone. He had an eye for talent and a talent for mentorship. E. Richard Hart was one of the young scholars Floyd brought to the American West Center beginning in the late 1960s. With a background in literature and a tenacious curiosity that found its home in the archives, Hart began working on research for the Pueblo of Zuni, eventually becoming the lead researcher and historian for the Pueblo's successful land claims against the United States. Hart went on to establish the Institute of the North American West, which hosted influential conferences on Western issues in Sun Valley, Idaho, during the 1980s, and then continued to an unparalleled career as a historical consultant for tribal nations. His essay in this volume illustrates the importance of careful historical research for tribes as they defend their land, water, and sovereignty.

Another of Floyd's early recruits was Gregory C. Thompson. A native of Durango, Colorado, Thompson came to the University of Utah at Floyd's urging to pursue graduate study. Beginning with research for the ongoing Duke project, O'Neil and Thompson expanded that vision to include the creation of comprehensive tribal archives documenting land use, water rights, and cultural knowledge. These archives became the basis for numerous tribal histories and curricular materials. After completing his own PhD, Thompson went on to become Associate Dean for Special Collections at the University of Utah's Marriott Library, where over the past four decades he has built one of the most important and heavily utilized research collections in the American West.

There were many more. John Alley, Laura Bayer, Clyde Benally, Thomas King, Kathryn MacKay, and Vincent Mayer, to name but a few, also began their careers at the American West Center under Floyd's watchful eye.

After Floyd's nominal retirement in 1996, several well-known scholars of the American West took the Center in new directions. The activities of the American West Center to some extent have always reflected the interests and training of its director. In 1996, the esteemed anthropologist and ethnohistorian Patricia Albers assumed the directorship. Pat's tenure was marked by an intensification of research for the Shoshone-Bannock Tribes of the Fort Hall Reservation, Idaho.

Daniel McCool, a political scientist, led the Center between 1999 and 2007, moving toward more research in environmental and natural resource issues, as well as initiating a World War II Veterans Oral History project that evolved into a long-standing effort to collect the stories of veterans of other conflicts. In 2004, the Center was the recipient of a major National Endowment for the Humanities grant that funded the digitization of the Duke Oral History collection.

Historian Matthew Basso succeeded McCool in 2007. Basso's interests in labor, gender, and Pacific studies were all reflected in the Center's work and programs. Arguably, the most important project undertaken during this period moved the Center back toward its roots but with a modern twist: the award-winning Utah Indian Curriculum Project and Utah American Indian Digital Archive (UAIDA). The project was a partnership between the Center, the Utah Division of Indian Affairs, and the Special Collections Department of the Marriott Library.

The success of the American West Center has also served as a model for several other regional studies centers, including those founded by two of the West's most revered historians. As a new assistant professor, Patricia Nelson Limerick made her way to the Sun Valley conferences that Richard Hart organized. There, she met Western history luminaries such as Alvin Josephy Jr. and William H. Goetzmann, witnessed the immediate impact of discussions between scholars, government officials, and corporate leaders, and was first introduced to the work of the American West Center. From this seed sprouted the Center of the American West at the University of Colorado, which Limerick cofounded with Charles Wilkinson in 1986. Today, Patty remains one of the most influential public historians and intellectuals in the American West and a vocal advocate of the applied power of history.

Richard White joined the faculty of the University of Utah in 1985. He quickly formed a lasting friendship with Floyd O'Neil and credited the American West Center with shaping his understanding of public history. During his subsequent tenure at the University of Washington, White became ever more deeply engaged in applied historical research, acting as an expert witness for Puget Sound tribes. Then, after he moved to Stanford University in 1999, he cofounded the Bill Lane Center for the American West. When it came time to celebrate the American West Center's fiftieth anniversary, it seemed fitting that Richard deliver the keynote. His talk, which sets the stage for this volume, is presented here as he delivered it, part tribute to Floyd and part reflection of the two men's humor and abiding friendship.

I first began working at the American West Center in 1988, and so when I assumed the directorship in the summer of 2012 this history of success weighed on my shoulders. I did not want to screw things up! Over the past nine years, the Center has stayed true to its roots while expanding its reach in several important ways. Working for and with Native nations remains a constant, but the Center's focus has also taken a turn toward public lands issues and projects with the National Park Service, Bureau of Land Management, and United States Forest Service.

Yet rather than concentrate on projects the Center has conducted during my time as director, I want to emphasize the third aspect of its mission statement as one of the Center's most important legacies: teaching and mentorship. Simply put, the American West Center gave me the opportunity to become a public historian. Today, new public historians are likely to have been trained in a public history program at the undergraduate or graduate level; at the very least they will have taken courses in public history or its allied methodologies. I did none of this. For me, becoming a public historian meant following a path more akin to that of a craft guild, where you learned by doing. At the Center, I edited and then recorded oral histories, I processed archival collections, and I conducted archival research and wrote contract reports. Along the way, I consulted with Native peoples and learned to really listen to their research needs and to respect their status as sovereign nations. There were few other centers like the American West Center at the time that offered such hands-on training. It was, and remains, in a very real sense a teaching institution that does not offer formal classes. This has been the legacy, bequeathed to me by Floyd, Pat, and Dan, that I think about the most and have sought to sustain.

So, what do I mean when I refer to a regional public history practice and how is that reflected in the essays that follow?

First, we need to settle on a definition of public history. This might be harder than it seems. When I ask students or even colleagues how they define public history, the most common response (if they have one at all) is that public historians speak to public audiences. While this is most often true, making scholarship accessible to nonspecialists should be a goal for *all* historians: public history cannot and should not be reduced simply to a matter of audience. Indeed, some forms of public history, such as the expert witness reports prepared by Hart and other consultants, are not intended for broad public consumption. They serve the very specific needs of the historian's client and are methodically written, usually in dense detail, to answer narrowly framed historical questions. And, in many cases, they remain the intellectual property of the community that commissioned them and are not widely available.

Nor should the role of the public historian be conflated with that of the public intellectual. Many an academic historian (including some of my own colleagues) has been heard to say something like, "Oh, don't we all do public history? I just did a talk down at the library last week." But doing a public talk or writing an op-ed for a newspaper does not make one a public historian (albeit many accomplished public historians also act as public intellectuals, such as the late Hal Rothman, profiled in this volume). For the most part, the work of the public intellectual is a top-down process. Public intellectuals tell the public what they, as the experts, believe that public needs to or should know. While this can be an incredibly valuable and impactful way to inform public discourse, the public usually has little or no input into what is deemed meaningful or necessary.

What truly distinguishes public history and connects the work of its diverse practitioners, then, is collaboration and application. In the inaugural issue of *The Public Historian* in 1978, Robert Kelley declared, "Public history refers to the employment of historians and the historical method outside of academia; in government, private corporations, the media, historical societies and museums, even in private practice."[3] Kelley emphasized the practical value of historical research and interpretation in a broad range of applications as well as the collaborative process of the historian working as part of a team to answer questions and solve problems. Today, the National Council on Public History (NCPH) reflects this formative definition with the concise statement "public history describes the many and diverse ways in which history is put to work in the world." It is also for this reason that the NCPH titled its blog *History@Work*.[4] So while public historians are museum curators, historical consultants, documentary filmmakers, archivists, historic preservationists, historical interpreters, and oral historians, it is not their occupations per se, but the application of their training and skills in collaborative projects that makes them public historians.

In order to put history to work for a public, a scholar must be willing to share authority in historical production. The concept of "shared authority" has been central to public history theory since Michael Frisch coined the phrase some thirty years ago.[5] Sharing authority does not mean ignoring professional responsibility or ceding methodological rigor. Public historians are first and foremost historians. Like all professional historians, they are bound by the discipline's core ethical and methodological principles. Sharing authority, however, demands that public historians begin by listening to the public, and allowing that public, as Kelley asserted so long ago and Richard White reaffirms in his essay here, to ask the first, most basic, and essential questions. Beyond this initial stage, public history ideally entails a reflective practice that requires historians to consciously assess their actions and assumptions and understand their effect on the process.[6] Done right, collaborations between historians and community partners or clients help to empower communities, inform public decision-making, protect heritage resources, and address the needs of public audiences.

Several of the essays here address the nature of public history practice and shared authority as well as the tensions between "academic" and "public" history. In addition to White's keynote, Leisl Carr Childers uses her own experiences to consider how historians might integrate the roles of public historian and public intellectual to do "public-facing history that provides a public service." Hal Rothman, one of the West's most colorful and influential historians, did just that, as Michael Childers demonstrates. Yet, Rothman came to public history not by design but out of necessity as he entered the job market during a hiring crisis in the early 1980s and "never truly considered himself a public historian." These long-standing tensions between academic and public history and their relative status in the larger profession still endure. For Steve Aron and Virginia Scharff, two historians celebrated for both academic and public work, "building bridges" has not been simply a matter of reaching public audiences but has also entailed a cultural struggle within the historical profession to build respect and value for the diverse career paths open to historians.

How then does region intersect with public history? If public historians everywhere employ common methodologies and approaches, the topics, issues, and questions they address can vary widely and are usually intertwined with place. A sense of place depends upon historical and emotional attachments that, as historian David Glassberg has argued, are inextricably tied to individual and community identities and understandings of the past.[7] For this reason, public history is most often a place-based enterprise that seeks to answer questions vital to local communities and individual clients. The details matter, and public history can thus be intensely local. Yet localities and local histories do not exist in vacuums. They are linked by larger processes and narratives that can enrich understandings of the local. And if a historian were to ignore these broader issues and forces, he or she would be doing a disservice to local communities. Because regions are defined by some combination of historical, cultural, and physiographic factors,[8] regionalism is also a place-based approach that can organize our understanding of the issues and themes that define regional public histories.

A useful example is found in American Southern history. In overly (and purposefully) reductionist terms, the South is the region defined historically and culturally by the institution of slavery and its legacies. Make no mistake, slavery was a national institution, and grappling with its meanings and effects remains an ongoing national struggle.[9] Nor do I mean to suggest that the South as a region does not have fuzzy boundaries or that other forces and factors were not at play historically. Indeed, the South was also shaped by the same processes of conquest and national expansion that removed Native peoples and erased histories that are viewed as fundamental for defining the West. Nonetheless, it is the "peculiar institution," the meaning of the Civil War, and the centrality of race in daily life that defines Southern history. As a result, these same themes dominate Southern public history. Controversies over the removal of Confederate monuments and memorials are simply the most visible manifestation of the battle over a dominant regional narrative. From addressing the causes of the Civil War at historic battlefields to ghost tours in Southern cities and on historic plantations, public historians at work in the South must constantly engage the histories of oppression, racial inequality, and violence that attended a region built upon the enslavement of human beings.[10]

As in the South, distinctive aspects of the region's history and culture shape the work of public historians in the American West. Unlike the South, however, the West lacks a singularly dominant narrative thread. It also presents a shifting array of subregions linked to cultural and environmental factors. Jedediah Rogers, coeditor of the *Utah Historical Quarterly*, has navigated these complexities as he and others have rethought the role of a state history journal at the intersection of the local and regional. Community-based public history projects can also reorient how we think about regions. Direct engagement can uncover community histories that have been overlooked or have not yet been written. Trisha Venisa-Alicia Martínez and Vanessa Fonseca-Chávez illustrate how an active collaboration between community members and scholars is documenting the historic migration of Hispanic New Mexicans, or Manitos, across the American West. The project reminds us that histories of migration and mobility are central to the region's past.

Instead of dominant narrative, then, a series of related and often interwoven themes animate Western public history. Some of these include the unique histories and sovereignty of Native communities and nations, the existence of vast expanses of public lands, and the power of the mythic frontier West in the national consciousness. These are certainly not the only issues and themes engaged by Western public historians, but they do provide a framework for understanding the essays presented here.

Asserting control over their own histories is essential for the West's Native peoples. Despite a brutal history of conquest, colonization, and genocide, tribal nations survive today as sovereigns with rights and powers rooted in historically derived treaty relationships with the United States. Sovereignty sets tribes apart from all other groups in American society and has deeply influenced the practice of public history in Indian country.

As sovereigns, tribes must guard their rights and must also interact with state and federal agencies, often in the context of land management. At the same time, Native peoples constantly struggle against stereotypes and misunderstandings of their histories and cultures that are often bound to mythic popular visions of the frontier West. These factors put a premium on solid historical research and effective interpretation. Essays by Yvette Tuell, E. Richard Hart, Brittani Orona, and Laurie Arnold illustrate the importance and complexity of Indigenous public history in the West. Hart's work has already been introduced. Yvette Tuell, an enrolled member of the Shoshone-Bannock Tribes and a long-time tribal official, recounts the lessons she learned "working on the dark side," that is, as a federal employee. A Hupa tribal member, Brittani Orona illustrates the importance of community activists and grassroots organizations in public history practice. Finally, Laurie Arnold, who directs Native American Studies at Gonzaga University, considers how models of community engagement and partnership drawn from public history practice might inform the development of Native American Studies programs.

Public lands are another defining characteristic of the American West and have loomed large in the work of public historians in the region. Today, the federal government owns and manages about 640 million acres, or approximately twenty-eight percent of the nation's total land area. The vast majority of this land—over 90 percent—lies in Alaska and the eleven contiguous far-western states. While Alaska contains over one-third of all federal acreage, several other Western states contain far more federal land as a relative proportion of their land area. Utah, for example, is over 63 percent federal land while fully 80 percent of Nevada is controlled by the federal government. Moreover, the management of most of federal land (615 million acres in all) is vested in just five agencies: the Bureau of Land Management, the Fish and Wildlife Service, the National Park Service, the United States Forest Service, and the Department of Defense.[11] History is an essential management tool for these federal agencies. Moreover, the dominant place of the federal government in managing Western lands has long been a source of conflict between it and many Western states and communities. Michael Childers and Leisl Carr Childers both speak to the critical role that public historians have played in both of these arenas. Then, Leighton Quarles assesses the importance of history as a management tool for the iconic National Parks of the American West.

Finally, much as public historians in the South must contend with romantic visions of plantations and the Lost Cause, public historians in the West must compete with popular, simplistic, and usually inaccurate narratives that celebrate the Anglo-American taming of the frontier and obscure the diversity and complexity of the region's past. Through their work at the Autry National Center, Stephen Aron and Virginia Scharff endeavored to push public understanding of the region beyond stereotypical notions of the Old West. Despite substantial success, their experience also reveals the political, financial, and professional obstacles of such bridge-building. In some cases, however, the mythic West presents opportunities as well as challenges. Some communities, such as Lake City, Colorado, have been able to capitalize on popular ideas of the Wild West. Yet, as Mette Flynt details, balancing economic development and historical preservation is not a simple matter. The economic rewards for such communities can be great, but making a community's heritage central to its economic survival always entails some level of risk to those very resources.

The themes, issues, projects, and communities addressed in the essays that follow illustrate just some of the significant ways that history is being put to work in the American West. They represent a cross-section of a regional public history practice, yet by no means do they constitute an exhaustive review of the subject. Public historians in the West are at work documenting and interpreting an endless range of stories, from the lives of the Chinese laborers who built the transcontinental railroad to LGBTQ communities in the urban West to the military's dominant presence in the region. These projects and the essays presented in this volume reflect the dedication, interests, and creativity of scholars and practitioners who understand the impact of collaborative and applied history and its value for communities. This spirit of public engagement has inspired the work of the American West Center over the past half century, and it is the vision that unites our contributors here.

CHAPTER 1

Posing the Question

What Makes Public History Public?

RICHARD WHITE

This is a more personal essay than I usually write, in part because I have been associated with the American West Center in one way or another since I taught at the University of Utah over thirty years ago and in part because so much what I think about public history has been shaped by the work of the Center. When I came to Utah, I considered both Floyd O'Neil and the Center old. I am now older than Floyd was when I met him, which may be the single most frightening thing I have ever written. It also makes Floyd a kind of human Permian strata. He doesn't so much age as slowly erode, constantly revealing new facets. He is our equivalent of Bryce Canyon.

When I was at Utah, there were few other centers devoted to the American West. Since then, they have proliferated. Most have much better funding than the American West Center, but very few are as good. And most have wisely chosen to try to expand on what the American West Center does, trying new things, rather than imitating it. It is inimitable.

When I first met Floyd, I had only the vaguest ideas about public history. It was what people did in museums. It was what was inscribed on historical landmarks. I was, and in some ways still am, a snotty academic historian. I figured most of what went on in museums and virtually everything on landmarks was wrong at worst and a half-truth at best. The American West Center taught me quickly enough that I did not know anything about public history. It also made me feel better about my ignorance: it was hard to be sure what public history was because in a real way Floyd O'Neil and the staff at the Center were in the midst of inventing it.

I don't know how things are now, but it used to be hard to grasp the rules at the American West Center. When I was writing a volume for the Oxford History of the United States, I ran across a quote, perhaps apocryphal (I have learned to preface all second-hand quotes as "perhaps apocryphal"), attributed to Thomas Edison. A new employee asked Edison about the rules of the lab. Edison replied, "Hell, there are no rules here. We're trying to accomplish something." Floyd had standards, and you better meet them, but the rules? They were up to you.

Watching the work at the Center, I eventually figured out what distinguishes public history from other kinds of history. It was certainly not a set of rules, nor was it a defined set of practices. It wasn't even a discrete set of topics or a different audience. Nor was it the questions per se—public historians usually pursue questions similar to those of other professional historians. All historians must meet the same evidentiary standards.

There are two key differences between public history and other academic history. I will take them one at a time. The first is who gets to ask the initial and most basic questions. In public history, the public gets to pose the question.

Much of the history I write as an academic historian stems from my own curiosity, from a consensus among working historians as to what the important questions are, or from a kind of vague sense of what people need to know or at least should know. What the public wants me to write about usually has little to do with it. As my wife would be the first to tell you, I take unreasonable pleasure in asking questions my audiences would prefer that I didn't ask. I blame this on nuns. Actually, as my wife can also tell you, I blame all kinds of things on nuns. I went to Catholic school for part of my education and learned that the sign of a good question was when the nuns told me either to shut up or that this was a mystery. Then I knew I was on to something. But I digress. My point is that in most of the history I write, I formulate the initial questions.

But I also write public history of the kind that the Center has produced for years. Public history arises from the premise that the public determines what it wants and needs to know. The historian still helps deliver an answer, but the answer is to the public's question.

The reason the Center did this better than other places was largely because of Floyd O'Neil and a legacy that passed on through Richard Hart, Pat Albers, Dan McCool, Greg Smoak, and others. Floyd taught high school before he received his PhD. Floyd knew Indian country, and he knew Mormon country. He knew the rural West, and he knew the urban West. He could get money from the Ford Foundation even when he couldn't get it from his own university administration. He thought that the advancement of knowledge meant putting books in grammar schools and high schools as well as in university libraries. He thought that because Indians had grammar schools and high schools, the university should serve these schools as much as any other schools. Floyd thought that the purpose of the Center was not to make the university a more comfortable place for academics but to put academics to work so that the West was a better place—better educated, more tolerant, more just. And he thought that people living in the West were the best guide to what they needed to know in order to do this.

The Center has done considerable work beyond its projects with Indian tribes, but work with the tribes has been at the heart of what the Center has done. Much of my own thinking about public history springs from that work. In the simplest version of working with the tribes, the tribe decides what it needs to know, and the historian produces it. But, as anyone who has ever done this work knows, this is the anodyne version of the process.

The tribes need historians because so much of the legal rights of American Indian peoples spring from their treaties, and those treaties are embedded in quite particular pasts. The legal standard is that the treaties need to be interpreted according to how Indians understood them at the time that they were negotiated. This means that treaty cases are inevitably historical. At issue in a treaty case are both facts and context, but the original question that leads to facts and context—at least in my experience—comes from within the tribe itself. Tribal members know the treaties in often impressive detail. There is a collective memory of unkept promises, disputed clauses, and unpaid funds. There is often a detailed, if scattered and partial, knowledge of otherwise forgotten events. And there is also a vernacular intellectual tradition in which tribal members have, to the best of their abilities, combed the archives for information and evidence. Dealing with the tribes is not only to deal with quite knowledgeable consumers of historical knowledge but also with impressive vernacular historians.

So why do the tribes need public history? Why can't they just testify about the treaties? In part, it is a question of credentials before the court, but this is not the only reason. Public historians are critical even when the consumers have a deep knowledge of their own past: public historians provide context. Public historians share the training of other academic historians. They have the ability to contextualize and to give meaning and potency to what might seem meaningless, trivial, or peripheral events. They can also keep things in perspective. They know when a mountain is a mountain and when a molehill is just a molehill.

Public historians, particularly those who do this work a great deal (and Richard Hart and Greg Smoak from the Center are two of them), bring to this work a knowledge of the archives that is absolutely essential. This is the kind of history where the devil is in the details. It demands the ability to trace documents and to look beyond the immediate sources. In a world that gets reduced to the internet, it is more and more important to master the archives. It is essential to know the gaps in collections and how they might be filled. I am a professional historian, and mastery of the archives is a skill I admire more and more as I age. I admire it perhaps because it is something that only comes with experience, and I am reaching an age where experience is about the only strong suit I can muster. Many of the very best archival historians tend to be public historians who, because of the nature of their work, need to be attuned to details, quite specific details.

And this leads to the second distinctive thing about public history. Academic historians work in the archives and know the archives. These are not places easily navigated by the public, but academic historians do not see creating wider access to archives as part of their calling. Public historians do. They make access to the archives easier by creating new archives through their own research. The cumulative work of public historians in treaty case after treaty case, tribal history after tribal history, water rights investigation after water rights investigation can, as the Center has done, create a formidable database that can be deposited with the tribes to be reused in other cases and recycled for other purposes.

The American West Center has helped create archives at many of the Pueblos, at Hupa, Lummi, and the Inter-Tribal Council of Nevada. They have created them for the Shoshone-Bannock, Southern Ute, Tohono O'odham, Uintah-Ouray, the Utah Navajo Development Council, Ute Mountain Ute, White Mesa Ute, and Zuni.

This democratization of the archives is an important thing. It is a work that has, until recently, largely taken place on paper but now takes place digitally. This is both a huge advantage and a significant challenge.

As part of the work I am doing with the Grand Traverse Ottawas in Michigan, Russ Overton, a public historian, and I had to create a GIS database that shows how every piece of land on the old reservation was allotted, sold, or otherwise alienated. We compiled the database with the help of Erik Steiner, a geographer at the Center for Spatial History at Stanford, whose inspiration came in part from the American West Center. The database and resulting digital map enabled the pursuit of claims cases because in court you need to specify what was stolen, when it was stolen, and who stole it. Generic accusations don't fly. When the tribal council saw it, they immediately saw its possibilities. But that was not what entranced them. For them the database was genealogical. They could locate relatives, place them on the land, connect them to other relatives, and put together a family as well as a tribal past. This had not been our intent, but then in public history we are not really in charge.

That is a minor example of how public history keeps historians grounded in a set of concerns—rooted in genealogy, community, local history, and lived identity—that, while they may go in and out of fashion in the academy, force us to deal with questions whose consequences are immediate, practical, and tangible for those using the history.

This immediacy occurs on a variety of scales, not just the familial and personal. I have done a lot of historical writing and have accustomed myself to recognizing that whatever influence my academic writing has, it will take years to be realized. But public history, particularly histories that influence courts or public agencies, can have almost immediate influence. Or rather, once the lengthy passage through the courts is over, it can have almost immediate influence. Things change. Indian plaintiffs get access to resources and funds. The funds produce housing, scholarships, land acquisitions, and more. This is true well beyond treaty cases. Public historians can influence public policy with an immediacy and directness that does not usually come with most historical writing. As the late, sainted, and always contentious Hal Rothman knew, reports on the origins, implementation, and context of the creation and operation of a national park or wilderness area worked themselves out in the here and now.

In focusing on the products and results of the Center's work, it is easy to miss the process itself—as well as its results. It is impossible to do public history without confronting either directly or indirectly the messiness of constructing a history. Public history is in my experience necessarily collaborative, which means historians need to operate outside the guild.

When doing a public history for a tribe, a community, or a public agency, a historian must work with people who are not historians. They are community members, lawyers, administrators, and students. All these people often possess a great deal of knowledge about the past, but knowledge of the past is not the equivalent of academic history. Academic history is a quite particular and quite powerful way of studying the past that comes from disciplinary training.

Academic history is what my colleague at Stanford, Sam Wineburg, has called an unnatural act. Interest in the past is natural: we all recall and narrate the past and listen and contest as others give accounts of the past. This happens every day. But what academic history does is to force stories about the past and evidence for them to submit to interrogation under quite particular disciplinary standards of evidence. This is not what people normally do when they consider the past.

In public history, the conflict is sometimes between different disciplinary standards and sometimes between academic and popular history. Lawyers, for example, have disciplinary standards that they use to evaluate the past. They judge historical evidence by legal rules of evidence, which determine admissibility in court. These rules are arcane, arbitrary, and to an historian, slightly cracked, but they are designed to create clarity. They yield answers to questions of what counts as evidence in a given case that are different from the standards that historians apply. This causes considerable tension between historians and lawyers.

There is a second set of tensions, however, that arise from working in the public sphere. Here, historians stand separate from both lawyers and the public that commissions a history. Lawyers are like historians in bringing disciplinary standards to bear, but they are unlike historians and like tribal members and community members in treating the past instrumentally. Lawyers and the public want a useful past, one that will allow them to achieve a desired end. Public historians, if they are doing their job, want to create histories that do work in the world, but they need to push against a narrow instrumentality. In part, we do this from our own instrumental reasons: it is our job to bring bad news because lawyers, tribes, and other clients can't protect themselves against what they do not know. But in part we are the bearers of bad news from disciplinary reasons.

These disciplinary reasons are often a subject of considerable confusion, embodied in the old debate about objectivity that was the theme of Peter Novick's *That Noble Dream: The Objectivity Question and the American History Profession*, which most American historians read in graduate school. But as Thomas Haskell has written in an article not nearly so widely read, objectivity has gotten confused with neutrality. No historian—no human being—is neutral. We cannot pretend we don't care about many of the things that happen in the world or have happened in the world. Historians have disciplinary rules precisely because none of us is neutral. It is the rules that produce the quality that we call objectivity.

The best way to enforce the rules is to operate as a community that produces knowledge. Truth, as American pragmatists recognized long ago, is collaborative and social. It is the result not so much of individuals but of communities of knowledge. Historians have to function as a community because singly none of us can be trusted. When I write public history, I am not neutral, but I am fair in the sense of following disciplinary rules. I am fair even if I sympathize with the tribes, the environmental groups, and the public agencies that I work with. If I did not, I would not work for them. But that does not mean that I tell them what they want to hear. My first goal is to meet the standards of my guild and profession. I know that whatever I write will be read by other historians as good as I am, and if they can show that I violated accepted standards, I am dead in the water.

In 1994, I was an expert witness on a shellfish case in western Washington. Years before that, during the late 1960s, I had been active in Indian fishing demonstrations at Frank's Landing on the Nisqually River. I was then twenty-one, a senior in college, from which I was frequently absent. It was the first time that I had lived with and known more than individual Indians. The Nisquallys did more good for me than I ever did for them, except, perhaps, providing them with unintended amusement. In many ways, the experience made me a historian.

Twenty-five years later, I testified for the Nisqually and other tribes. During the deposition, when the State of Washington began to lay the basis for challenging my credentials, its lawyers did two things. First, they attacked my master's thesis, which, for good reasons, I never published, particularly the sections written in high dudgeon and that my advisor suggested I delete. I should have listened to him. I did not take them out, and I now had to disavow them in the deposition. I had written that treaties were a sham, dictated documents, which was precisely the State's contention in seeking to strip them of legal force. In response, I said I was then learning to be a historian, I was not yet one, and I had not only not published the thesis but had consistently written the opposite for twenty-five years.

A second line of attack went to my involvement at Frank's Landing. The State argued that I was an advocate rather than a dispassionate expert. Here I did not disavow anything. My answer went to the distinction between neutrality and objectivity that I have just outlined. I sympathized with the Nisqually and the other tribes, and the tribe got to ask the basic questions that they wanted me to answer, but they were not hiring me to produce the answers that they wanted. My answer in the deposition was that my task was to deliver the news, good or bad, and as a professional historian the check on my behavior is that my work will be examined and, if necessary refuted, by other historians.

Lawyers are hired to win the case and provide only the evidence that helps them to win. Historians doing public history seek to produce a history that can stand up to the criticisms of other historians. A key disciplinary rule is that we cannot deliberately leave out anything that, if included, would falsify or change our argument. The easiest way to discredit an academic history is to cite some piece of evidence that can change the meaning of the story. And this was what I told the opposing counsel: I might sympathize with the tribes, but my job was, as Bernard Bailyn has put it, to deliver the news. Whatever I wrote had to stand up to the only community that could make or break me—other historians.

All of this is important because there has been a kind of reaction against the public history done by the Center and other public historians. It has occurred largely because this history has proved so helpful for the publics—particularly the tribes—that have requested it. The criticism is a kind of backhanded compliment. Until recently, the tribes have usually won in court, and there has been a complaint that they did so because they hire historians whose sympathies are with the tribes. These hired guns are better than the state's hired guns and deliver the histories that tribes need. The charge, sometimes explicit, sometimes implicit, is that these historians bend the histories to benefit their clients.

This is a critique, that in my experience, is a combination of sour grapes and a willful ignorance of how fraught public history can be. Indian tribes and other communities are hardly homogenous, and they do not grant academic historians the right to deliver verdicts on their past, no matter how useful those verdicts often prove in court. They are not always, or usually, grateful. I expect to be resented both by the officials of the states that the tribes sue and by the tribes. I expect to have my motives questioned and my conclusions challenged. I cannot take a job with the tribes without recalling Floyd O'Neil's counsel years ago regarding work with them, and which he has most likely forgotten. "Just remember," he told me, "this will probably not end well." When tribal councils turn over, the first move is often to fire the lawyers and experts. The long and tangled story of the Center's relation with the Zunis is a history in itself.

This challenging of what historians do, and this questioning of our motives forces us to defend not only what we do but why we do it. And this is a good thing. There is a kind of casual cynicism in much of the American public—and among many of my students—that the world is a collection of opinions. You have your opinion; I have mine; and who is to say who is correct? Public historians are in this sense on the front line of arguing that some things are far more likely to be true than other things and getting this right matters. A public history is written to give information and interpretation that a public has requested, often to form the basis of a decision designed to shape the way part of the world operates. It should not be written simply to please the public.

The collaborative nature of public history is a critical element of the enterprise. The American West Center is precisely that, a Center. It brings together professional historians, scholars in other disciplines, graduate students, and undergraduates. It works with community members, lawyers, and government officials. That collaborative aspect makes the Center a great teaching tool. The best teaching that I ever saw at Utah was in the Center, and the best teaching that I ever did at Stanford was in the Spatial History Project, which, like the American West Center, was collaborative.

This collaborative aspect has also shaped other centers that have been inspired by the American West Center. Today, there are a plethora of West centers, virtually all of them doing public history. There is the Center of the American West at the University of Colorado, run by Patty Limerick. It has long been concerned with federal governance in the West but over the last few years has focused more and more heavily on land, water, and energy use, interjecting itself into public conversations and disputes over water, mining, and, above all recently, fracking. This is a topic that can make working with the tribes seen like a vacation on an isle of tranquility.

There is the Autry National Center, whose research arm is headed by Steve Aron and one of whose key figures, Gingy Scharff, focuses on popular history and the cultures of the West. It has done so by starting with a West that the public knows and is curious about. Instead of hectoring the public, it contextualizes and explains that West—clearly, smartly, and entertainingly. The Autry National Center does so around material objects—an astonishing variety of art and artifacts put together in combinations that usually manage to teach without lecturing. These exhibits do not always give messages that the public—or *New York Times* reviewers—want to hear, but they are engaging enough to capture the audience.

There are also western and regional centers at the University of Washington, University of Montana, University of Wyoming, University of New Mexico, Stanford, and more. Each has a particular niche, but all owe something to the American West Center.

The flourishing of public history in the West is not and does not need to be confined to centers. Jon Christensen at UCLA made *Boom* one of the most interesting, if not the most interesting, publications focusing on the West—in this case California. It combined public journalism, photography, and scholarship to examine issues of public concern.

I cite these other examples to underline my major point here: the core of public history lies in who asks the questions rather than in who gives the answer. This definition is somewhat different from the usual definition of the field, which often settles for a kind of history aimed at the public, as if historians were marksmen and the public a target. Such a definition is, I think, insufficient because a wide variety of history—academic and popular—seeks a public audience. But more than that, such a definition is insufficient because unintentionally it diminishes public history by drawing an artificial line between academic history (which becomes real history) and public history, which becomes a watered-down lesser history.

There is no good reason for this demeaning of public history within the academy as a lesser endeavor, something with lower standards, less prestige, and less consequence than academic history. As I have argued, in terms of methods, rigor, and standards, public history is the same as other academic history. Public historians are not part of a separate breed. They are trained academic historians, and what they do is a branch of academic history. Many of its practitioners are respected academic historians who do not abandon their standards or skills when they turn to public history. I do not change my methods or standards when I do public history, and thanks to Floyd O'Neil I have been doing it for forty years.

CHAPTER 2

Taking a Public Turn

Public History as Public Service in the American West

LEISL CARR CHILDERS

As someone who specializes in public lands history, a meaningful and often highly charged topic in the American West, I have had occasion to think deeply about how I operate as a scholar when working on public lands issues for nonacademic audiences. In some cases, I have served as a public intellectual speaking with journalists and providing comment on current issues; in others, I have done public history in collaboration with journalists; and in some instances, I have engaged in applied history to inform political discussions. Despite the lines that we often draw between the work of the public intellectual, engaging in applied history, and doing public history, there is a distinct common ground between these modes of operating. Rather than view them as largely different, we should consider the ways in which they are interrelated descriptors of how we as historians can deploy history to better affect and serve the world around us. The common ground these activities occupy illustrates what it means to take a public turn with our work and bring history to bear on the world as a public service.

SERVING AS A PUBLIC INTELLECTUAL

In late April 2014, I watched with growing irritation the news surrounding events as they unfolded between Cliven Bundy, along with his family, and federal officials directed to round up the family's trespassing cattle near Bunkerville, Nevada. I was particularly incensed by Sean Hannity's treatment of the situation. On April 9, Hannity interviewed Bundy on his television show, using the rancher as a foil for his typical attacks on the perceived overreach of the federal government. Hannity goaded Bundy saying, "This is public land. It's not being used. In my mind, and I'm not a rancher, but I would think the federal government would be thankful because you're cutting the lawn for free, and they're charging huge amounts of money to let your cattle graze there with these fees?" Bundy, his voice stuttering on camera as he held a wireless microphone in his hand, agreed with Hannity's points. This was precisely why he was being interviewed on the conservative political commentator's Fox News show.[1]

As the conversation continued, Hannity deftly positioned Bundy to make a very frightening pronouncement. "Let me ask you one more question, Cliven," he said, "You talked about a range war with the federal government. There is a lot of people out there, now that they are taking your cattle, that are fearful this is another Waco situation. Ruby Ridge has come up in some articles. What do you mean by range war? How far are you willing to take this?" Bundy responded, "My statement to the American people, I'll do whatever it takes to gain our liberty and freedom back."[2]

Hannity was not the only one turning Bundy and the situation at Bunkerville, which was escalating by the day, into fodder for their ideologies or increased viewer numbers. At its height, the standoff between federal land management and law enforcement officials on one side and the Bundys and their armed militia supporters on the other nearly caused a terrible, violent outcome to a lawful cattle roundup. Everyone from Fox News to the Sierra Club took a position on Bundy's actions, making the situation just another vehicle for political conservatives to blame the federal government for overreaching environmental regulations and for environmentalists to blame ranchers for degrading public lands and federal officials for not doing their job.[3]

I have grappled with this pattern of public lands management throughout my academic career. My first book, *The Size of the Risk: Histories of Multiple Use in the Great Basin*, was an attempt to explain how this kind of conflict was neither political nor ideological, however much it might appear to be on the surface. At the time of the standoff at Bunkerville, I was neck deep in copyedits for the book and passionate about how "seemingly inconsequential populations" that lived in rural areas of Nevada and Utah had been historically forced to "grapple with national interests and pressures" because of their proximity to "a vast concentration of public lands" and the astounding ignorance of place many land managers, scientists, and politicians demonstrated.[4] In the Bundy situation at Bunkerville, I did not see government overreach or environmental degradation so much as I saw echoes of my research on the past in the present. In a sense, I knew the Bundys, having interviewed ranchers just like them. I knew the historical context in which they operated. So, I set my mind on writing a piece for a nascent blog on the American West that I and four other colleagues had created to serve as a public forum for historical discussion of current issues in the region.

Six months earlier, one of those collaborators, Kent Blansett, had published a piece on the Canadian Indigenous movement Idle No More that generated tremendous public interest on the heels of a massive protest against the Texas-based Southwestern Energy Company's search for shale gas deposits on the Mi'kmaq reserve.[5] Blansett's essay served to clarify and contextualize the movement in the moment in which it occurred. Similarly, I generated a post that tried to cut through the media white noise around the events at Bunkerville and offer some insight into the Bundys' actions.

"Right-wing pundits, wildlife activists, and a host of others," I wrote, "have turned Bundy and the misery of his situation into anecdotal proof of the justness of their various ideologies." I argued, "Bundy is no ideologue, despite his language about protecting his rights and liberties. His adoption of politically charged rhetoric is a defense mechanism and not a real identity." Where Hannity and others had worked to "contextualize Bundy's experience within the framework of an overreaching federal government," I offered to provide "a little more about Bundy's history and what he means when he says that his family has ranched in the area since the late nineteenth century."[6] Bundy's crime at Bunkerville was opposing federal officials with firearms. Federal agents were at Bunkerville to round up his trespassing cattle, and I thought the history of his family's ranch went a long way toward explaining how those cattle came to be in trespass in the first place. That context explained the rancher's perspective and commitment to hanging onto his operation.

Bundy, it turned out, had been part of the Sagebrush Rebellion in the late 1970s, a movement in the American West supported by ranchers and many who worked in extractive industries to wrest public lands out of federal hands. At that time, I wrote, he had "supported state oversight of public lands as a way to alleviate the administration of his grazing range from the pressures of national interests." I asserted that "federal retention of public lands ensured that they would be managed in the interests of the

American people, but this subjected them to a wide variety of sometimes-conflicting uses and often required reductions in traditional uses." Bundy and the other Sagebrush Rebels did not succeed in transferring public lands to state administration, but their advocacy of such a transfer certainly drew attention to the plight of ranchers in the early stages of the 1980s economic depression called the Farm Crisis. At Bunkerville in 2014, Bundy had lost his ability to ranch cattle. My estimation of that incident, relative to his decades-long endeavor to improve his situation, was, "All that is left to Bundy is some semblance of his dignity, which is quickly being eroded on national television. He should not be made into the mascot or villain in anyone's cause and we should not be so quick to condemn him. Rather, Cliven Bundy deserves a little bit of empathy since it is we who have asked him to continually adapt."[7]

Putting the Bundy piece out in public was one of the best professional decisions I have ever made. The post generated a handful of comments, some of which offered praise, such as "this may be the best single piece I have read on this whole affair," and some of which suggested I was absolutely wrong.[8] Three fellow historians, Ann Little (Colorado State University), Christian Harrison (a doctoral candidate at the University of Nevada, Las Vegas, at the time), and Joseph Taylor (Simon Fraser University) even weighed in and offered alternative perspectives. Taylor commented, "I think Leisl overstates the case when she argues that 'Bundy is no ideologue.' Cliven Bundy's (and Sean Hannity's) ideas may be inconsistent and undoubtedly confused, but there is certainly ideology driving him as well."[9] These comments led to further conversations with Taylor, Harrison, and other historians at conferences and via email. The post itself, along with the release of my book nineteen months later, fueled interest from journalists who began contacting me for comment. This became especially true after January 2016 and Bundy's sons Ammon and Ryan, along with several dozen militia members, seized and held the headquarters of the Malheur National Wildlife Refuge near Burns, Oregon.

I was not the only academic writing about the Bundy family. Nancy Langston (Michigan Technological University), who had written a book on the Malheur refuge, published an opinion piece in the *New York Times* that emphasized the importance of understanding the history of the place. She argued, "Equitable futures for Western public lands won't be achieved when ideologues swagger in, brandishing guns and taking over federal buildings."[10] The *New York Times* itself commissioned a panel of historians and other experts in a segment entitled "Who Should Control the

West?" to address the events at Malheur during the early stages of the takeover. Historians Patricia Limerick (University of Colorado, Boulder Center of the American West) and Louis Warren (University of California, Davis) weighed in on the issue, as did legal scholar Deborah Donahue, Paiute Chairwoman Charlotte Rodrique, public policy scholar Robert H. Nelson, and economist Terry L. Anderson of the Property and Environment Research Center.[11]

The six short pieces offered the paper's readers different perspectives on the problems posed by the Bundys and militia members at Malheur. It was refreshing to read their work and that of Langston at a time when finding historical context for the situation at the refuge was hard to come by. Historians who are willing to engage with current situations as public intellectuals offer nonhistorians clarity on issues by building and articulating historical context, sometimes by providing a necessary critical voice. Ta-Nehisi Coates, a hard-hitting public intellectual, has described himself and those he admires as sharp interlocutors who communicate *to* a larger public.[12] Similarly, psychologists John Issett and Duncan Jackson (both from New York University), in their study on public intellectuals, have described them as thinkers, experts, critical dissenters, and revealers of truth.[13] In other words, public intellectuals offer their expertise, and also their authority as experts, to the general public in order to influence audiences through criticism and dissent.

Adam Sowards (University of Idaho) has transformed his academic career on this basis. In addition to creating a new regular column in *High Country News* entitled "Reckoning with History," he has been a regular contributor to the magazine's "Writers on the Range" series and an author on *History News Network* and *The Conversation*. His articles are timely and provide critical insights into public lands management issues and employ his expertise in order to provide greater understanding and clarity. His first piece for the new column succinctly reminded readers of the sad but normal state of affairs in the Department of the Interior under bad political appointees. Albert B. Fall in the 1920s, James G. Watt in the 1980s, and then Ryan Zinke in the late 2010s all utilized their position to take ethically questionable actions and exploit the nation's resources for personal profit.[14]

Sowards's piece was the perfect reminder of the political context in which the departments have always operated. It is hostage to the political appointees that lead it. By reminding us of this context, Sowards served in a critic's or dissenter's role and asked readers to rethink their position on Zinke's actions. This is a valuable contribution. As Issett and Jackson explain, "In order to identify the spirit of our times, judge its worth, relevance, origins, and futures, we must ourselves be dissenters from that spirit." [15] That is the greatest public service public intellectuals can provide.

WORKING AS A PUBLIC HISTORIAN

As I became more practiced at providing comments to journalists, I had opportunities to engage in a deeper level of dialogue with them. In December 2016, I received an email from Abby Ellis, a *Vice News* reporter and producer with the Public Broadcasting System's *Frontline* series. By this point, I had a tenuous working relationship with two other journalists: Tay Wiles, an associate editor at *High Country News*, and Leah Sottile, a freelance journalist published in the *Washington Post*, *Vice News*, and the *Atlantic*.

Matthew A. Pearce (then at the University of Oklahoma) had given my name to Wiles, who contacted me in April 2016 for information on public lands grazing in Nevada. She had read my essay "The Angry West: Understanding the Sagebrush Rebellion in Rural Nevada" in an anthology edited by noted agricultural historian David B. Danbom and published by the Rural West Initiative at Stanford University's Bill Lane Center. In it, I had attempted to clarify the specific experiences of the public lands ranchers in Nevada who had helped engineer the Sagebrush Rebellion.[16] I found Wiles to be incredibly articulate, curious, and very much a scholar of the past. Sottile contacted me in November 2016 in support of an article she was writing on the takeover at the Malheur refuge marking its one-year anniversary. She also was interested in discussing the Sagebrush Rebellion.[17] I enjoyed talking with Sottile and found her to be equally passionate, engaged, and appreciative of my time.

Speaking to both Wiles and Sottile, I discovered that although they treated me as an expert on the past, there was a lot I could learn from them about the present. I also found that my initial fear that these journalists were only looking for juicy soundbites to support their theories was utterly incorrect. They were seeking understanding. For every word they quoted in their articles, we dialoged thousands more. From this I learned that the most important aspect of working with journalists was not which of my statements they ended up using but the conversation that had led to those statements. It became increasingly important to me to be available to talk to these journalists.

Abby Ellis, like Wiles and Sottile, was a smart, young professional who asked excellent questions and was willing to take the time to talk through theories and concepts. I found her completely dedicated to her work and committed to developing the most accurate story possible. In her email introduction, she indicated that Joseph Taylor had recommended she get in touch with me. In the time since I had written the blog post, Taylor and I had opportunities to dialogue several times at academic conferences about the Bundys and the incidents at Bunkerville and Malheur. Commenting on the piece when it appeared, he had said, "I think we can romanticize Bundy's attachment to the land a bit too much. The loss of two ranches in one century would be a wrenching dislocation, one I'm not about to diminish, but it seems to me equally important to point out that the loss of those grazing permits would also amount to a devastating diminishment of the capital value of the family improvements to the property."[18] This was why Taylor had recommended Ellis contact me and why she had followed through. I had addressed this idea in the blog post, book, and chapter essay. She hoped I could speak to why the Bundys might be so adamant about their grazing "rights" and their ranch for a *Frontline* episode entitled "American Patriot" focusing on Ammon Bundy.[19]

The conversations I had with Ellis spanned six months, from December 2016 to May 2017. I traveled to Las Vegas in February and New York City in April to do on-camera interviews, but most of our dialogue occurred via email, telephone, and text message. Though the episode focused on the most charismatic member of the Bundy family, my role was to contextualize the family and their ranching operation. As our conversations evolved, I began providing Ellis with as much source material as I could find. Instead of simply answering her questions, I worked to provide raw information that we could then discuss and interpret. The process also went the other way. When Ellis found interesting or compelling sources, she sent them to me for evaluation, and we talked about what they meant. In this way, my interactions with Ellis felt very much like what we do as public historians when we work collaboratively with nonhistorians to produce new historical interpretations.

After our first phone conversation, Ellis read my "Angry West" essay and then emailed several follow-up questions about grazing fees. I sent her two scholarly articles on the subject with some explanatory material on the creation and the scale of various public lands ranch operations in Nevada during the twentieth century. It was particularly important for me to emphasize how property worked in these operations. I wrote, "When ranchers talk about their property, they are not necessarily referring to their grazing ranges. They are referring to their water rights, which anchor their grazing ranges. Those water rights typically mean that no one else can be permitted on that grazing allotment."[20]

This opened the door to a flood of questions, and we spent the next month discussing how to think about the relationship between grazing permits and fees, water rights, business expenses in ranching operations, and the global beef industry. I worked with her to develop a framework of thought about this system, both as it existed in the past and what it has become today. By the time we scheduled the first recorded interview, I had spent nearly five out of the eight weeks since our first conversation on the phone with Ellis.

At the interview, it made me nervous to think that my words would be broadcast to PBS audiences globally. In fact, at one point, I became nauseated. Ellis and her partner Rick Young, a veteran *Frontline* cameraman, worked hard to put me at ease during the videoed interview session. We had convened for lunch the day before the interview so we could meet in person and talk about their vision for the project. They had chosen a pine-forested oasis at the southern edge of the Great Basin, the Mt. Charleston Lodge in the Spring Mountains just northwest of Las Vegas, as the first interview site. Just prior my departure for the interview, Ellis had texted me to ask whether Cliven Bundy, Ammon's father, was indeed the last rancher in Clark County, Nevada. I made a frantic search of my files and the Bureau of Land Management's online permit system to answer her question. The answer was both yes and no. Technically, Bundy was not the last rancher in Clark County to hold a permit, but truthfully, there were far fewer ranchers running cattle in the county than there had been at the end of the twentieth century. As the interview started, I hid my hands underneath the table to keep from gesticulating and tried my best to answer their questions without using scholarly jargon. When they asked me about Bundy being the last rancher, I responded, "The Bundys are among the last ranchers in Clark County."[21]

In the succeeding weeks, Ellis sent me additional email inquiries. Some were designed to test the accuracy of statements made by other journalists; others focused on clarifying Cliven Bundy's background as the episode began to take its final shape. A few of the questions tested interpretations that Ellis and the executive producers of *Frontline* had drafted. At one point, Ellis inquired in a text message about an interpretation that made the Bundy family's difficulties out to be a federal bureaucratic problem instead of the outgrowth of the complex urban expansion of Las Vegas in Clark County. For television, Ellis said, the story needed to be simple, but it was "a very complex problem." This tension between the complexity of history and the attention span of a television audience sat at the core of our discussions. I responded, "True that. But making it a bureaucratic problem obfuscates the fact that it is a people problem, as in volume of people."[22]

Our dialogue had an impact. This conversation produced an interpretation that framed the entire show. In the program that aired, narrator Will Lyman intoned, "For twenty years, the government had been trying to phase out ranching in Bunkerville to deal with development and environmental issues."[23]

I was not the only historian who worked with Ellis on "American Patriot." Joseph Taylor also gave Ellis and Young an interview. Taylor's on-camera material, even more than mine, helped drive the first half of the episode. But in speaking informally with Taylor about his experience, I realized that mine had been significantly different. Besides providing source material and perspective to supplement Ellis's own research, I also assisted with fact checks and even provided some editorial remarks to their script. In one email, Ellis asked how best to state the dollar amount Bundy owed on delinquent grazing fees and the associated fines. I suggested that she avoid making a political statement about the amount owned and not reference American taxpayers as so many other media outlets had. I said, "I think it is safe to say that Bundy does owe in excess of $1 million."[24] In another, she inquired how I felt about a particular line in the script that served as a starting point for the Bundy family's situation. I responded that it was "a clear and accurate statement."[25] The lines they crafted to tie these ideas together opened the episode. Lyman began, "In the fall of 2013, Ammon Bundy's family lost a decades-long legal battle with the federal government. They'd been refusing to remove their cattle from public land near Bunkerville, Nevada, and owed over a million dollars in fees and fines."[26]

Working with Ellis on "American Patriot" was incredibly satisfying professionally. It also afforded me the broadest exposure as a scholar I have had to date. More than the sales of my book and distribution of any essays and articles I have written, more than the museum exhibit on the National Finals Rodeo I curated in 2008 for the fiftieth anniversary of that event, my contribution to crafting this episode reached a broad public audience. At the end of 2017, PBS rated "American Patriot" the seventh-most-watched film in the *Frontline* series that year.[27]

The episode was not without its critics. On *Frontline*'s Facebook page, the comments were colorful, beginning with one that declared "Haha, what a crock of sh*t."[28] But whether audiences agreed or disagreed with the interpretation and no matter the reasons for their opinion, undeniably, the show made an impact on public audiences. That outcome is what public historians desire most and speaks directly to the utility of our profession and the public service we provide.

Noted public historian Robert Kelley (University of California, Santa Barbara) has explained that "Public History refers to the employment of historians and the historical method outside of academia." He once wrote, "Public Historians are at work whenever, in their professional capacity, they are part of the public process."[29] Barbara J. Howe and Emory L. Kemp (both at West Virginia University), in one of the first introductory textbooks on public history, argue, "Public history by its very nature is a multidisciplinary activity, demanding a team approach to projects which have well-defined and often limited objectives."[30] Thomas Cauvin (University of Luxembourg), in a more recent text, has suggested that one of the purposes of public history is to "touch a public as broad as possible."[31]

If we broaden Kelley's definition to characterize doing historical work outside of academia as those activities that historians engage in with nonacademics, regardless of where those historians work, public history then becomes the collaborative, multidisciplinary endeavor done by *any* historian who works with nonhistorians in order to reach as broad a public as possible. This is the epitome of history as public service.

DOING APPLIED HISTORY

Another outgrowth from releasing my blog post on Cliven Bundy into the public sphere and publishing my first book and other pieces on public lands has been to move further into endeavors that not only put my historical expertise to work but also put me in a position to speak directly to those making decisions about public lands policy. One warm, sunny morning in December 2017, I found myself at the Biltmore Hotel in Phoenix sitting with my hands in my lap nervously waiting my turn to address a panel of western governors and a moderately crowded room of administrators and political staffers. I was one of four historians at the Western Governors' Association (WGA) Winter Meeting invited to speak to the attending state executives about the historical relationship between the federal government and the states.

On my right was Sarah S. Elkind (San Diego State University), who specializes in how local politics affect federal policy, and to her right was Peter Onuf (Emeritus Thomas Jefferson Memorial Foundation Professor of History at the University of Virginia), cofounder of the history radio show *BackStory with the American History Guys* and a prolific scholar of the early American republic. We joined Patricia Limerick (Director of the Center of the American West at the University of Colorado, Boulder), who had organized our panel and had a reputation for fearlessly putting her skills as a historian to use in political settings. Our panel waited on stage with the governors under the watchful eye of Joe Rassenfos, WGA Communications Director who served as our liaison, Utah Governor Gary Herbert, who chaired our panel, and WGA Executive Director James D. Ogsbury, who according to Rassenfos was "a driving force behind our work to re-set the state-federal relationship" and the author of the WGA resolution on the subject slated for adoption at the end of our panel.[32] That resolution was the reason for our presence.

Under Ogsbury's leadership, the WGA believed, "The inauguration of a new Administration and the start of the 115th Congress presents an unusual opportunity to realign the state-federal relationship." With the resolution, western governors sought to "work in true partnership with the federal government and call upon the Administration to engage them in the development and execution of policy that impacts state authority."[33] A collaborative endeavor between the WGA and four other western regional associations, the resolution emphasized the frustrations state and local officials had with overlapping and intersecting federal mandates, policies, and agencies. The resolution declared, "In the absence of Constitutional delegation of authority to the federal government, state authority should be presumed sovereign."[34]

In this narrow view of the federal government's enumerated powers, the governors desired that "each executive department and agency should have a clear and accountable process to provide states with early, meaningful and substantive input in the development of regulatory policies." They also believed, "Where authority has been delegated by the federal government to the states, states should be granted the maximum administrative discretion possible and should be treated as co-regulators."[35] Limerick, Onuf, Elkind, and I each sucked in our collective breaths as we read this most recent assertion of states' rights.

Our "adventure in Applied History" with the WGA, as Limerick called it, entailed fine-tuning our normal historical understanding of states' rights to resonate with the sentiments of the attending governors.[36] In other words, we were in the unenviable position of figuring out how to do good history in a political setting, for a particular audience. However, Limerick is a master of this type of endeavor. In a set of poignant instructions, she directed us to consider that the WGA "has an impressive record of bipartisan problem-solving," that "there is not always an exact and precise match between forthrightness about historical understanding and the furthering of bipartisan common cause," that there was more than one way to make a historical point, and criticizing elements of the resolution that did not conform to good history was not going to be as productive as helping the governors facilitate "'innovative governance,' appreciation of 'state expertise,' 'true partnership,' 'authentic collaborators,'" and generally achieving a better relationship with the federal government.[37]

This advice is what sits at the core of understanding what Limerick has called applied history, a term used in the early twentieth century by Benjamin Shambaugh, the first superintendent of the State Historical Society of Iowa, a professor of political science at the University of Iowa, and an early public historian. Shambaugh envisioned applied history to be the "practical application" of history, much the same as he saw the growing practical application of botany, chemistry, physics, geology, and other academic disciplines at the University of Iowa. "Why not," he asked in a short article entitled "Applied History" in the *Mississippi Valley Historical Association* proceedings, "apply the scientific knowledge of history to the practical affairs of today?"[38]

Rebecca Conard has described Shambaugh's vision of applied history as "collecting, preserving, publishing, and using history for the greater good of the state."[39] Shambaugh believed, "To wisely use the results of all these experiments in efforts to solve the problems which confront each generation is to carry out a program of Applied History."[40] His foundation for Applied History focused on the production of reference reports detailing the history of policy and governance in Iowa. Though it overemphasized the scientific aspects of historical study and the concept of historical continuity, Shambaugh's applied history pointed to the discipline's pragmatic usefulness.[41] Applied history was inherently oriented toward state and local history but had potential application at the federal level.

Applied history also serviced the present and focused on impact. To urban historian Joel Tarr (Carnegie Mellon University) in the early stages of his career, "history was important and useful," and "like a lot of other intellectual tools" could be deployed in service of a social problem. There were, he argued at the first national public history symposium, areas of intellectual work where historical insights and materials could help solve particular problems. Applied history, according to Tarr, sought to approach and help solve those very contemporary problems.[42] Thomas Cauvin has concurred, stating, "Applied history refers to the history applied to present issues, interrogations, audiences, actors, and policies. It is, therefore, problem-solving oriented," its purpose "to apply historical methodology to the production of narratives for a corporate demand and/or more specific audiences."[43]

Patricia Limerick herself hoped to develop "practices that transcend the conventional turf fights between 'academic history' and 'public history,' uniting them in the strenuous and satisfying work of 'applied history,' which she described simply as the "application of historical perspective."[44] According to writer Ian Frazier, Limerick "believes that history, skillfully applied and deeply understood, can save the world."[45] Indeed, it has that potential. Or if not save the world, it could at least provide thirteen governors at the WGA a better framework of thought about the federal-state relationship.

After Governor Herbert gave each of us a very kind introduction that emphasized our personal connections with his state, Limerick transitioned from a brief panel introduction to each of our topics. We had only five minutes to make one, maybe two, poignant statements to the governors. Peter Onuf emphasized that the history of the United States is a history of federalism itself and that although it does help to understand the context in which the nation's founders functioned, their ideas and actions can only be said to address the issues of their own time. Limerick followed these comments with an emphasis on the how leaders of the early republic did not have the West in mind when the early federal-state pattern evolved. "New institutions came into play," Limerick said, "to deal with the vast, rugged, often arid landscapes of the West." Sarah Elkind provided a brief, cogent statement on the interplay between local interests and federal policy, emphasizing that "federal policies still reflect the bottom-up process." It was only during this past century that "lots of Americans went from seeing governments as protectors of liberty to the biggest threat."[46]

My statements focused on the federal-state relationship in public lands management, a contentious topic with state executives at best. I reminded the governors that public lands management was a story of "trial and error" that lacked any inevitable outcome. Public land laws codified activities in which Americans were already engaged. At the behest of such individuals, who were ranching, mining, and logging, their political representatives had legalized these activities. I also reminded the governors that federal oversight had been "necessary where realities of rugged and arid lands were being sparsely populated" and that federal support was required in order "to see that public lands could be used to still have economic value to the nation."[47] Limerick concluded our remarks by emphasizing the importance of asking questions of the past in order to better grapple with our present.

During our statements, it was clear that several governors were unappreciative of our perspectives on the past. The governors of Arizona and Idaho in particular seemed largely uninterested, even annoyed, sitting just to Limerick's left. Governor Herbert, however, was attentive and asked a challenging question. If our nation's founders were not thinking at all about the West, to what extent, he asked, is the past at all applicable? This question could have been understood either as an attack on the utility of the historical profession or as a sincere attempt to redefine his understanding of historicism. If we understand his question as the latter, this is precisely the moment that applied history seeks to achieve: to bring to bear our historical expertise on a particular present issue that causes the individuals we are dialoging with to come to a new understanding of that issue. We could have answered Herbert's question a number of ways, but the best path was to provide him with a better framework of thought about the federal-state relationship.

Working in applied history for the WGA panel required that we listen to those who seek our help more than we speak, look for points of consensus more than conflict, and go easy on the criticism. Rather than make our statements complex and highly textured, we made them brief, yet precise. As opposed to serving a political agenda, we sought to serve and clarify the governors' understanding of the past. Instead of correcting their facts, we gave them a way of thinking about the past.

We are accustomed to thinking about applied history in terms of policy and governance, and that is certainly how Shambaugh thought of it, but we should also think of it in terms of particular audiences and finely tuned responses to bring our expertise to bear in public service with policy makers. Jean-Pierre Morin (Indigenous and Northern Affairs Canada and Carleton University) has similarly advocated for how "we will need to learn how to produce the documents used by policy makers: the brief, the position paper, the policy report. We aren't speaking their language [yet], so it's time for us to start speaking theirs and showing them why history matters."[48]

TAKING THE PUBLIC TURN

In 2014, the American West Center invited noted historian Richard White to deliver the keynote address at their fiftieth anniversary symposium, "Western Lands, Western Voices: The American West Center at Fifty." In a room packed with western historians who were scheduled to present their work in the subsequent days of the symposium, White cogently articulated and advocated for public history. This came as a surprise to many in attendance.

Seven years prior, White, as the president of the Organization of American Historians, had offered a harsh critique of doing history in public in an opinion piece in the group's *OAH Newsletter*. He wrote, "I have begun to worry that public history and public intellectuals are in danger of becoming oxymorons." His piece attacked a "lazy" and "embarrassing" political rant, entitled "The Necessity of Public Intellectuals," that Todd Gitlin had recently penned for the Rutgers University journal *Raritan*.

Though not opposed to either the work of public intellectuals or even public history, White argued, "The best public interventions by scholars are when the stars align and a matter of urgent public interest corresponds to topics to which we have been giving considerable thought and research." "Though historians," he wrote, "have a responsibility to speak out no matter how unpopular our positions might be," we could become "too public," too hostage to the moment.[49]

Jack Holl, former Department of Energy historian during the Reagan Administration and a retired professor of history, emailed White after his article appeared and asked him how he really defined public history. Concerned that White had misunderstood the often-tenuous position of public historians, particularly those working in professional capacities for federal or state agencies, Holl asked him to clarify. For Holl, "To whom one speaks and how, in addition to the process, scale, and form, divides the ground between practicing professional historians and academics." Historians working inside the academy, he thought, had little common ground with those "practicing professionals" such as himself who had to adapt history to serve the needs of their employer.[50]

In answer, White wrote, "I consider public history the work done by those working for nonacademic institutions and addressed to either the general public or to the specific constituencies of those institutions. Second, I consider public history as all history aimed at either a general public audience (as distinct from academics), all history, no matter the intended audience, whose primary intent is to achieve a public purpose, and all history produced for the use of a public or private institution."[51]

Holl found White's description to be "generous, thoughtful, and revealing" but worried that the scholar believed "that the highest responsibility of all historians [was] 'to speak out no matter how unpopular our positions might be.'"[52] For Holl, there was a clear divide between public and popular history. "History without historians," he wrote, "is like biology without scientists, trials without lawyers, healing without physicians, and war without soldiers. All are possible, but from the point of view of a professional, they are disconcerting."[53] Public history to Holl was not popular history, and neither did it refer to public uses of history.

White's early definition of public history and Holl's response to his statements reflect the work these men chose to do as academically trained historians in public-facing settings. For White, it was applying his expertise in historical inquiry for the benefit of a particular nonacademic group; for Holl it was producing professional historical products to serve the needs of his employer. Both men oriented their public-facing work from the position of their academic expertise but eschewed the role of the public intellectual and feared the consequences of advocacy-driven public pronouncements.

Now, more than a decade removed from his essay on the danger of public historians becoming public intellectuals, White provided an even more refined definition of public history in his keynote speech. He differentiated public history on the basis of who gets to ask the driving questions, its collaborative nature, and the benefit historians can provide to communities, governance, and policy making. He declared public history to be sympathetic, engaging, sometimes entertaining, and an outright necessity. In fact, White alluded to public history as if it were a fundamental public service where emphasis is placed on "who asks the questions, rather than who gives the answers."[54]

White's revised definition of public history placed emphasis on its utility and contribution and expanded upon his earlier idea of intervention. This was a much more satisfying definition to the public historians in the room. As I listened to him speak, his explanation set off a buzz of ideas that caused me to reevaluate how I had been delineating the work of academics, public intellectuals, and professional historians from public history. Rather than draw boundaries between these different activities, I was more interested in stitching them together under one banner and taking a public turn in my work.

The public turn is doing public-facing history in the public sphere as a public service in ways that transcend the various definitions of public history and how academics operate. Producing history in public as a public intellectual can stimulate engaging and necessary conversations about difficult current events. Public historians largely interpret the past in ways that are designed to reach broader public audiences to shape the discourse about them. Applied history shapes frameworks of thought for public officials who have to grapple with these events. The core relationship between all three endeavors is centered on skilled expertise grounded in historical methodology, which always requires deep historical research and interpretation and an absolute commitment to the integrity of that process.

The public turn is a purposeful effort to put history to use in the wider world with both broad and targeted intent. Engagement in the public sphere, however, means risking criticism, overcoming the belief that history has a limited utility, and enduring the accusation that it is biased and dishonest if done for pay.[55] So I have three basic observations about how I have had to adjust as a historian employed in an academic position in order to take this public turn.

First, it takes an awful lot of trust to work with nonhistorians and do historical work. Regrettably, when historians produce books, articles, and essays, we often think of that work as noncollaborative. It most certainly is collaborative in terms of how these products come into being with the assistance of our peers through the review process and with the support of editors at the presses that publish them, but that is not the same as working with those in other disciplines or professions who may not share our understanding of history as a discipline that creates historical interpretations. Working with journalists, communities, policy makers, and governing bodies requires us to take a more macroscopic view of the past and relinquish some of the nuances. Sometimes historical interpretation is better when it is less complex.

The second observation is that there is no room for self-consciousness in this type of work. Hal K. Rothman (University of Nevada, Las Vegas), one of the more prolific scholars who took a public turn with his work, savored shooting smart, savvy analyses into the public sphere in the latter part of his career. Rothman initially launched his career as a historian working in public history, but with his academic appointment at UNLV soon began doing applied history as an expert witness and became one of the American West's most prominent public intellectuals. He was not at all self-conscious about his weekly column with the *Las Vegas Sun*. In one of his more memorable pieces on public lands management, he told Secretary of the Interior Gale Norton, "Stuff it, Madam Secretary." This was in response to her suggestion that the money generated from land sales under the Southern Nevada Public Land Management Act be used to pay off the national debt.[56] Nor did he fear criticism from either his peers in history or from public audiences. In fact, he welcomed the debates that his colorful language generated. Regardless of how we choose to engage, we ought at least to strive to do so unapologetically.

The final observation is that all of these activities take time. As an academic housed within a university, I ostensibly have time to engage in research. But when I engaged in these activities, it was within the context of a regional comprehensive university, as opposed to a research institution, and it is debatable how much time I actually got to produce scholarship. Even at a research institution, there is not enough time. In addition, most tenure and promotion guidelines in university history departments do not consider working with journalists, speaking to governors, or writing blog posts to be anything but peripheral activities. I have published a peer-reviewed book and several articles and essays, the important elements for tenure and promotion within a university context. Sometimes these activities can be packaged under a category entitled service and sometimes engagement, but I think those labels do a disservice to what is actually accomplished. Rather, there should be a category for public-facing scholarship and collaborative, interdisciplinary engagement.[57]

This is what taking the public turn entails. It is a commitment of time and energy to deploying engaged, impactful historical scholarship into the public sphere so it can be utilized by nonhistorians and sit in dialogue with experts in other areas. It is a feedback loop that propels a scholar from being a public intellectual to working as a public historian to doing applied history in service of addressing current issues and public needs. These elements will come about differently for each of us. What is most important is that we engage in them. History has a vast and prolific utility in the public sphere, and it is time we put it to work.

CHAPTER 3

Rothman's West

The Education of a Western Public Intellectual

MICHAEL CHILDERS

"I always cringe when people from the rural West tell the rest of us how to live. There's an arrogance to their pronouncements, a foolhardy pretension that they are real and that the ninety-five percent of us who live in Western cities somehow don't matter," growled Hal Rothman in a short editorial for *High Country News.* Continuing, "The truth is hard but clear. The rural West has become a playground, a colony the rest of us visit when we want to relax or indulge our fantasies."[1] It was classic Rothman. Provocative, defiant, and unapologetically opinionated, especially when it came to the West. He lived for the combat of ideas, telling both colleagues and students that he preferred to run through things rather than dance around them. A prolific writer, Rothman's numerous books, articles, and essays drove straight at the reader, challenging them to engage, to argue, and to think. As a professor of history at the University of Nevada, Las Vegas, he loved the moments of enlightenment in the survey and the push and pull of the seminar room.

Yet, it was in the public arena where Rothman flourished as both a historian and public intellectual. Never shy with an opinion, he strongly believed scholars held a much greater obligation in shaping public understanding and discourse than simply penning academic books and articles. He was an example of what a public intellectual could become by promoting a deeper understanding of place, helping bring the past to bear on the present, and, most importantly, inspiring and fostering the next generation. Rothman explained in a 2002 interview, "If we do not engage the public on its own terms—if we do not create the ears with which to hear us—then we abdicate an important part of our obligation as scholars."[2] It was an obligation Rothman took seriously. Whether in one of his newspaper columns, on his radio show, as a talking head in a documentary, or in a television appearance, he always showed the same enthusiasm that shaped his scholarly work. Often, it was difficult to tell the difference between the two.

To Rothman, the modern West was a paradox between old and new. It was the country's most densely urban region but also home to the majority of its public lands. The West's urban dynamism was what now drove the region's economic motor, he argued. The romance of cowboys on the open range, small towns, and high-paying, extractive-industry jobs were little more than illusions of the past. "Service and leisure have mostly replaced extraction and herds, cities dominate, and people wearing cowboy hats sit in traffic in SUVs, with glorious sunsets behind the nearby mountains that most never visit," he wrote in the *Denver Post* in 2006.[3] It was an opinion born out of nearly two decades of tireless thinking and writing on the region's national parks and monuments, tourism, and most particularly his adoptive hometown of Las Vegas.

Throughout his career, Rothman wrote on everything from environmental politics to cities of the future. He reminded us that tourism matters in understanding the American West and that national parks and monuments have always been something more than mere symbols of conservation.[4] He emphasized the importance of cities in a region often defined by its rural spaces. "He changed the way we thought about things we thought we knew about: tourism, urban development, the power of the West as a cultural motif in American history," recalled Char Miller, Rothman's longtime friend and collaborator.[5] But most significantly Rothman reminded us of the importance of community and our shared responsibility in joining in public discourse on the West's future.

Rothman embraced public history less by design than by need. After graduating from the University of Texas, Austin, where he worked with Alfred Crosby, Rothman struggled to find a university post and so took a job with a private research firm. But the company's shaky financials caused it to shutter rather quickly, forcing Rothman to look for a new way to make ends meet. With a dissertation on national monuments and experience as a contract writer, he knocked on Melody Webb's door at the National Park Service's Southwest Regional Office in Santa Fe. As Regional Historian, Webb was swamped with projects but no staff to complete them. Seeing potential in the energetic but inexperienced historian, she hired Rothman to write an administrative history of nearby Bandelier National

Monument. After moving his young family, Rothman dove into the project with his usual zeal. Webb read numerous drafts, patiently molding both the history as well as the young historian. "It was a wonderful experience and made me even more of a devotee of the National Parks," Rothman later said of his work on Bandelier. And the parks would remain at the center of his life's work.[6]

The National Parks were a relatively overlooked topic by historians at the time. What scholarship did exist was either outdated or romanticized. Seeing an opportunity, Rothman hung out his shingle and began bidding on national park administrative histories and historic resource studies. It proved to be a rather timely decision. Few academically trained historians considered contract work a viable career choice, a view Rothman somewhat shared. But as the next two decades would prove, such work could be both compelling and highly lucrative. Working with fellow historians Don Holder and David Sproul, as well as an army of graduate students, Hal K. Rothman and Associates produced numerous administrative histories, historical resource studies, and other gray-literature projects for the National Park Service. These included administrative histories of Navajo National Monument, Pipestone National Monument, Fort Scott National Historic Site, Golden Gate National Recreation Area, and Death Valley National Park.[7]

But while such contract work paid the bills, Rothman continued to desire an academic post. Dismayed over his initial failure to secure a university position, he eventually landed a tenure-track job teaching public history at Wichita State University. It was an odd fit. Rothman never truly considered himself a public historian, and the department held just the most general ideas of what public history was. In truth, few university history departments understood, or even fully supported, public history, somehow believing it to be less rigorous. Rothman's hire as a public historian was one of many by history departments across the country seeking to train historians for jobs outside the academy.

Within a few years of moving to Kansas, Rothman published his first book. Based upon his dissertation, *Preserving Different Pasts: The American National Monuments* chronicled their early history.[8] Reviewers praised Rothman's tackling of the overlooked topic, offering only slight criticism of his "penchant for zealous overstatement" and lack of a clear thematic argument.[9] While taking the criticism of a need for a clearer theme to heart, Rothman never truly gave up his penchant for hyperbolic prose. Published that same year in the *Western Historical Quarterly*,

"'A Regular Ding-Dong Fight': Agency Culture and Evolution in the NPS-USFS Dispute, 1916–1937" fully cemented his standing as an academic historian.[10]

But it was his second book that provided the foundation upon which he would build the rest of his career. Published in 1992, *On Rims and Ridges: The Los Alamos Area since 1880* traced the history of the Pajarito Plateau in New Mexico. Based upon his *Bandelier National Monument Administrative History*, the book was both prototype for converting contract histories into scholarly works and exemplar of an important shift within environmental history. Building upon Crosby's *Ecological Imperialism,* Rothman argued the plateau's transformation from a cultural and economic backwater to the home of a national monument and the Los Alamos National Laboratory "meant significant changes in the way people utilized the land, the way they perceived it and its importance, and in the character of the land itself."[11]

With *On Rims and Ridges*, Rothman joined a small but growing cadre of historians redefining the field of environmental history. While historians such as Crosby, John Opie, Donald Hughes, Susan Flader, and Roderick Nash had delved into environmental topics, few described themselves exclusively as environmental historians. Robert Righter noted as much when he warned Rothman as a graduate student that no one found work as an environmental historian; instead, you had to sneak it into whatever you got hired to teach. Yet, environmental history had a dedicated number of practitioners, a journal, a biannual meeting, and a small academic association.[12]

Established in 1977, the American Society for Environmental History, or ASEH, sought to solidify the nascent field's legitimacy. "I think some people thought of it as a kind of joke, or a phenomena [*sic*] of the '60s, as well . . . and not a legitimate field. And one of our agendas was certainly to establish credibility," explained John Opie, one of the association's founders. To that end, the newly formed association launched its first academic journal, *Environmental Review*, in 1976. Meant to be interdisciplinary, the quarterly published articles by historians, geographers, scientists, and even poets. Slowly, membership grew, allowing the ASEH to hold its first conference in 1982 on the campus of the University of California, Irvine. "Irvine was a real turning point for us," Opie later said, "because it was clearly identified as an environmental history meeting, and only an environmental history meeting, at that point." Nearly two hundred people attended the conference, surprising even Opie, who later joked, "We didn't realize that there were that many environmental historians out there."[13]

Despite such interest, the association struggled to find its way over the next decade. Interest did not necessarily translate into membership dues. Reliant on subscriptions, *Environmental Review* rarely operated in the black. Yet, by the end of the 1980s, the journal's financial woes began to ease. Serving his second stint as editor, Opie asked Rothman to stand in for him as interim editor while Opie went on sabbatical. The temporary position would last a decade. "If I'd knocked over a liquor store that day instead of accepting John's offer," Rothman later joshed, "I'd have been out on parole long before now."[14] Nevertheless, Rothman's taking over the editor's chair marked a generational shift.

Determined to reshape the field, Rothman flattered, cajoled, and simply conscripted works from historians he believed could help break the field free of its advocacy roots. Char Miller was among those whom Rothman first targeted. A cultural intellectual historian teaching at Trinity College in San Antonio, Miller attended his first ASEH meeting in Houston in 1991. Spotting Miller across the room, Rothman bulled his way over, thrust his hand out, and declared, "You must be Char Miller." Stunned, Miller smiled, nodded, and replied that he was indeed. Rothman insisted Miller revise and resubmit his article on Gifford Pinchot, which Miller had submitted years prior and had simply left unrevised after review. "What was amazing was that he had had the pragmatism to go back through all of the submitted articles," Miller remarked of the encounter with Rothman. Following Rothman's advice, Miller quickly revised and resubmitted the article, and Rothman published "The Greening of Gifford Pinchot" the following year.[15]

Miller's experience was far from unique. Rothman solicited articles from historians such as Robert Gottlieb, Dan Flores, and many others based simply upon discussing their work in person. "It reflected Hal's interest in several new strands of environmental history that were just then coming together in articles and books," said Gottlieb of Rothman's transformative role as editor.[16] Flores's "Place: An Argument for Bioregional History" came from conversations between Rothman and Flores over the concept of bioregionalism and its applicability to environmental history. "Hal and I had both already written bioregional books, and there were others in print," Flores said, "So the idea was floating around but without any codified articulation."[17] Such articles embodied a broader shift within environmental history.[18]

Subscriptions grew steadily during Rothman's tenure. Finances, however, remained unsteady, constantly threatening the journal's ability to publish. A solution to the money problems presented itself in 1995. For years, Forest History Society President Harold "Pete" Steen had wanted to replace the society's *Journal of Forest History* with a more scholarly journal. Published since 1957, the journal was an in-house publication. While it had a loyal readership, Steen believed it too insular. Seeing an opportunity, he reached out to ASEH President Susan Flader with the idea of merging *Environmental History Review* with the *Journal of Forest and Conservation* to create *Environmental History*. Such an arrangement would provide the FHS with a more scholarly journal and the ASEH with solid financial grounding.

Rothman remained as editor of the new journal, steering it through a tumultuous first year. Long-time *Journal of Forest and Conservation* subscribers complained the new journal ranged too far from forestry, and a handful of university libraries tossed the journal's first issue into the trash, not understanding that it replaced the older Forest History Society publication. A budget shortfall added to the chaos, but by its second year, *Environmental History* was on solid financial as well as scholarly ground.[19]

The first issue included William Cronon's seminal essay "The Trouble with Wilderness: Or, Getting Back to the Wrong Nature," with responses by Tom Dunlap, Samuel Hays, and Michael Cohen. It proved a lively debate, reflecting the current tension within the field over method and approach. Cronon's central argument that wilderness, and by extension nature, was no more than a cultural construction rankled the three historians. Hays called Cronon's deconstruction of wilderness "well off the mark," attacking for its disregard of work done by wilderness devotees. Cohen took a more diplomatic approach, noting Cronon's essay discussed human perceptions of place rather than concrete places. Dunlap accepted Cronon's argument, though admitted that he was unsure where it would take a field so long grounded in environmental activism.[20]

"We could not advance as a field until we differentiated scholarship and advocacy," Rothman explained of the seismic shift occurring within environmental history. The new journal's publication of Cronon's "The Trouble with Wilderness" marked an unmooring of the field from what Rothman termed the "tragedy school" of environmental history. Epitomized by Roderick Nash's 1967 classic *Wilderness in the American Mind* and Donald Worster's *Nature's Economy: A History of Ecological Ideas* (1977), the "tragic school" often focused on declensionist narratives of disastrous human interactions with the physical world. Such works left the field open to criticisms of self-righteousness and ignoring issues of race, class, and gender. By building upon postmodernist themes of cultural construction, environmental historians sought to move beyond such a narrow focus within the work, a shift Rothman fully embraced as editor.

Articles on borderlands, Native Americans, and global topics added to the field's breadth. In the journal's third issue, American colonial historian Alan Taylor described the mutual relationship between environmental and social history. He wrote, "By reading that landscape historically, we can see the unfolding of American society with its manifold divisions."[21] Taylor was correct in pointing to environmental history's possibilities in adding greater depth and understanding to all periods, a fact not lost on a number of historians.

"Environmental history's promise has always been a redefinition of the boundaries of the discipline of history," Rothman noted in his farewell essay as editor in 1992. Environmental historians are not advocates of the environment, he argued, but rather advocates of including the environment in the story of human evolution on the planet.[22] While not everyone agreed with his vision of the field, they could not question his influence in transforming environmental history from a minor subfield to one of the most dynamic approaches to history. By the time Rothman stepped down as editor, *Environmental History* had become the third most frequently cited journal of history, surpassed only by the *Journal of American History* and *Pacific Historical Review*.[23]

Rothman warned, however, that despite such successes environmental historians should not become complacent. The lure of orthodoxy remained a constant threat to the field's vitality. "As other historical fields have shown, an orthodoxy, even when it is revisionist, stagnates a field, stifles its creativity, and makes it puerile," he wrote.[24]

As environmental history was undergoing a generational sea change, so too was Western history. Seeking to tell a "longer, grimmer, but more interesting story," a growing number of historians began publicly calling out the field's narrow focus on the frontier.[25] Works such as Patricia Nelson Limerick's *Legacy of Conquest: The Unbroken Past of the American West* and Richard White's *"It's Your Misfortune and None of My Own": A New History of the American West* challenged what they believed to be the field's devotion to Frederick Jackson Turner's 1893 frontier thesis, which, in part, argued American identity grew out of the nation's frontiering experience.[26] Branded as the New Western Historians, younger scholars attacked what they saw as the field's uncritical eye toward issues of race and gender and a failure to move beyond the "closure" of the continental frontier in the late nineteenth century.[27]

Critics railed against what they believed to be the new scholarship's overtly negative view of American History, often in a tactless manner. Renowned Western historian and Holocaust survivor Gerald D. Nash decried the New Western emphasis on race as reminiscent of Nazism and criticisms of capitalism as suggestive of Stalinist totalitarianism. Fellow historian William Savage joined Nash in condemning what he saw as the younger generation's self-absorption, calling New Western Historians self-promoting "whores to fashion."[28]

Such heated language quickly attracted the attention of the national media. Newspapers including the *Los Angeles Times*, *Arizona Republic*, and *Denver Post* cast the academic debate as yet another example of revisionist university professors destroying a treasured American fable. Western novelist Larry McMurtry joined in, writing a scathing denouncement of New Western History in the *New Republic*. He called the new scholarship "Failure Studies" conducted by Yale-trained historians, a point he no doubt took from Nash's linking of the university's graduate programs with fascism. But what most offended the Pulitzer Prize-winning author was the New Western Historians' rejection of the romantic West, a West where his father and brothers were playing out their calling as cattlemen, not as part of some faceless industry. "From Zebulon Pike to Louis L'Amour, no Westerner has wanted to think that the West of imagination was lost," McMurtry argued, concluding, "For if that West is lost, then it's all just jobs."[29]

That the acrimonious debate over the nuances of academic historiography captured the public's attention spoke to a broader anxiety gripping the region. Western cities and counties ranked as the fastest growing in the nation. This rampant growth was erasing the West's open space and replacing it with strip malls, office parks, and subdivisions. Political crises over traditional sources of friction—such as water, access to public lands, and transportation—took on a new intensity as millions migrated to the region's suburban fringes. As real estate costs rose, so too did the animosity between long-time residents and newcomers. Underscoring this clash of cultures, the question of who owned the West played out on the opinion pages of local and regional newspapers. Even *Time* joined the fray, chronicling how "Range Rover-driving yuppies" were replacing cowboys and lumberjacks throughout the Intermountain West. The same was true across the eleven Western states, where the historical promise of a better life met a new economy based on technology and the service industry.[30]

Having chronicled such struggles in his work on New Mexico's Pajarito Plateau, and recently moved to Las Vegas, Rothman took a keen interest in the region's transformation, making it the center of his work for the next two decades. "Hal was just like a dream come true," Limerick recollected on the importance of Rothman's work in highlighting the significance of the twentieth-century American West.[31] He found little use in the emotionally charged debate over western history, however, calling it both silly and missing a more important truth about the region. The West's history was not about "process" or "place," Rothman argued, but rather about its transformation into the nation's most dynamic and metropolitan region.

From Santa Fe to Seattle, Rothman understood that most westerners now lived in suburbs, not rural ranching communities. This signified an important reality overlooked by many historians. The New West, he believed, was the point when the service and leisure industry supplanted resource extraction as the region's primary economic and cultural motor. This made places such as Olympic National Park, which had been built atop an established extractive economy, critical in understanding the West's changing economic and cultural landscapes, where service-industry jobs were rapidly replacing timber, ranching, and mining. Yet, Rothman's West remained reliant on the romantic vision that it was, in the words of William Kittredge, the last best place, where wide-open vistas offered the promise of opportunity. Nowhere was this more apparent than in Las Vegas.[32]

The fastest-growing city in the fastest-growing state in the fastest-growing region of the country, Las Vegas resembled what writer Mike Davis would later call "a hyperbolic Los Angeles, the land of sunshine on fast forward."[33] In this manner, Rothman's move there was a sort of homecoming. He exuded the city's frenetic energy and drive. "Las Vegas and Hal Rothman were a marriage made in heaven," his colleague Andy Kirk told the *Los Angeles Times*. "He was this brash prodigy with incredible energy who wasn't afraid to express his ideas. . . . He was a great spokesman for the city. He embraced it and made it his own."[34] In Vegas, Rothman saw the forces reshaping the American West in high relief. Chiefly, it was the supplanting of the region's extractive industries by the service and leisure industry. In this manner, he argued, Las Vegas held the key to the region's future.

Throughout the 1990s, the Las Vegas skyline changed daily. The city held no qualms about destroying its architectural past.[35] Older casinos were leveled to make way for newer resorts. The opening of the Mirage in 1989 began a land rush that quickly overran Las Vegas Boulevard. Within a decade, seven new resort casinos arose along the famous Strip. Sprawling over hundreds of acres, new resorts such as the Excalibur, the Luxor, and New York, New York offered more than craps tables and slot machines. Caesar's massive Forum Shops mall included high-end boutiques, restaurants, and an animatronic fountain that performed the fall of the mythical city of Atlantis every hour on the hour. Treasure Island's mock sea battle Buccaneer Bay drew crowds of pedestrians, while audiences packed the resort's massive theater to watch Cirque du Soleil's newest show, *Mystère*, every night. Swimming pools, nightclubs, restaurants, and shopping malls all added to Las Vegas's allure, helping draw millions of visitors annually.

As throngs of tourists flocked to watch the Bellagio's fountains, visit the Forum Shops at Caesars Palace, and sunbathe beside Mandalay Bay's pool, many people were also relocating to Las Vegas. Drawn by low taxes, cheap real estate, and good-paying service jobs, millions moved to the communities of Henderson, Spring Valley, and Summerlin. By the end of the century, subdivisions sprawled across the valley floor, creating a vast metropolitan expanse. Outsiders viewed Las Vegas's mercurial growth with unease, calling the booming city "sinful" and based on a "vulture economy."[36] But such criticisms failed to halt Las Vegas's draw.

Like its city, the University of Nevada, Las Vegas, Rothman's new academic home, was also undergoing its own resurgence. The university's beloved Runnin' Rebels men's basketball team national title run in 1990, and subsequent undefeated season—losing only to Duke in the NCAA Championship game—garnered UNLV national attention. Increased donations, primarily from local casino and real estate magnates, financed a campus building boom. Enrollment soared, surpassing upstate rival University of Nevada, Reno, by several thousand. While northern Nevada continued to view the Reno campus as the center of the state's higher education system, there was no denying UNLV's rising prominence.[37]

It is rare for a work of academic history to reach a popular audience. Yet Rothman's third book *Devil's Bargains: Tourism in the Twentieth-Century American West* did just that. His simple-yet-poignant argument—that despite its promises tourism often failed to meet the expectations of those western communities that embraced it to solve their economic woes—put into shape a sentiment that had been floating around rather loosely for years. Calling tourism the most colonial of colonial economies, *Devil's Bargains* sought to shift the conversation away from the West's well-worn narratives of extraction by placing the region at the center of the twentieth century's postindustrial revolution. "The embrace of tourism triggers a contest for the soul of a place," Rothman wrote on tourism's economic and cultural power.[38] From Yellowstone and the Grand Canyon to Aspen and Las Vegas, he pointed out tourism's inescapable transformative influence on the region, arguing that tourism was the marker of the modern West.

The first overarching study on tourism in the American West since Earl Pomeroy's 1957 *In Search of the Golden West*, *Devil's Bargains* marked the beginning of a wave of new works on tourism's historical importance. Historians John Sears, Cindy Aron, and Marguerite Shaffer had each helped frame tourism as an integral part of the national experience. Tourism quickly grew into an important topic of study, particularly for historians of the American West. Historian David Wrobel and sociologist Patrick Long's anthology, *Seeing and Being Seen: Tourism in the American West*, joined *Devil's Bargains* in seeking to understand tourism's effects on both tourists and the western places they visit. Geographers William Riebsame and James Robb's *Atlas of the New West: Portrait of a Changing Region* pointed to tourism's role in defining the New West. A new generation of scholars including Annie Gilbert-Coleman, Connie Chiang, Lawrence Culver, and William Philpott soon followed in adding their own examinations of tourism.[39]

Devil's Bargains also struck a chord in western communities experiencing the very shifts Rothman described. Journalists, city planners, and scores of others used Rothman's thesis in framing their communities' struggles with growth and changing social and political landscapes. "Who truly profits from growth in a mountain resort community?" asked Harry Williamson, editor of the *Winter Park Manifest*, after reading *Devil's Bargains*. The weekly newspaper for Colorado's Fraser Valley, home to Winter Park Resort, which had just been purchased by corporate giant Intrawest, the *Manifest* chronicled daily the very transformations Rothman described. True, tax revenues were up, property values were skyrocketing, and business was booming, Williamson noted, but housing remained scarce, which made it nearly impossible to find employees. And while you could sell your house or condominium for far more than you bought it, you could never replace it if you wished to stay in the valley. "Are locals happier, more relaxed, working less, more satisfied with their lot in life in the Fraser Valley? If so, who are you talking to? I would like to talk to them," wrote Williamson on Rothman's clear analysis of tourism's cost to rural communities.[40]

Nevertheless, *Devil's Bargains* was not without its faults, a fact Rothman readily admitted. Most reviewers noted Rothman's overall negative tone toward tourism. Many observed that the book's heavy focus on skiing and gaming provided a limited view of tourism's broader history throughout the region. Others noted Rothman either failed to mention or spent little time discussing large swaths of the West, particularly California, the Pacific Northwest, and the Great Plains.[41]

Furthermore, his focus on destination tourism ignored the impacts of day-use tourism in areas adjacent to the region's burgeoning metropolitan areas. Rothman agreed with such critiques, and, in typical fashion, sought to address the latter two in his book *The New Urban Park: Golden Gate National Recreation Area and Civic Environmentalism*. Arguably his most comprehensive study, Rothman combined his work in environmental, national park, and tourism history in telling the story of one of the nation's most complex and compelling national recreation areas. In it, he argued that unlike Yellowstone or Yosemite, Golden Gate was at once a historical, recreational, and natural park, making it the model for national parks of the twenty-first century.[42]

Perhaps most importantly, *Devil's Bargains* marked Rothman's evolution as a writer. While the majority of the text was densely academic, he took on a more journalistic voice in the book's preface by placing himself into the center of the story. Opening with his family joining the hordes of tourists flocking Maui's Lahaina Harbor to witness the annual humpback whale migration, Rothman described how own his experience had reinforced his identity as a tourist. Written after he had completed the manuscript, "Maui Redux" marked Rothman's transition from academic historian to public intellectual and his embrace of a popular voice in his writing.[43]

His next two books further reflected this shift. Coedited with fellow writer and historian Mike Davis, *The Grit Beneath the Glitter: Tales from the Real Las Vegas* offered a wide portrayal of life in the city. Contributors included historians and journalists, sociologists and union members, and locals. Aimed at a general audience, the anthology sought to move beyond the Sin City narrative to ask how residents of the fastest-growing city in the United States felt about their home. Rothman's contributions included his essay "Colony, Capital, and Casino," which denounced the colonization of Las Vegas and by extension Nevada. "The most basic reality of Nevada is that the state is a colony," he wrote, "a point driven home by a trip to Hoover Dam, where vehicles inscribed with the insignia of the Los Angeles Municipal Utility District sport Nevada license plates."[44]

Rothman spent the next five years thinking, writing, and talking about Las Vegas, railing against both outside and local forces that kept his beloved hometown from earning the respect it deserved. But it was in *Neon Metropolis: How Las Vegas Started the Twenty-First Century* that Rothman firmly established himself as a public intellectual. Las Vegas epitomized the new American Dream, he wrote, a postmodern city built upon the promise of consumerism and entertainment, nestled in a desert valley where critics wrongfully argued no city should exist. A hard city, it offered a place for many to reinvent themselves, he argued, where low-skill union jobs could still offer a comfortable middle-class lifestyle and libertarian views of government meant you could be and do whatever you wanted; you just had to take the opportunities presented. As in "Maui Redux," Rothman placed himself at the center of *Neon Metropolis*, acting as tour guide and critic to readers in an often-lively romp around the city. From cruising the Strip to passing through the growing suburbs sprouting up across the Las Vegas Valley, he drove home the argument that here, in this hot and isolated place, was the future.

By the time he began writing *Neon Metropolis,* Rothman had become a media darling. His gap-toothed smile and machine gun quotes made him the go-to for a quick statement or in-depth interview on everything Las Vegas. "The media calls a lot these days, mostly on short notice," he quipped in *Neon Metropolis*.[45] Rothman's prolific and often brash views on Las Vegas and the West landed him appearances on television and radio, and in daily newspapers and national magazines. He became Las Vegas's defender, explaining to viewers and readers, as he told CNN in 2002, "Las Vegas isn't really about gambling anymore. It's about entertainment. And gambling is probably the entree on that menu. But there are many, many appetizers and many side dishes and many deserts."[46] He carried his argument that the region's future lay with Las Vegas onto the pages of *High Country News*, the *Los Angeles Times*, and the *Las Vegas Mercury*. "Rothman always nurtured hope for Las Vegas," remembered William deBuys, "He hoped, in fact, that as a critic and commentator he might nudge the city toward a future that was healthier in all dimensions, more just and vigorous, better."[47]

In the summer of 2005, Rothman began writing a weekly column for the *Las Vegas Sun.* Covering a wide range of topics, including immigration, retirees, right-wing militias, water, and nuclear waste, he sought to enrich public debate at a time when discourse was stunningly shallow. Each column focused in some manner on issues of community, the environment, or Las Vegas's place in the wider American culture. They reflected Rothman's understandings of history's importance in the much larger conversation over the future of Las Vegas, the American West, and the nation. "History has a tremendous significance in the postmodern world. The problem with journalists is that they operate in a vacuum. They have no knowledge of or appreciation for context. That's what historians bring to the table."[48]

As aggressive and prolific a writer and thinker as he was, Rothman treasured working with others, especially those beginning their careers. In reality, this was Rothman's true legacy as a public scholar. In the closing of *Devil's Bargains*, Rothman notes, "Despite my efforts here, most of the great monographs about tourism in the American West remain to be written." He hoped that the book offered a road map that younger scholars would, in the best scholarly tradition, soon discard for their own.[49] Whether encouraging them to submit an article to *Environmental History* or offering them a contract to write their first administrative history, Rothman believed deeply in fostering work that he saw as reimagining the field. "He took me seriously and showed real interest in what I had to say as a graduate student," recalled William Philpott, whom Rothman had sought out to comment on his early drafts of *Devil's Bargains*.[50]

Many of Rothman's students found themselves working on, if not directing, one of his dozens of contract projects. "Hal was conscious of the limitations of academic history," said David Sproul, "that we need another kind of training that was not purely academic history." Just a year after starting his PhD work, Sproul found himself as the lead researcher and writer for the Rainbow Bridge Administrative history. It was quite a lift for a rather inexperienced historian. "I had no idea what I was getting into, but it was classic Hal—sink or swim," he noted. Initially, Sproul did more sinking than swimming, but after begging a reprieve to conduct further research he completed the manuscript. "It exposed me to a whole world of the profession that had nothing to do with the academy," he said. Currently Historian and Cultural Resource Manager for the Department of the Navy in San Diego, Sproul spends much of his time researching and writing historical compliance reports. It is important work—work that is reliant on solid research, deep historical analysis, and sharp writing. Reflecting on what lesson he took to heart from Rothman, Sproul stated, "Hal always pressed that history should always answer the question, So what? Does it answer the mail?"[51]

It is an important question, one that sat at the center of Rothman's final graduate seminar in which he laid out what he hoped would be the future of the profession. Calling the debate that had so captivated Western history in the 1990s "archaic and silly," he argued that the field was moving rapidly into far more interesting territory. "As you'll see, much of the reading here is decidedly NOT about the American West. If this seems perverse, it truly is," he wrote in the syllabus. Rather, he offered a list of books that he believed would stimulate students' imaginations about the region and its issues. Among the eighteen assigned books were works on the movie industry, marketing, Indian gaming, and immigration. Rothman preached that we should be forward-looking and should use history to explain the world in which we find ourselves.[52]

As always, he remained energetic and combative, demanding that students challenge his assertions, reject them if necessary, but be prepared to defend their own assertions. It was a challenge few initially took on, often looking on in horror as Rothman's longtime graduate assistant unashamedly called out his advisor on his interpretation of a point, only to have Rothman press back. Soon, the seminar took on Rothman's personality, students verbally jousting over how immigration, commercialization, race, and the environment were reshaping the American West. "My favorite has always been interaction in the classroom," Rothman later said, reflecting on his career in the classroom. "I was never one of those guys for whom students had to repeat what I said to do well. My thing always was, 'Agreeing with me and $3.11 gets you Starbucks. Disagreeing with me with a cogent argument earned you my respect.'"[53] If Rothman held a central philosophy, this was it. He lived for the combat of ideas, and wholeheartedly believed that history was a perfect medium for understanding how to view the world.

In the summer of 2005, Rothman noticed a twinge in his forearm while visiting Israel to work with a group of scholars on the country's first environmental history. Later completed by Char Miller, *Between Ruin and Restoration: An Environmental History of Israel* continued Rothman's frontward approach to history.[54] He understood that environmental history needed to expand beyond North American topics and become more global—a view that has come to fruition in the past decade. After returning from the Middle East, with a brief family vacation in Paris, the twinge became more pronounced. Relenting to a friend's insistence that he see a neurologist, Rothman was diagnosed with ALS, more commonly known as Lou Gehrig's Disease. The malady slowly erodes motor function, leading to difficulties in walking, speaking, and eventually breathing. Rothman met the news much as he had met life—head-on.

With a graduate student acting as his hands, he continued to write his columns and even produced three more books before passing away in his Henderson home. "Truthfully, I got forty-seven perfect years," he said in one of his final interviews. "Everything broke my way. That's a hell of a lot more than most people get."[55] His death shook the history profession. Obituaries recalled his boundless energy, sharp mind, and combative nature. Speaking from the floor of the U.S. Senate, Nevada Senator Harry Reid said this of Rothman, "Hal was an outstanding ambassador for Las Vegas and to a larger extent Nevada. He was our front man. He was our image. He was our voice to the world. Nevada has lost one of its favorite sons, and Hal will be forever remembered as a tireless advocate for Las Vegas."[56]

Asked what his legacy should be after his decade-long tenure as editor of *Environmental History*, Rothman replied, "It is hard to think about legacy, but near as I can tell, my legacy has been to take the field from the founding generation to the successor generation." That, he explained, was what inspired him to foster the work of younger scholars. "I like to think that I had a better appreciation of what they were trying to do than most."[57] Rothman's legacy is more than as an advocate of the city he called home. And his belief that the past has a purpose and we have an obligation to the next generation continues to resonate.

CHAPTER 4

Mythic Spaces, Real Places

Thoughts on Administrative History in the Western National Parks

LEIGHTON M. QUARLES

This chapter considers National Park Service administrative history through the lens of Western history. It is my assertion that at its heart the national park system is quintessentially Western, statistics notwithstanding. Thus, it is important to explore the interplay between myth and history in the park system, zeroing in on administrative history as an essential tool for park management. Examples from my own administrative history project at Zion National Park serve throughout to illustrate broader points. The chapter concludes with a look at the turbulent present that national parks in the West occupy and reiterates the importance of administrative history to management and understanding.

America's national parks claim a significant space in the national geography and imagination. Park units cover 84 million acres, 85,000 miles of rivers and streams, 43,000 miles of shoreline, 12,000 miles of trails, and 8,000 miles of roads. They also encompass 68,000 archeological sites, 27,000 historic structures and 150 million museum objects.[1] When one looks at a map, national park units in the East cluster near population centers and encompass tremendous diversity, from Civil War and other battlefields to marine monuments divorced entirely from land to urban historic preservation and interpretation projects. Park *units* may concentrate in the East, but the sheer volume of NPS acreage lies in the West, particularly if one includes Alaska.[2]

And so does its image. The National Parks are, for good or for ill, peculiarly Western in the national—and international—imagination as well as in their geography. Yellowstone, Yosemite, and the Grand Canyon are international icons, mythic symbols with tremendous power to represent and simplify not only arresting monumental landscapes but American history and the nature of American society.[3] The manifesto for the 1984 conference "Parks in the West," called at the behest of the National Park Service, asserts that "the values represented in the establishment of parks in the West have an importance to all citizens of this country, and to much of the world."[4] Visiting the famous Western parks can have overtones of religious pilgrimage, even to self-conscious recollectors. Writer and conservationist David Harmon names the defining event of his Ohio boyhood as a vacation when his family "lit out for the mythic spaces of the West," and he found a transcendent moment on the North Rim of the Grand Canyon.[5] Such is the power and perceived importance parks hold in the national imagination.

Western parks are also caught in the middle of, and sometimes central to, problems as old as the "winning of the West," as in the case of Grand Staircase-Escalante National Monument and its newly created sibling Bears Ears National Monument. Conflict over control of public lands, attempted erasure of Native American habitation and territorial claims, and concerns with water, range, fire, and wildlife management all make Western parks particularly visible components of what Patricia Limerick calls the "legacy of conquest." These legacies of conquest range from conflicts over treaty rights to hunt Yellowstone buffalo to interpreting history at the Whitman Mission National Historic Site, a park unit expressly devoted to commemorating American colonial expansion.[6] Moreover, the growth of the environmental movement throughout the twentieth century has always been closely tied to the parks, with an accompanying rise in complexity of management and fraught relations with local and state governments and individuals. As such, Western parks require particularly careful interpretation and management. Such care in turn calls for an attention to the importance and production of administrative history.

HISTORY IN THE PARKS

"The origins of the NPS," historian Ari Kelman reminds us, "lie in Progressive Era conflicts over the future of the West's wild places."[7] The NPS's now-famous dual mandate exhorts the Service to

> promote and regulate the use of the Federal areas known as national parks, monuments, and reservations hereinafter specified by such

> means and measures as conform to the fundamental purpose of the said parks, monuments, and reservations, which purpose is to conserve the scenery and the natural and historic objects and the wild life therein and to provide for the enjoyment of the same in such manner and by such means as will leave them unimpaired for the enjoyment of future generations.[8]

Promotion and regulation. Preservation and access. The Park Service's founding mandate is broad, and the agency's focus has long since widened to encompass battlefield stewardship, development of recreation areas, and historic preservation of the built environment as much as or even more than conservation of the great outdoors, as the numbers in this chapter's introduction demonstrate.

The NPS has a daunting historical mission, and a two-pronged one: to ground itself and its units in place and time, and to interpret that place and time to an ever-increasing number of visitors from around the world. The Park Service has a tremendous interpretive program, itself made up of hundreds of subprograms at units around the country. While interpretation at national park sites occasionally leaves something to be desired, it is usually good, sometimes great. But it is hardly produced in a vacuum. The Park Service has long-running ties to the academy, and not just in the natural sciences.[9] NPS retired chief historian Robert M. Utley has been a regular collaborator with academic historians for over fifty years and was a founding member of the Western History Association.[10]

Partly due to funding concerns, regularly cited as a significant reason for NPS's perceived failures regarding its handling of history, individual parks and regional offices may not maintain such close ties with the academy. But those same funding and personnel shortfalls have for decades prompted NPS administrators to turn to contractors, often academically trained or, as in the case of arrangements made through the Cooperative Ecosystems Studies Units (CESUs), university employees to handle historic site reports, resource studies, administrative histories, and many other gray-literature projects. Thus, NPS units are rarely without an outside perspective on the production of history, whether for internal or public consumption.[11]

Interpretation is part and parcel of the national park idea. It is the outward-looking process of educating the public and promoting its appreciation for parks—in essence, fostering "the benefit and enjoyment of the people."[12] Bookstore materials, ranger-led programs, summer camps, informative signs, and all the panoply of display, advertisement, and education at a park unit fall under the rubric of interpretation.

Administrative history, by contrast, is the internally focused production of history to aid and inform management decisions. This process of looking at past successes and failures, building and maintaining institutional memory, and endlessly contextualizing development is of tremendous importance and is symbiotically related to interpretation. Administrative history informs interpretation, which in turn informs administrative history. At its root is the inescapable reality that for effective management and interaction with the public a park must know its history.

Parks in any locale exist in the context and cultural milieu of local history, and that history, as an increasing number of Southern sites commemorating the Civil War and antebellum area demonstrate, is often fraught. Western parks more directly embody the tensions inherent in settler-colonial expansion. Indeed, Western parks owe their very existence, in large part, to invented conceptions of virgin land and either its protection from or its rightful exploitation by farmers, miners, timbermen, and other developers of the West.[13]

Dwight Pitcaithley, former chief historian of the National Park Service and champion of the value of administrative history, argued in 2003 that administrative history had particular significance in the West. He pointed out the growing NPS commitment to the practice and significance of history in general, a milestone being the 1989 Congressional mandate to study the "causes and consequences" of the Civil War rather than carefully avoiding contextual material surrounding battle sites. The addition of Manzanar National Historic Site, the Sand Creek Massacre National Historic Site, and many other park properties representing diverse and often deeply troubling moments in the American experience also thrust the NPS into a more overtly interpretive role. Pitcaithley characterizes that interpretation as shifting to "offer more than simple descriptions of events, more than 'happy face' history."[14]

The same might be said of administrative histories. Administrative history as imagined in this century represents an attempt to internally engage in "new ways of looking at a past presumed to be comfortable, and comfortably past," in Pitcaithley's words. It seeks to equip managers in a more richly contextualized way to conduct their parks into an uncertain future characterized by tremendous upsurges in visitation accompanying acrimonious debates over the future of public lands and the effects of climate change. Pitcaithley argues, "Presenting history in and about the American West is filled with opportunities to teach history to a public eager to learn about the past but unclear, or even hostile, about its relationship to the present."[15] Western parks in particular are in some sense mythic ideals overlaid on the land and their scenery. Built environment and interpretation tend to mask history in favor of myth. As NPS historian William E. Brown wrote, "Parks and other preserved lands in the West are reliquaries where the old myths find sanctuary."[16]

Western parks exist, and often interpret their history—even for internal management decisions—in the context of the frontier myth articulated by the influential historian Frederick Jackson Turner at the turn of the twentieth century. Richard West Sellars and others have written on the Turnerian style of wildlife management, including the influence of the settler-colonial ideal in the creation of the groundbreaking 1963 *Leopold Report*. *The Leopold Report* asserts that "a national park should represent a vignette of primitive America" and that managers should work with "the utmost in skill, judgment, and ecologic sensitivity" to achieve that end.[17]

The same applies to the mere existence of sites such as Homestead National Monument in Nebraska and Whitman Mission National Historic Site in Washington. At Zion National Park, the very name "Zion" periodizes and privileges an Anglo-American, Mormon view of the land at the expense of the Native. Mukuntuweap National Monument was named using John Wesley Powell's understanding of a Paiute word. But in 1918 Congress renamed it Zion and a year later elevated it to national park status, specifically enshrining a conception of "sanctuary" that could please Mormon pioneers, for whom Zion was very much a physical space in which to manifest God's kingdom on earth, and Protestant Anglo-Americans comfortable with such imagery. This "kingdom of god" aspect resurfaced in the early 1990s when white supremacist Johnny Bangerter told reporters that he planned to make Zion National Park into a fortress for his version of the future United States, "an ancestral homeland for the kingdom of Yahweh."[18]

Zion National Park, of course, is part of someone's ancestral homeland. So is every park in North America. The Park Service holds as a core tenet John Muir's aphorism that "everybody needs beauty as well as bread."[19] Beauty for some was bought at the expense of bread for others—Western national parks were carved out, in multiple instances, not merely from the federal domain but from Native American domain as well. There was no room in Yellowstone National Park for the Crows, for the Blackfeet in Glacier, for the Havasupais in Grand Canyon, or for the Tlingits at Glacier Bay.

Thus, as historians from Theodore Catton to Karl Jacoby have pointed out, "America's best idea" is also a living example of settler-colonialism, white America's better sort indulging in scenic nationalism for the sake of its own spiritual uplift while engaging in some practical land and watershed preservation. We might not have the Sistine Chapel or even St. Paul's, went the thought at the turn of the twentieth century, but by God we have monumental scenery on a scale even a Swiss might respect—and we can manage it too. National parks had no place for Native habitation and as such were built on a combination of Indian removal and erasure. At a place like Glacier or Yellowstone, "dispossessing the wilderness," in Mark David Spence's memorable phrase, required active political and military intervention.[20]

At Zion, Mormon pioneers had already done the dirty work. Note the language in the legislation changing Mukuntuweap to Zion National Monument. The bill argued (erroneously) that the North Fork of the Virgin River canyon "was named 'Zion Canyon' by Mormon settlers many years before the name 'Mukuntuweap' was given to this region because it was regarded as a safe refuge in the event of Indian attacks on neighboring settlements."[21] Before it was ten years, old Zion National Monument had lost its only visible connection to the Southern Paiute people who had used the canyon for centuries.

For most of the twentieth century, Zion's managers ignored the Southern Paiutes. Even the 1982 administrative history casually dismissed Indian presence or use, uncritically regurgitating a Mormon folk-history claim that Paiutes feared to enter the canyon, the place where "Wai-no-pits the devil lived."[22] Oral histories make clear that the only reason Zion's management changed their approach was the simultaneous growth of a dedicated cultural resource program and the fortuitous appointment of a cultural resource specialist predisposed to work with Native people.[23]

Zion currently enjoys a relationship with a number of Native American stakeholders, prominently features Indian attitudes and material culture in its museum and interpretive materials, and issues Southern Paiutes unofficial permits on an as-requested basis to harvest willows on the banks of the Virgin River. Its current superintendent is closely involved with interagency and intertribal cultural preservation and growth efforts and champions Native access to parkland. But the fact remains that the park's founding myth and management for much of the twentieth century so thoroughly excluded Native people that they were treated not as persons with a legitimate claim to the land but as a now-gone historical curiosity, one more component of the mythos of Zion.

The connection between parks and the various myths underpinning Anglo-American civilization has been well documented by scholars such as William Cronon and Roderick Nash, and NPS historians have also worked to address such narratives, but the connection persists, nonetheless. Getting past Native erasure and dispossession, ideas of wilderness and frontier, is easier said than done. For example, the NPS in my own limited experience, perhaps echoing broader themes in American environmentalist thought, turns a somewhat deaf ear to conceptions of wilderness as a human construct, even as it unself-consciously promotes environmental manipulation to create and maintain the same "wilderness."[24] Public Employees for Environmental Responsibility (PEER), for example, a group often closely associated with National Park Service employees among many others, frequently takes a stand reminiscent of Alaska historian Morgan Sherwood's when he angrily reformatted Turner and the U.S. Census Office's definition of "frontier" from denoting a quantity of people per square mile to a quantity of bulldozers per square mile.[25] Likewise the Southern Utah Wilderness Alliance recently ran an antidevelopment television ad campaign featuring a Maverik gas station sullying a pristine red rock nature scene. Nature here stands in for the frontier and is in imminent danger of destruction.

Administrative histories must, then, grapple with conceptions of the frontier, with the legacies of Indian removal and erasure, with the myths of the garden and of Paradise-always-in-danger-of-being-lost so prevalent in environmentalist rhetoric. But they must also recognize and capture nuance and value, in lived experience, in myth and memory. Zion National Park exemplifies the powerful aesthetic appeal of a "crown jewel" national park and its effects on the imagination. The park's tremendous natural features are labeled with awe-inspiring spiritual references to Protestantism, Mormonism, and Paiute religion as well, from the Court of the Patriarchs and the Great White Throne to the Temple of Sinawava and the Kolob Canyons. The Colorado Plateau as a region holds transcendent natural beauty. John Wesley Powell thought so, as did Clarence Dutton, Stephen Mather, and many others.

But Western parks are also associated with the demonic, the improbable, and the merely undesirable. "Colter's Hell" still resonates in Yellowstone country. Interpretation at Bryce Canyon cheekily plays off pioneer cattleman Ebenezer Bryce's dry and perhaps apocryphal remark that Bryce was "a hell of a place to lose a cow."[26] Indeed southern Utah, that land of striking vistas, sorghum cane, and violent flooding celebrated in Utah pioneer culture, so appalled a pioneer songster with its aridity that he wrote, "Oh, I was mistaken, and so I went away; / For the red hills of November looked just the same in May."[27] Even Wallace Stegner uneasily described southern Utah as "that geological charnel-house."[28]

Nonetheless, the administrative historian would be wrong to conclude that, as the Park Service and more than one academic historian have assumed, early settlers found no beauty in the land that became a national park. Joseph Black, one of the first Mormons to live in Zion Canyon, evidently irritated his neighbors enough with his paeans that they dismissed the canyon as "Joseph's Glory."[29] Local son and federal surveyor Leo A. Snow in 1908 recommended the site become a national park, albeit in the driest terms possible.[30] Writing the history of a place that in one breath is a sacred homeland to not one but two groups of people, in the next an unforgiving wasteland in severe need of "improvement," and in the last a veritable church for neurasthenic seekers of sanctuary from civilization amid terrible beauty is a tall order.

Along with the mythology and often powerful sense of place, Western parks share a host of management concerns that require good administrative history to handle sensitively and with an eye to past decision-making. Resource extraction and development concerns threaten physical resources such as water flow and quality and less tangible values like viewshed and park area integrity. An administrative history of Zion National Park for example, this author's dissertation topic, must cast a wide net and study the undeniably (if not solely) Western themes of intersection of religious settlement, Native dispossession, irrigation-based economy and settlement patterns, federal exploration, "traditional" western resource uses such as farming, ranching, and timbering, and, peripherally, mining and oil and gas exploration along with the manipulation of flora and fauna aimed at maintaining a "natural" environment. It must consider long-running and complex relationships with gateway communities such as Springdale and Mount Carmel Junction and "pioneer" neighbors and inholders, with whom relations are not, despite the tone of public lands reporting since the 1970s and increasing tensions around the region, uniformly hostile. It must also chart the development and control of water resources in a park featuring the intersection of high plateaus and the edge of the Great Basin and Mojave Deserts, a growing regional population, and an agricultural economy that long predates the park, not to mention relations with the state of Utah and local governments.

And a Zion administrative history, just like a history of Yellowstone or Grand Canyon, must also give ample room to real and perceived threats to the park and its values from major mining and power generation initiatives, frequently pitched in utopian tones at the outset and degenerating into ugly rhetoric of despoliation and colonialism. After the failure of the proposed Kaiparowits power station in the 1970s, a megaproject that would have featured a company town with thousands of residents and that spurred heated debate on the national level, angry locals in Kanab, Utah, burned effigies of environmentalists and federal agency representatives.[31]

These and a host of other concerns inform the complex administrative history of Zion National Park, which, despite its tremendous recent visitation numbers, remains a geographically small park unit by Western standards and enjoys a modest staff. Any major park unit's administrative history is similarly complex, if not more so.

PROBLEMS WITH ADMINISTRATIVE HISTORY

The National Park Service has had a long and rather ambivalent relationship with its own history. The NPS endlessly struggles with a sort of feedback loop: attempting to manage parks scientifically while shaking one's head at those poor benighted souls of yesteryear who aggressively suppressed fire, fed bears for public spectacle, and ranched bison as though they were cattle. National parks historian Joan Zenzen has recently written persuasively on both the importance of administrative history and its suffering and neglect. The Park Service's own guide to administrative history writing declares, "High-quality administrative histories do more than recount a narrative of events. They provide valuable historical context. They tell us what was behind certain decisions and policies and explain their significance. Understanding where we have been often provides insight and perspective on the present and future. Like all good history, they describe and evaluate people, events, and actions in the context of their own times."[32]

But park administrators and NPS officials leery of conflict emphasize sterile narratives featuring "the facts" rather than the rich, contextualized documents the guidelines call for, when they use or ask for administrative histories at all. And therein lies the rub. Administrative history in particular, and historical gray literature in general, has been remarkably difficult for researchers to access. The NPS is peripatetic in its pursuit of administrative history, which somewhat dovetails with its pursuit of scientific management.

Scientific management has, at least on the surface, become the gospel, whereas history is rather less well provided for. But the real problems remain access and visibility. These are not unfamiliar problems. As Anne Mitchell Whisnant et al. noted in 2011 in their critical but hopeful report, *Imperiled Promise: History in the National Park Service*, "The agency's most significant investments in new historical research often produce very high-quality administrative histories, historic resources studies, cultural landscape reports, and other studies that sit on shelves, unread by colleagues, unused by other scholars, and inaccessible to the public."[33] The report's authors not only mention the obscurity of the rich body of gray literature the NPS generates almost constantly for interpretive and compliance-related purposes but also pointed up the insular and vault-like nature of the NPS's own often-excellent archives, which even the service's own personnel struggle to access.[34]

Indeed, despite excellent intentions and years of improvements, a quick glance at the NPS's potentially invaluable Park Histories webpage reveals distressing and uneven dissemination of the resource to parks, leaving Zion, among many others, badly underrepresented. Park units are not equally, or particularly understandably, provided for, and available resources appear to correspond very little with either geographical size or popularity—with two salient exceptions.

A word-search survey of resources on several of the most-visited national parks today, among them Great Smoky Mountains, Grand Canyon, Zion, Yosemite, and Yellowstone, reveals a decidedly lopsided body of what NPS terms "park history."[35] Yellowstone appears 58 distinct times, Yosemite 27. But Grand Canyon, without contest the second-most visited national park, appears only 15; Great Smoky Mountains—the most-visited park in the nation by a cool 5 million visitors—appears 8; and perhaps most dismayingly, Zion, which has historically received top-ten visitation billing and in 2017 pulled into third place, appears only once. That one history is a 1937 typescript draft of Angus Woodbury's 1944 *A History of Southern Utah and Its National Parks*.[36] The problem relates directly to the recommendation the authors of *Imperiled Promise* made that some mechanism—any mechanism—be put in place to allow and encourage scholars to upload and thus make visible the valuable work they continually produce for the NPS.[37] Clearly this process is still underway.

Institutional history at Zion provides an excellent example of administrative history's importance and neglect. It has lagged significantly behind popular history, leaving managers a confusing jumble of reports from a century of operation. A real problem is the endless reinvention of the wheel. Documents from the 1970s and before contain various unattributed brief histories of the park, published material such as Woodbury's notwithstanding. The administrative history completed in 1982 simply sat on a shelf, unapproved and undistributed, for thirty-five years, even as a companion report was widely employed. Every master plan, every foundation document, every GMP rehashes the park's history, each in a slightly different and largely uncited (although excellent) manner. There is no historical baseline from which material can be pulled. An extremely conscientious and careful ranger compiled a timeline, but without citation, and even this was not the first timeline.

Historical documentation at Zion National Park is a palimpsest of overlapping documents, each created, one suspects, because of a dearth of institutional memory or practical framework. It is hard to find meaningful news and interpret it properly when constantly delivering the same thing and reinventing the wheel in the process. While one might laud folks for constantly returning to primary sources, this frequency may reflect the lack of available histories.

The tremendous work done by a small, contracted public-history organization, Western Heritage Partners, in the late 1970s and early 1980s demonstrates the vital importance of gray literature and accessible archives, even as it points up the confusing nature of what happens to the material produced under contract. The team produced various reports, among them a full administrative history that carried park history to within a year of publication and an in-depth but less chronologically lengthy history of the park's primary concessioner. Perhaps incidentally, they also generated an enormous, carefully organized file of primary source documents while compiling their reports. These source documents, some drawn from the park archives and some from around the country, have paradoxically had a far larger influence than the administrative history and serve as the building blocks of much of the material generated since, as attested by notes made in differing shades of fading highlighter.

And yet the narrative document combining those sources is almost entirely unused. Dena Markoff's 1982 "An Administrative History: Decision-Making That Shaped Zion National Park, 1909–1981," was never adopted or published. Certainly, the document has its flaws. The *Yosemite*

News's bibliography of national park administrative histories (itself a fine example of the need for better gray-literature visibility) criticized Markoff's history for lack of internal organization and adequate editing, and for overlooking two salient issues in the park's history, even as it praised her candid assessment of previous superintendents' "personal problems."[38] Whatever its problems, Markoff's report could be a valuable tool for park managers. Instead, it has languished in gray-literature limbo for thirty-five years, the original, unaccessioned copy simply residing in the capable but greatly overworked curator's office. Public access relies on photocopies from university archives abroad and the Park Service's Harpers Ferry Center. At Zion, longtime resource management personnel, the closest thing the park has to historians, know of the admin history's existence but subscribe to a sort of park legend that it is of no use and probably not around anyhow.

All attention focuses on Markoff's 1980 history of the park's longtime Union Pacific Railroad-owned concessioner, "The Dudes Are Always Right: The Utah Parks Company in Zion National Park, 1923–1972," which is thought to contain the same information as the administrative history, despite the fact that nearly 200 of its 216 pages focus on the period between 1923 and 1950, concentrating almost exclusively on the concessioner's activities rather than the park's administration. This focus is so complete that Zion's 2017 State of the Park Report lauds "The Dudes," as it is known internally, as "a great step toward an administrative history," in the same breath lamenting, "As a 34 year old document, it constitutes the only attempt of historical analysis and park establishment."[39] The lack of an administrative history at Zion is keenly felt. But it need not be.

ORAL HISTORY: A WAY FORWARD?

If the National Park Service should pay more attention to administrative history, there is also one element of historical practice with potential to substantially deepen it—oral history. Since the 1970s, the NPS, along with the U.S. Forest Service, has embraced oral history as a practice and a method of building institutional and community memory. Peculiarly, oral history seems to be the one form of historical practice that consistently finds support in park budgets. It is even easier to find oral history resources on the NPS's gargantuan website than it is to find park histories. Interpretations of oral history's purposes borrow directly from the

Oral History Association's best practices. In stark contrast to its administrative history, Zion National Park has been the subject of no less than four oral history projects, all spanning the last forty years and including one with Park Service grand old man Horace Albright. These projects range from interviews with park employees, past and present, to folklife-oriented histories of members of the local community. An ethnographic overview and assessment of the Zion/Pipe Spring area works hard to add long-excluded Native voices.

But this fixation on oral history, while a valuable corrective, especially to more than a century of attempts to erase Native people, has a decided drawback: oral history projects require extensive presentation before they can be useful to managers, interpreters, or the public as anything more than another primary-source collection. As a primary source, or even on its own, oral history is often useful in substantive, concrete ways, but it really excels in lending richness and context to a narrative. For example, when asked to characterize relations between Park Service personnel and southern Utahns in the 1970s, Robert Heyder, retired superintendent of Mesa Verde, Zion, Bryce Canyon, and Capitol Reef National Parks, described an encounter at a gas station in Escalante, Utah, while on his way to a public lands meeting. "He says, 'You with the Sierra Club?' I said no," Heyder remembered. "Well then he started talking to me. He says, 'Who are you with?' I says, 'National Park Service.' And he's just shaking my hand, and then he went over and washed his hand."[40] Heyder's anecdote might be funny or depressing, depending on one's point of view. But used in an administrative history—given the opportunity to inform the present—it might also give a park manager a small example of past experiences other park managers had and contextualize the history of public relations.

CONCLUSION

National Park Service units saw 307 million visitors in 2016. Western parks in particular experienced unprecedented demand, perhaps due to the NPS's "Find Your Park" centennial campaign. At the time of this writing, officials at Zion National Park were considering limiting visitors to Zion Canyon, the park's main attraction, in an attempt to mitigate impacts to the canyon's delicate desert environment. While the park system struggled to meet visitor demand and protect the nation's shrines, funding levels remained insufficient to meet demands and seemed likely to decline significantly.[41] At the same time, even as enormous new monuments such as Gold Butte and Bears Ears entered the national park system, conflict over public lands rose to a fever pitch unseen since the Sagebrush Rebellion. Nevada rancher Cliven Bundy's standoff with federal agents in 2014 was hardly over before militia members seized the Malheur National Wildlife Refuge and held it for forty-one days.[42] The sheriff of Garfield County, Utah, threatened to arrest Bureau of Land Management personnel.[43]

In the West, park units are both mythical national shrines *and* visible representations of the power of federal land management agencies. Thus, they have a distinct need to understand their own history and place in this frequently contested and increasingly heavily trafficked environment. Administrative histories hold the dual burden of breaking and enriching the power of myth, of explicating the origins, development, and context of each wilderness shrine, each battlefield site, each component of what senior NPS administrator John Maounis called "the largest network of museums in the United States."[44] Administrative history has a distinctive place in western parks, because the West has a distinct position in the nation. Public lands and imagination inform every aspect of the Western park experience. Administrative history is valuable everywhere. But in the West, it is critical.

CHAPTER 5

Prospecting the Past

How Public History and Tourism Remade Lake City, Colorado

METTE FLYNT

Lake City, Colorado, was a skeleton of its former self in 1972, the only community left in a county of ghost towns with more deer than residents.[1] Like many Westerners dealing with dying mining and ranching industries, Lake Citians thought tourism could revive their economy. The town's potential for tourism remained extensive but untapped. In addition to outdoor recreation, Lake City offered tourists the chance to visit a place seemingly frozen in time. It still had dirt streets, no bank, and few downtown structures built after the Panic of 1893.[2]

In many Western towns, tourism pitted residents against tourists, preservationists against corporate developers, and purveyors of the authentic against promoters of Disney-inspired vacations.[3] Lake Citians' experience did not fit within this narrative. For this reason, it challenges scholars to rethink the binaries that often describe the dynamic between public history and tourism. The residents and tourists who founded Lake City's first public history organization, the Hinsdale County Historical Society (HCHS), hoped that the town's "timelessness" would increase its tourist appeal. The society, as well as other public history organizations and initiatives, shaped and redefined Lake City's sense of place—the ways in which people have bonded over time with the area's landscape.[4] Residents and tourists worked together to save Lake City's history and economy. Their efforts illustrate how public history and tourism can remold individuals' sense of place and belonging in the American West. Public history institutions helped people hold on to the fading past as they developed a more inclusive community identity rooted in tourism. The stories of Lake

City's HCHS, National Historic District, and Alpine Loop Backcountry Byway—stretching from the early tourism years of the 1970s through today—provide a template for reimagining this dynamic through local history.[5]

HINSDALE COUNTY HISTORICAL SOCIETY

As tourism increased in the 1970s, residents worried about the disappearance of the past and began planning a historical society and museum. With the nation's bicentennial as the decade's centerpiece, Americans became increasingly interested in history and nostalgia.[6] Founding HCHS member, Grant Houston, explained how this trend manifested locally. First, many tourists and residents saw historic structures as lumberyards with free construction materials. One family even moved whole cabins from the ghost town of Sherman to Lake City, repurposing them as tourist rentals. Tourists scavenged ghost towns for souvenirs, too. Thus, the objectives of tourism and preservation often conflicted. In 1973, Lake Citians met to create a historical society that would slow this physical erasure of local history. Members thought that they could protect the town's heritage by giving people a place to donate items, so they established the Hinsdale County Museum. The museum's first exhibits, events, and tours centered on nineteenth-century mining life.[7]

The founding of the HCHS and its museum marked a turning point in the relationship between tourism and history in Lake City. It represented a conscious effort to protect material evidence of the past, both for its historic value and its potential to attract tourists. Moreover, the society's decision to collect materials primarily related to nineteenth-century mining shaped community members' definition of history. It also influenced which histories they included and excluded in tourism marketing. The goals of tourism boosters and public historians did not conflict.[8] In the 1990s, the HCHS and the tourism industry became more codependent. At the same time, the society broadened the chronological and thematic focus of its exhibits, special events, and tours.

Curators reimagined museum exhibits, making twentieth-century stories the focal point. Summer curator Chay Rees Runnels moved the HCHS in this direction. Her exhibit, "Finding Paradise," examined the history of tourism. Runnels highlighted overlooked parts of the society's collections, including gambling machines and travel albums.

Hinsdale County Historical Society and Bureau of Land Management volunteers replace the roof of the Capitol City Post Office in 1992. Located nine miles from Lake City, Capitol City's founders thought they were building the future capital of Colorado in 1877. The post office is one of the only remaining structures at the former boomtown. Collaborative roofing projects were essential in preserving the ghost towns around Lake City. Photo Courtesy of Grant Houston.

She acknowledged that to early tourism boosters, the twentieth century did not seem historical. Yet, she argued that more recent events were as important as the distant past.[9] Runnels's experience as a local tourist influenced her perspective. She explained, "Because I had been a tourist myself, and because my mother had previously worked at VC Bar Ranch tourist resort in Lake City in the 1960s, I was fascinated with the history of tourism in the area. I was also very interested in what drew tourists especially from Texas back to Lake City year after year."[10] Tourists, such as Runnels, framed history and place through different lenses than residents.

Other exhibits during the late 1990s and 2000s covered midcentury honky-tonk culture, the local filming of *Cariboo Trail*, and patriotism during the mining and tourism eras. Tourism was entangled in the exhibits' creation. Curators not only historicized the tourist experience but also integrated tourists' oral histories and personal collections into narratives. In this way, their exhibits contributed to a more participatory sense of place and of history. Tourists were more invested and engaged in their seasonal home since the HCHS recognized that their histories are local histories, too. By writing tourists' stories into the community narrative, HCHS members enhanced Lake City's inclusivity.[11]

In a similar vein, special events at the museum not only connected tourists with the HCHS but also relied on their expertise in telling a more complete history. As seasonal resident and docent Adolph Assenheimer observed, these events "make the museum alive for the public."[12] For instance, the society acquired a dilapidated caboose from the county and moved it to the museum for renovations. Volunteers, who were primarily seasonal residents, spent months restoring it. Seasonal resident Bob Lozano created a tour of Lake City's former railroad sites, based on the research he conducted with longtime resident Margaret Rawson Pitney. Lozano and his son, Michael, produced a map showing the old railroad lines on the contemporary landscape. Like the caboose restoration, Lozano's educational programs not only connected seasonal residents with the community but also provided another means for visitors to develop their own sense of place.[13]

Museum volunteers used other special events to rewrite Lake City's mining history. They brought New Western History to a local audience, highlighting the forgotten through bottom-up narratives.[14] The museum's theatrical production exemplifies this pattern. Grant Houston and local author Mary Stigall wrote the script for *Scarlet Belles*, a play about late-nineteenth and early twentieth-century sex workers. Whereas business owners and miners left behind a tangible past, the homes where these women lived have been lost to fire or demolition.[15] Their presence in written sources is also limited. As historian Carol Kammen suggests, leaving their stories out of community narratives would only perpetuate existing archival silences. With this in mind, Houston and Stigall shared these women's histories. Actors included year-round and seasonal residents of all ages.[16] While some objected to the subject matter, Houston and Stigall did not romanticize the sex workers' lives and instead told the kind of difficult stories that historical societies too often avoid. Houston explained the logic behind the play, saying, "There's almost a religion to honoring people who would otherwise be forgotten . . . you are honoring people whose lives mattered. Whether you agree with the way they lived is inconsequential."[17]

The society's cookbook project and Helen's Garden represent a similar impulse, focusing on the lives of housewives, cooks, and truck farmers. To capture the fading culinary past, volunteers contacted the families of people who had left town or who were tourists, along with longtime local families, to develop a collection of old recipes. Tourists were the cookbook's target audience and a source for its content. Recipes imparted the town's isolation, locally sourced diet, and ethnic diversity. At the same time, the cookbook did not include recipes from communities who had left a century earlier, particularly those of former Italian American and Jewish residents.[18] The project culminated in a community potluck cooked by both year-round and seasonal residents. As a whole, the cookbook project forged stronger community ties and illuminated the experiences of people often excluded from the dominant narrative.[19]

Helen's Garden represented an attempt to capture forgotten fragments of social history. Dana Lozano and her aunt, Helen Ewart, drew inspiration from the garden that their ancestor, Mette Ewart, once raised in town. It reproduced the gardening techniques and plants of early twentieth-century Lake City. An annual tea transformed Helen's Garden into a community space. Lozano gave a forgotten historical landscape—still evident in the poppies and rhubarb growing in each yard—new meaning in the tourist era. Moreover, the garden advanced the objectives of tourist promoters, who sought more aesthetically pleasing landscapes downtown.[20]

While these special events were relatively new, the HCHS has organized walking tours since the 1980s. The evolution of the tours' content and participation represents another facet of the relationship between public history and tourism. In 1984, the society offered historic district, cemetery, and interior home tours. Guides showcased the stories of the wealthy and middle-class residents who owned the historic buildings that many tourists admired.[21] HCHS guides have changed the tours since then. In 2007, they added midcentury tourist cabins to the interior home tour. They started a modern interior home tour that engaged with the tourist experience. With seasonal residents as their guides, participants toured contemporary homes.[22] These changes illustrate new perspectives on what constitutes history and who should narrate it.

The ghost tour, nearly unchanged since its 1995 premiere, remains the most popular HCHS event and reflects a rising national interest in dark tourism.[23] Guides integrate history and folklore by relating the stories of deceased residents who allegedly haunt local sites. These stories are a hook for sharing histories of alcoholism, racism, and extralegal violence. For many, the tour is an annual tradition. Like other dark tourism sites, it appeals to individuals anxious about the pace of recent change. The tour's ritual—the order of stops, the guide's tone, and participants' storytelling—is perhaps more important than its content. Some participants even resist new content or contextualization. Historians David Glassberg and Tiya Miles comment on this pattern, claiming ghost stories allow tourists to form a "simplified and depoliticized" sense of place.[24] For most participants, the ghost tour is less about connecting with a distant past and more about connecting with a personal past, grounded in memories of family and vacation in Lake City. The tour is simplified in that participants often use the difficult aspects of local history as a backdrop for an enhanced tourist experience. As a whole, the tour shapes tourists' emotional connection with the city, which is inseparable from their sense of history and place.[25]

On the other hand, the tour of the National Historic District lacks the same following and expectations, meaning participants are more open to new tour content. I have guided this tour since 2004 and have rewritten its content as I have gained a deeper understanding of history. The original tour focused on the mining era, particularly the lives of those who could afford to build sturdy, lasting buildings. Years later, participants began to question the stories that I told. Could everyone afford a Queen Anne home in 1880? What happened to the Italian American families who used to live in town? These questions and my public history training led me to reframe the tour. It now incorporates new historical structures, including tourist cabins and the erased spaces where the working class and people of color lived: a garden planted by the formerly enslaved Williams family; the buildings of the red-light district; and the remnants of a Chinese laundry shop. Most recently, I organized a special tour, "Lost Lake City," in response to an avalanche cycle that forced the museum to close. Participants learned about environmental justice and erasure through the history of local natural disasters.

These new exhibits and programs not only retold Lake City's history in a more participatory way but also forged a broader public history community. Seasonal residents still serve as the foundation of historical interpretation.[26] The society's dependence on tourists is both a consequence of and contributing factor to tourism. Retired museum coordinator Steve Priest claimed that without tourist dollars and volunteer hours public history projects would not exist in town.[27] Most residents earn their annual income during the summer months, leaving few free to volunteer at the museum then. Volunteers continue to draw more tourists to the area through the programs they support. In short, tourism and public history have a symbiotic relationship.

LAKE CITY NATIONAL HISTORIC DISTRICT

Lake City's National Historic District reflects a similar transition toward more inclusive and community-oriented public history initiatives. Three periods define this process: creation of the district in the late 1970s; conflict over the town's historic school in the 1980s; and a reimagination of preservation in the 2000s.

The district's history mirrors that of the HCHS: it emerged from a desire to salvage a disappearing past, shaped a new sense of place entwined in tourism, and eventually related a bottom-up story of the past. The district's evolution differs from that of the HCHS because the interests of tourism influenced it more strongly from the beginning. Property owners wanted the tax breaks that came with a historic district listing. They also thought that improving Lake City's curbside appeal would attract more tourists. Realtor Bob Hall and business developer John Parker pushed the district's designation. Parker funded the necessary historical survey, while Hall assured property owners that the new status would enhance, not limit, economic growth. Some opposed the district's National Register nomination, thinking it would restrict what they could do with their property. Regardless, the nomination received the necessary community backing and approval from the Colorado State Historical Society.[28] In its letter of support for the district's nomination, the HCHS described Lake City as the "gem of Colorado" because of its many historic buildings and few "modern intrusions."[29] The same supposed timelessness that made Lake City appealing to tourists also propelled its listing onto the National Register. Shortly after the designation, the municipal government passed ordinances to safeguard the town's nineteenth-century buildings.[30]

While these measures preserved some of Lake City's deteriorating structures from the mining era, they did so at the expense of buildings from the recent past. This resulted, in part, from the National Register's requirement that qualifying structures generally must be at least fifty years old. Residents also defined the town's identity around mining history, not midcentury tourism. Their sense of place was both a response to tourist expectations of an Old West town and residents' own sense of what constituted history. One resident said, "Once we lose it [historic buildings] the cost to reproduce it will double. The old historic town is part of what draws tourists, which is why I can live here."[31] In short, the tourism industry shaped the direction of preservation efforts. Renovations of the midcentury Matterhorn Motel reflect this mindset. To match the town's "unique character," the Matterhorn's owners hid the hotel's mid-century façade with shingled siding, gables, and decorative exterior beams characteristic of the mining era.[32]

The town's interpretative plaques illustrated a similar perspective. They highlighted structures associated with the town's founders, prominent businesspeople, and churches. The plaques perpetuated the idea that history ended when the mines closed. They transformed marked buildings into "preserved antiquity . . . adrift in a modern sea."[33] In addition, preservation proponents gave some homeowners plaques to win their support for the proposed historic district designation.[34] Few who read the plaques, however, knew that the plaques had their own historical and political context. For instance, many tour participants stopped to read plaques, questioned why homes with plaques were not on the tour, or assumed that those with plaques had more significance. This reflects the power of interpretive plaques in remembering and forgetting the past.

The debate over Lake City's school in the 1980s exposed fissures in the relationship between public history and business and pushed citizens toward more inclusive interpretation. By the late 1980s, Lake City's century-old, structurally unsound school had undergone so many renovations that only the original foundation remained. Yet students still attended classes there. When school board members proposed demolition, their plan uncovered divisions regarding how to best preserve Lake City's history. Demolition supporters noted the school's structural problems and said a new school would promote economic growth. In contrast, the HCHS wanted the building to become a museum. Most opponents expressed the idea that the school remained significant to Lake City's sense of place. Their activism represented the grassroots nature of the town's ongoing conversation about the appropriate direction of historic preservation. For instance, Hazel Whitton observed that newcomers did not value the school building because they lacked a connection to place and to history.[35]

Critics countered that sentimentality had no place in the discussion. Carol Drake stated that only four percent of visitors mentioned history as a significant factor in their tourist experience. How could the board justify preserving the school when that was the case? Houston responded, "Surely it was sentimentality which was largely responsible for establishing the Lake City Historic District, sentimentality which reared its ugly head and caused so many of our Victorian homes to be restored, that demon of sentimentality has continued to bring generations of families back to Lake City year after year."[36] This discussion highlights the recurring themes of emotional connection, memory, and tourism in shaping historic preservation. While the board ultimately demolished the building, Lake Citians remained unsettled on whether the objectives of public history and business were complementary.[37] The town maintained a cohesive historic district, yet individuals' interpretation and attachment to that place was not universal.

As tourism grew, community members forged a more unified vision for the place of the past in local identity that integrated diverse experiences and perspectives. First, the emergence of a new organization, Downtown Improvement and Revitalization Team (DIRT), represented an attempt to harmonize the objectives of historic preservation and business development. Like many local organizations, DIRT relied on year-round and seasonal residents for support. As part of the Main Street America program, it sought to maintain the town's "authentic historic district" and "rare sense of community" while cultivating unique, sustainable businesses.[38]

DIRT's early projects included the reconstruction of downtown boardwalks and placement of historic photos in vacant storefronts. DIRT depended on a group of children, known as YouthCorps, to support many projects. By drawing these students into preservation and promotion, DIRT director Kristie Borchers hoped to engender in them a sense of place, making them stewards of local history.[39] Like HCHS members, DIRT volunteers saw youth programs as a means of forging new connections to the past within a shifting tourist economy. DIRT's Marketing Committee embodied the impulse to find a mutually beneficial relationship between the historic landscapes of local memory and the imagined landscapes of tourist expectation. In its 2008 marketing plan, DIRT's board described the historic district as "the most authentic" in the state, offering an "old-town experience flavored by the 'Old West.'"[40] To maintain this culture, DIRT developed a buying guide for historic property owners. It produced an audio tour of nineteenth-century buildings, too. These efforts made history more accessible to the broader public and encouraged people to visit downtown businesses. In this instance, business and preservation complemented each other.[41]

In tandem with DIRT, the Town of Lake City and the HCHS redefined the historic district and, consequently, how people engaged with history. In the late 2000s, the town broadened the scope of its interpretive plaques. New sites included midcentury tourist lodging, the red-light district, and a car garage. Town administrator Michelle Pierce described the importance of the new plaques in 2009: "We hope to establish an emotional connection and strengthen the audience's relationship with the historic district of Lake City, resulting in longer and repeat visits by heritage tourists, and better buy-in to the well-being of the historic buildings."[42] Borchers echoed Pierce, saying DIRT hoped to "develop a local 'sense of place' and thereby create more connections, relevancy, and a historic preservation ethic."[43] Both comments reflect a desire to shape new relationships with the historic landscape, bound to tourism and preservation.

Expansion of the district's contributing buildings list imparted a similar vision. Like HCHS members, town leaders sought common ground between the objectives of tourism and public history. Historians and municipal leaders saw the resurveyed district, which included early tourist and midcentury buildings, as a means of integrating tourists more fully into Lake City's historic identity. In doing so, they protected the perceived timelessness of Lake City that appealed to tourists and residents, while also capturing the town's postmining history.[44]

This resurveyed district, which counted 216 contributing buildings, included more than tourist structures. It also recognized the everyday life of late-nineteenth- and early-twentieth-century residents through the inclusion of seventy-six outbuildings. These ranged from large mule barns to outhouses. In 2007, many of these buildings were at risk of collapse. The loss of a few buildings would undercut the historic district's status. In response, the municipal government applied for state grants to save the outbuildings. State funding for this type of preservation was unprecedented. Pierce explained that the outbuildings' historic and economic value made them significant. Community members had created the district to preserve a disappearing landscape, but once they accomplished that goal, Pierce said, "We find that there is a very important tourist element that is specifically attracted to national historic districts."[45] In other words, the outbuildings' preservation bolstered tourism without undermining public history efforts.

In 2010, the town gained a spot for these outbuildings on Colorado Preservation's Most Endangered Places List. Pierce said, "The secondary structures which serviced these more grand buildings—outhouses, garages, and woodsheds—have largely been forgotten."[46] Similarly, Houston said, "A historic district such as Lake City isn't just made up of fine homes, it's the back of the buildings which actually tell the story of how our ancestors lived and worked . . . these buildings illustrate how homes were heated, how people traveled, and how they handled basic sanitation."[47] By acknowledging these buildings' importance in the mining and tourist eras, Lake City residents recognized the ties between these two periods and told a more inclusive historical narrative.

ALPINE LOOP BACKCOUNTRY BYWAY

The Alpine Loop Backcountry Byway illustrates yet another facet of the relationship between tourism and public history. The loop became a national Scenic and Historic Byway in 1989 and is administered by the Bureau of Land Management (BLM). As the primary local tourist attraction, the loop connects Lake City to two former mining towns, Ouray and Silverton. Ninety-six percent of Hinsdale County's land, including most of the loop, is public, which has slowed the pace of change on the loop and created an impression of timelessness.[48] Private organizations, government entities, residents, and tourists collaborated on history education and preservation for the loop. Lake Citians made the loop central to a new sense of place rooted in both tourism and history. Three periods demonstrate how they fused promotion and preservation: the early push to save mining structures during the 1980s and 1990s; restoration and new interpretation in the 2000s; and recently, the creation of a heritage park at the Ute-Ulay Mine.

The first organized push to save the loop's deteriorating historic structures coincided with the creation of the scenic byway in the late 1980s. A combination of human and nonhuman forces had erased many ghost towns and historic mines on the loop, alarming stakeholders at the HCHS and BLM. Their concern reflected how essential these historic areas were to Lake City's economic and social fabric. It also stemmed from the management plan for the area, which prioritized the preservation of historic sites. The HCHS and BLM first collaborated on renovating historic loop structures and facilitating private land transfers to the federal government. A BLM newsletter explained the reasoning behind local partnerships: "The Alpine Loop is not just spectacular alpine scenery and hair-raising jeep roads; the numerous historic mining structures and other evidence of past mining activity provide visitors with a cultural channel to the past."[49] These efforts foreshadowed the 1986 Alpine Triangle Recreation Area Management Plan (ATRAMP), which reiterated the twin objectives of preservation and recreation. The BLM expanded interpretation on the loop, creating programs, interpretative plaques, and a revised *Alpine Explorer* guide that promoted education and heritage tourism.[50]

The revised 2006 ATRMP, however, acknowledged the difficulties in preserving historic loop structures. It pointed out that forty percent of loop structures had collapsed in the previous fifteen years. The BLM expected another forty percent to collapse in the coming five to ten years. The destruction of the Empire Chief Mill legitimized this concern.[51] Once heralded as a top loop attraction, the mill was in an avalanche chute. In fact, an avalanche ran through the mill and killed several miners in 1929. The BLM began stabilizing the structure in 2000, after successfully nominating it to the National Register in 1999. It placed a new interpretive plaque at the site, which detailed the historic avalanche and complemented an HCHS exhibit on the 1929 slide. Ironically, an avalanche destroyed the mill again in 2008. Rather than rebuild the site or remove its remnants, BLM officials left the structural timber in place. BLM archaeologist Liz Francisco explained this decision: "In its current state, the Empire Chief shows the powerful force and the dangers avalanches posed to miners . . . visitors can now see the exposed massive timbers and construction methods used to build the mine."[52] This strategy enabled the BLM to convey the region's environmental history through a powerful example of nature's dynamism.

The Empire Chief project signified a divergence from the community's longtime attempts to preserve a seemingly timeless mining past. Yet, it also motivated stakeholders to prevent a similar fate for other compromised structures. Grant Houston pushed for better preservation on the loop in a 2008 editorial. He called for a "multi-organizational" and "proactive approach," warning that a metaphorical "avalanche is building and all could be swept away."[53]

The BLM addressed these concerns through historic preservation and education during the 2010s. BLM Outdoor Recreation Planner Jim Lovelace commented on this two-pronged approach. He said, "You hear the phrase loving our public lands to death . . . but in the case of the Alpine Loop, collective efforts have been essential to historic buildings' survival."[54] He mentioned that this management has been a "never-ending balancing act" supported through regulations, such as a ban on camping within 150 feet of historic structures. Lovelace observed that education is vital because "regulations without education are pretty empty."[55] People must understand why structures are important so they will be informed stewards of the area's historic and environmental resources. The restoration of the Golconda boardinghouse and compressor building, completed in 2015, exemplifies this perspective. The BLM worked with HistoriCorps and the Southwest Youth Conservation Corps to restore and reconstruct portions of the complex. In the end, the collaboration represented another phase in heritage tourism in which volunteers developed a connection with historic landscapes through working vacations.[56]

The BLM's Junior Explorer program focuses on developing a sense of place and stewardship among another set of stakeholders: visiting children. Similar to YouthCorps, this project teaches children about the region's history through engagement with cultural resources. In particular, children become Junior Rangers by completing tasks in free Junior Explorer booklets. Content includes lessons on Ute ideas about weather and on differentiating trash from artifacts. The explorer program emphasizes children's ownership of public lands and conceptualizes the loop as a "storybook" for local history.[57] Like adult-centered preservation programs, it cultivates a sense of belonging and history for both residents and tourists.

The planned heritage park at the Ute-Ulay complex exemplifies an expanded vision for collaboration in preservation, tourism, and education on the loop. Known as the "mine that made Lake City," the Ute-Ulay was deteriorating in the early 2000s. Its privately owned buildings—some of which teetered over a steep canyon—were intriguing but unsafe for visitors. When an avalanche blocked the creek flowing below the mine and forced the town's water source to run through the Ute-Ulay's toxic tailings, residents rethought their hands-off approach to the site. The county's limited resources necessitated collaboration with stakeholders outside the area. Federal, state, county, and private agencies searched for a better management plan that would protect the Ute-Ulay and the community's health. Ultimately, environmental protection was the county's top priority. Heritage tourism was an added benefit. Working with DIRT, the HCHS, and BLM, the county accepted donation of the Ute-Ulay from its owner.[58]

Stakeholders created a management plan that complemented different needs, or as scholar Wilton Corkern said, formed a "nexus between recreation and scholarship—the place where the 'public' in public history meets the 'history' in public history."[59] Casey Carrigan, a representative of the local Lake Fork Valley Conservancy, called the Ute-Ulay "part of who we are."[60] Speaking broadly about balancing the economy, preservation, and environmental protection, Lovelace observed that tourism had replaced mining as the driving force behind local growth. In his view, recreation-based tourism did not affect the environment to the same extent as "the furious decades" of mining.[61] These comments reflect the increasing importance of stewardship and a preservation ethic in defining individuals' sense of place.

Recent developments at the Ute-Ulay impart this blended sense of place. First, the BLM opened the site to visitors. Previous owners had warded off visitors with a sign stating, "No trespassing. Shotgun enforced."[62] The BLM partnered with the Environmental Protection Agency to enhance the safety of the tailings location.[63] Visitors now could walk through the site. The Colorado Art Ranch also made the site more inviting. The ranch's visiting scholars brainstormed ideas for the complex's future, interviewing a cross-section of residents and tourists to pinpoint the Ute-Ulay's meaning for the community.[64] Their approach embodied the theory that planners create the most impactful programs when they combine insight from artifacts, history, and memory.[65] Moreover, this collaborative strategy bridged the common gap between authenticity and authority. This divide exists between experts, whom the public often associates with authority, and the individuals who know a place through experience and have authenticity.[66] Integrating local voices empowered Art Ranch scholars to find a middle ground. After considering the scholars' proposals, county officials planned a Ute-Ulay heritage park.[67] The Ute-Ulay's upper level is now open for self-guided tours. Brochures place equal emphasis on the Ute-Ulay's nineteenth-century heyday and its twentieth-century cycles of decline and rebirth. The brochures acknowledge residents' sense of place by using unofficial local names to identify buildings.[68]

By developing public history and tourism in tandem, Lake Citians forged a participatory sense of place informed by engagement with the HCHS, historic district, and Alpine Loop. The HCHS worked with tourists and residents to write a more inclusive historical narrative. Historic district advocates preserved a diverse built environment, saving the "quaint charm" that often shapes tourists' first impressions of Lake City.[69] Lastly, the Alpine Loop reflects how abandoned mining sites continue to affect Lake City's economy and its understanding of history.

Lake City's history provides a model for sustainable programming that supports the objectives of tourism and public history initiatives. Yet, these initiatives continue to challenge Lake Citians. Organizations dependent on volunteers are constrained in their growth, the pioneer narrative still dominates some interpretation, and the threat of "loving places to death" looms. Nevertheless, one former ghost town offers a template of hope for public history in the tourist West.

CHAPTER 6

Finding and Building Community on the Manito Trail

TRISHA VENISA-ALICIA MARTÍNEZ AND
VANESSA FONSECA-CHÁVEZ

> At the heart of the modern Nuevomexicano identity formation is the paradoxical condition of being simultaneously displaced and place-based: a dispossessed, diasporic, deterritorialized yet landed people.
>
> —Sylvia Rodríguez

INTRODUCTION

In 2007, the seeds for what would become the Following the Manito Trail (FMT) project were planted by Levi Romero, who took a group of students from the University of New Mexico along what he referred to as a Manito trail, the stretch of the Interstate 25 corridor that runs from Albuquerque, New Mexico, north through Colorado to Cheyenne, Wyoming. The FMT project is an interdisciplinary, ethnographic project that examines the migration experience of Manitos—an endearing term deriving from the diminutive form of *hermano* (Manito) or *hermana* (Manita) and used to express kinship among Hispanic New Mexicans—from the mid-nineteenth century to the present. This migration is part of a larger internal diaspora taking place among Mexican/Mexican American/Manito peoples of Greater Mexico. Romero relates the story of his Manito relatives who moved to Wyoming, California, Colorado, and Utah to find work in agricultural fields, on the railroad, in the mines, or in sheepherding.[1] He remembered these stories into adulthood and, during a trip to Riverton, Wyoming, to visit the family of his wife, Jeana Rodarte Romero, he sensed an affinity for her family that reminded him of his own home in northern New Mexico. The story of his wife's family migration to Wyoming echoed that of various people from his home, the Embudo Valley. As a result of similar experiences during invitations to read his poetry in Cheyenne and Rock Springs, he wrote, "Someone really should do an oral history documentation project on New Mexico Manitos who now call Wyoming their home."[2]

Artistic carving of a woman graces an Aspen tree in the Routt National Forest in southern Wyoming. At the turn of the twentieth century, sheep-herders from New Mexico flocked to this area of Wyoming in search of opportunity. Over the decades, they made their mark on the forests here, filling the aspen groves with names, dates, and artistic carvings. Photo courtesy of Adam Herrera.

Six years later, in the fall of 2013, Vanessa Fonseca-Chávez found herself in her first academic position at the University of Wyoming in Laramie as an Assistant Professor of Latina/o Studies and English. As a Manita from Grants, New Mexico, she too felt called to Wyoming. The elevation, cowboy culture, and open spaces were not dissimilar to her own hometown, which had itself experienced an influx of newcomers during the thirty-year uranium boom that began in the 1950s. Fonseca-Chávez's family was also familiar with economic migration. Her paternal grandfather's family moved from Mexico to Kansas to work on the railroad and later found themselves in California. One of her maternal great-grandfathers was a sheepherder in northwestern New Mexico, and her father worked throughout New Mexico, Washington, California, and Nevada in construction jobs to support their family. She experienced her first out-of-state migration when she left New Mexico in 2008 to attend

Emilio Vigil smokes a cigarette near his home in Riverton, Wyoming. In 1986, after years of neglect by the city, Vigil and other Riverton barrio residents took it upon themselves to pave their own streets. Photo courtesy of Adam Herrera.

a doctoral program at Arizona State University, and in 2013 she was back on the Manito trail heading to Laramie.

It didn't take long for Fonseca-Chávez to find a Manito community in Laramie. She remembers visiting the Ace Hardware store in town and seeing a woman who exhibited features like those of her own mother's family—dark skinned with salt and pepper hair and a typical New Mexican accent. She started a conversation with the woman, who said excitedly that she had just returned from Mora, New Mexico, and laughed about the lingering *mocho* accent she brought back with her. Fonseca-Chávez smiled and felt thankful in that moment. Although she was far away from New Mexico, this encounter served as a reminder of Manito kinship across geographic spaces.

Fonseca-Chávez first became aware of Romero's work on the Manito trail from speaking with a mutual friend at a conference in Denver. She later contacted Romero to ask if he wanted to work together on the project by using Wyoming as a proof of concept, and in 2015 the FMT project began with Romero and Fonseca-Chávez serving as codirectors.[3] The project team now includes producer Adam Herrera, research scholar Trisha Martínez, and consultant Troy Lovata. With the exception of Adam Herrera, all of the team members are fellow Manitos who are interested in documenting the migration stories of their own families and others who were called to Wyoming over the years.

In Trisha Martínez's family, old stories tell of her great-great-grandfather Antonio Valdez, who would travel to Wyoming to hunt buffalo. In the early 1900s, many of the men in her family embarked on the Manito trail to pursue seasonal labor opportunities, cultivating crops and herding sheep. In the 1930s, her great-grandfather José Victor Sánchez began herding sheep in Hanna, Wyoming, and eventually worked for the city of Cheyenne. After years of traveling back and forth on the Manito trail, the entire Sánchez family decided to relocate from New Mexico to Wyoming, as was the case with many Manito families. Martínez was born in Cheyenne, but her familial roots in Sapello (maternal) and Valdez (paternal) resulted in frequent travels along the Manito trail. Over the years, such family connections and cultural traditions have fostered the survival of strong ties to New Mexico.

Martínez learned of the FMT project shortly after beginning her doctoral program in American Studies at the University of New Mexico. Romero shared with her details of the project, and she immediately signed on as a research assistant. Her initial assignment was to listen to the oral interviews conducted by the students in his 2007 summer English course. To Martínez's surprise, the first oral history she heard was a very familiar voice, that of her grandmother Alice Martínez. This was the beginning of a fruition of knowledge and experiences left for Martínez to discover through her own journey on the Manito trail. The cultural remnants of the Manito trail legacy continue to serve as a source of inspiration for the FMT project team as a whole, encouraging their collective energy and excitement for documenting the depth of the Manito diaspora.

This chapter begins with a contextualization of the Manito networks that have brought the FMT team together in community. We have often referred to this project as a labor of love. As scholars and Manitos deeply rooted in New Mexico, we are grateful for the opportunity to highlight the stories of those who have migrated over time and who have worked to maintain their *querencia*, their sense of home and love of place, despite the geographic distance to the place of their *antepasados* (ancestors). Knowing the land or, as Martínez would describe, being one with the land, is vital to one's sense of self and querencia because much of a person's identity is shaped by memories and day-to-day experiences in a particular place. Consequently, to be displaced ultimately influences constructs of identity, culture, and community.

Throughout this project, our aim has been to bridge the fragmented history of Manito migration with the stories and cultural expressions of Manitos in their homeland and in the diaspora. We recognize that the movement of people from one locale to another draws upon the foundational cultural and communal values of their respective homelands. Moving across borders, generally speaking, is a form of social movement. When viewed alongside studies of (im)migration, the FMT project offers insight to the shared experiences of inhabitants of the U.S. Mexico borderlands and the ways in which mobility serves as a means of survival among communities that are often set apart and economically displaced from their homes. This study, in particular, accentuates the experiences and stories of Manitos who are commonly alluded to in New Mexico scholarship but rarely covered in depth or detail.

BORDERED REALITIES

"Changing one's place of residence in the eternal quest for a better life is a common historical phenomenon," state Francisco Balderrama and Raymond Rodríguez.[4] This, of course, includes the movement of people across state and national borders. For the inhabitants of the U.S.-Mexico borderlands, many of these movements stemmed from intentional acts of displacement and the pressures of failing economies. Although the border has imposed boundaries and restrictions on the inhabitants of the borderlands, it has remained porous to the influence of people, economies, and the politics of both nations. William Hewitt documents Mexican settlement prior to and during World War II. He writes, "The sugar beet industry drew many Mexicans to Wyoming in the early 1900s. Mexican Nationals and Mexican Americans provided a ready supply of labor for the sugar companies."[5] Hewitt acknowledges the significant role the railroad played in dispersing migrant groups, outlining a migratory trail that laborers traveled beginning in the border town of El Paso, Texas, and moving north through the Rocky Mountain states of Colorado, Wyoming, and Montana. As the FMT project has documented, Hewitt highlights the bleak conditions in which the migrant laborers found themselves, receiving low wages and encountering discrimination and poor housing conditions in their new locales.[6] It is likely that Hewitt does not include New Mexico as a migratory labor stop because, like Mexican workers, Nuevomexicanos were also involved in outward economic migration and often worked alongside Mexican laborers. Pivotal to the work of the FMT project is the documentation of state and national politics that attempted to curb Mexican/Mexican American opportunities, combined with protest efforts to combat workplace discrimination.

In the fields, mining camps, and factories, as well as on the railroads, immigrant workers from Mexico became a significant source of labor for the United States. Various streams of Mexican and Mexican American migration, flowing toward economic opportunity, have run throughout the Southwest and the Intermountain region. These experiences of (im)migration are well documented. Scholarship on the specifics of Manito migration and the context of those experiences, however, remains limited, due to a focus on Mexican immigration. Yet, it is important to acknowledge the conflation of Mexicans, Mexican Americans, and Manitos as one culture and community. Historical documentation found in government and economic reports is often from an Anglo perspective and highly generalized in description. Zaragosa Vargas writes, "Anglos did not distinguish between the newcomers from Mexico and Mexican Americans. Both were perceived as foreigners, even though the latter's ancestry had been in the United States or had become Americans with the Treaty of Guadalupe Hidalgo. Mexican immigration reinforced and intensified both the external Anglo hostility and the internal pressures within Mexican communities."[7] We build upon this analysis in acknowledging the notable experiences of Manito migration across U.S. state borders and distinguishing their migration experiences from their Mexican counterparts.

To understand the Manito experience, it is imperative to recognize the influence of racialized processes and politics that influenced their daily lives and worldviews. The myth of New Mexico as a tricultural state has led to a number of misunderstandings about how myriad groups came to call this region home. Though the complicated history of New Mexico has inspired a rich cultural knowledge of mixed heritages, politics of race and blood often are used to distinguish communities, depending on the context of the conversation and generational perspective. However, what remains true is that the skill sets and culture of Nuevomexicanos are inspired by the mixed, Native-Hispano practices of their forbearers. Despite efforts toward division, community has been essential to survival and can be distinguished by Manito traditional values and expressions. One of the primary goals for the FMT project is to flesh out the distinct qualities of Manitos within the scope of their migratory experiences. To this end, we are interested in the very practices and characteristics that have sustained Manitos generationally across borders, while we also analyze the effects of migration on Manito communities.

LOCATION HOMELAND(S) ON MANITO TRAILS

Fixed routes are established throughout the Nuevomexicano landscape. As part of everyday experiences, Manitos had pathways to various areas and places that were essential to survival and as a means to engage community. For example, foot trails connected one *vecino*, or neighbor, to another and pathways led to the village church. Established routes linked villages to towns and to the nearby Pueblo communities, where Manitos were able to conduct trade with their Native neighbors. Trails led down to the river, and routes ran to and through the *monte*, or mountain. Manito trails throughout the homeland are many.

As a result of bordered realities brought forth since the Spanish colonial period and later intensified by the Treaty of Guadalupe Hidalgo, Manito trails began to branch out from the homeland. In this era, Manitos traveled by bus from Mora and Taos to work as sheepherders in Wyoming;[8] wartime industries attracted working-class Hispanos to California's aircraft industry and naval shipyards;[9] some traveled to the Colorado mines and sugar beet fields; and there is evidence documenting Manito trails extending into Arizona, Texas, Utah, and other parts of the U.S.

Sarah Deutsch has argued that Hispanic migration became the dominant strategy of survival on an intercultural frontier. She notes that a "regional community describes the mutual dependency of migrants and villagers and the extended village that dependency created. It describes both a strategy and a geographical area, a migrant system and the routes those migrants traveled."[10] By following the Manito trail, we can trace an extended Manito community through a continued flow and exchange of people and culture beyond bordered realities. This approach to the study of Manitos allows for a consideration of the various factors that link Manito communities on localized and national levels. It provides the opportunity to examine the reasons for migration, Manito experiences within the diaspora, and the contemporary conditions of their culture and community as it persists beyond the homeland.

In our own work on the FMT, we take a diasporic approach to Manito migration to better understand the dispersal of Manito communities and the conceptualization of the Manito diaspora. This framework permits a realization of the homogenizing effects of power structures that tend to generalize varied experiences and qualities of distinct groups. It also provides the flexibility to respond to the processes and practices of identities in motion that bring together community through overlapping histories, goals, and experiences. By following the Manito trail, we can identify the roots and routes of Manito identity across generations, maintained through ties and connections to New Mexico, the Manito homeland. As the FMT project demonstrates, the link between Manitos and the villages of their particular Nuevomexicano homelands remains pertinent in maintaining cultural values and a sense of ethnic identity in marginalized spaces. This connection inspires recognition of a Manito diaspora and the ability to trace its various trails.

Considering Manitos' migratory experiences, it is important to critically engage with their ties or attachment to place, particularly the ways they have maintained and regenerated their querencia in New Mexico and beyond. According to community scholar Juan Estevan Arellano, from Embudo/Dixon, querencia is "that which gives us a sense of place, anchors us to the land, and makes us a unique people."[11] Sylvia Rodríguez explains, "From the verb *querer* (to want, love), querencia is both a physical place or location and the subjective feeling that ties a person or a people to that place."[12] In the articulation of Manito identity within the diaspora, we argue that the cultural landscape of a person's place of origin injects a set of values and distinct qualities that create a strong sense of identity, enables community, and serves as a social form of resistance in marginalized spaces.

While many perceive the homeland as a territory to which the people of the diaspora hope to return, that is not always the case. William Safran demonstrates that while many diasporas maintain a "myth of return" not all participants are interested in returning to the homeland.[13] This is evident in the numerous Manito families that have established permanent residency within the diaspora. In many cases, it was not possible for Manitos to return to their homeland, as was the case with Avelinda (Lindy) Arguello Paskett, a Manita who lives in Riverton, Wyoming, who dreamed of returning to New Mexico to live on the land her father deeded to her and her sister. Though she was not born in New Mexico, she fondly recalls traveling there with her grandpa and connecting with everyone he knew. Even though they only went back about once a year, she noted, "Between the two of us, we never knew a stranger."[14] This land was part of her querencia.

When Romero and Fonseca-Chávez sat down with Lindy and her mother, Cleotilde (Cleo) Medina, Lindy told the story of the land she held on to for many years. She had visited the homestead a few years prior, a small plot of land whose adobe house had only two walls standing. Yet for Lindy, this served as an important link. She says, "My connection to New Mexico was that I still had land in New Mexico. . . . It was tiny, but I loved it."[15] When a woman called her with a similar story, she regretted never taking the time to go back to New Mexico. She was from Denver and wanted to return to the valley near Mora. The woman was buying an adjacent plot and told Lindy, "I want that land, I want to go back to New Mexico."[16] In a tearful interview, Lindy expressed her sadness in eventually agreeing to sell the land. Although she always had the memories of her trips there with her grandfather and her father, she didn't want to impede someone else's dream of returning home when she couldn't. She said of the woman, "When she told me her story, it was just about the same story as mine. And she was doing something about it."[17]

As a public-facing project, we find tremendous value in learning about a marginalized community's history and a diasporic identity that exists outside dominant archives and materials. And we often see our own family experiences echoed in the stories community members share. The significance of memory and orality resonates across marginalized and diasporic communities in ways that force us to consider how archives have silenced the less powerful and less fortunate.

From 2014 to 2016, the Following the Manito Trail team conducted approximately forty interviews with Manitos living in Wyoming. In those interviews, there was an overwhelming sense of community and culture. It was not difficult for families to remember the small New Mexico towns of their *antepasados*, their ancestors. This was due to the connections they maintained over the years by traveling the I-25 corridor back to their homeland for fiestas, family reunions, and other holidays. And despite the number of generations removed from New Mexico, many of our interviewees, including Ida La Febre, continued to identify strongly with their New Mexico roots. Ida stated, "Even though we live here [Laramie, Wyoming], so much of our hearts are part of New Mexico still, you know? And, so, it's just ingrained in us that that's who we really are, we're New Mexicans."[18] An additional source of cultural and linguistic pride was palpable at the home of David and Sibilia Apodaca, who both spoke a pristine dialect of New Mexican Spanish, despite having lived in Riverton, Wyoming, since the 1940s. At the beginning of our interview with David and Sibilia, Romero and Fonseca-Chávez established a linguistic kinship with them that set the tone for the interview to continue in Spanish.[19]

The recent scholarship produced by the FMT team engages with literary and cultural texts that Manitos produced while in the diaspora;[20] reflections on the first year of the FMT project;[21] and visual markings of place on sheepherding trails.[22] Of the work we have completed thus far, there are three particular projects that highlight the importance of our community engagement and that demonstrate a clear commitment to diversifying public history efforts in Wyoming. In 2015, Romero and Fonseca-Chávez met Annie Vigil Mejorado, a Manita from northern New Mexico whose family moved to Wyoming to work in the sugar beet fields. In Riverton, a small town west of Casper, a Manito enclave was established in the South Park barrio. During our interview with Annie, she spoke about a community activist moment in 1986 when Manito residents of South Park spoke repeatedly to city officials about the notable neglect in their barrio. The neighborhood lacked such basic services as "running water, sewer mains, streetlights, and paved roads."[23]

Because the city of Riverton was largely unresponsive to their requests, Annie, along with other Chicanas and Chicanos from the barrio began to write grants for funding to address the problem on their own. After being denied a number of times, they took it upon themselves to pave the streets and install curbs and gutters in their neighborhood. In an FMT documentary, Annie explains how an everyday conversation with her brother launched a community project that would forever affect the residents of South Park. Using their knowledge of Manito communal ways and traditional practices, a labor-intensive project naturally emerged. Her brother, Emilio Vigil, quit his job and became the project foreman. This was a form of Manito labor to which the community was well accustomed. The women also pitched into collective effort. Annie reflects on how she solicited their contributions: "Okay gals let's see what we can do to help. We can't be out there shoveling and doing this heavy work. We'll do the cooking."[24] With the hands and support of many, the project was underway. Emilio recalls how the larger community contributed to their efforts. Some businesses gave discounts for material and donated cement and tools, while other companies provided food and drinks to the South Park barrio residents. After advocating for the improvement of their community for more than a decade, it only took two months to complete the work. While many people doubted that the South Park community could complete such an endeavor, Manitos proved that community activism and hard work were values driving their identity.

Perhaps the most impressive aspect of this endeavor was Annie's ability to serve as a community activist and archivist. When we spoke to Annie about organizing a thirtieth anniversary celebration in honor of their accomplishments in 1986, she pulled out scrapbooks and VHS footage of the paving process. She masterfully narrated the details of the project, including noting the street names, dates, and the names of the individuals present in the documentary footage. This demonstrates the effort put forth by community to preserve their past through various forms of documentation and allows them to look back on their formation as a community dedicated to the improvement of their alternate homeland.

On July 23, 2016, residents of the South Park Community united to celebrate the thirtieth anniversary of their barrio accomplishment. Members of the FMT project organized the event and worked with the community to photograph families, conduct interviews, and participate in a communal Manito gathering space. At the celebration, Annie shared a few words, touched by the project's continuing resonance for the community. "Anything can be accomplished if everybody works together," she stated. "And I realize most of the people who were the workers out here are gone, but their children are here, and they can learn by what we did. Anything is possible as long as you set your mind to it and you got a lot of people who are with you."[25]

This community struggle and accomplishment is well documented through Annie's home recordings and photographs. Susana Vigil—Annie and Emilio's sister—also contributed greatly to the archival process by compiling all of the related materials for a project assigned in her Chicano Community Organization class at the University of Wyoming. A three-ring binder is filled to capacity with correspondence, legal documents, financial grant requests, maps, and other documents related to the persistent plight of the South Park barrio residents. These materials, along with the oral histories conducted by the FMT research team emerged as a documentary, produced by FMT member Adam Herrera. Viewing the video footage of the thirtieth anniversary celebration juxtaposed with original footage of the road pavement project has a profound effect, as it speaks to the struggles and labor efforts of the Manitos from Riverton. It represents a determination to maintain querencia and underscores the significance of community collaboration that solidifies a Manito legacy for generations to follow.

The "Riverton Paving Project" documentary is one of three documentaries produced by the FMT team. It recognizes and honors the power of community archives and activism in telling stories of Manito migration. While these stories often are fraught with struggles for inclusion and equality, there is a resonating Nuevomexicano spirit of community determination and perseverance that is not always reflected in the official archives.

In 2016, Fonseca-Chávez, Herrera, and Lovata received a grant from the Wyoming Institute for Humanities Research to explore the Sierra Madre Mountains in southern Wyoming to document aspen carvings left by Manito sheepherders in the early twentieth century. Our attention had shifted to sheepherding narratives when Lovata came across an item in the Cultural Resource Inventory of the state archeological database that identified arborglyphs left by New Mexican sheepherders as early as 1905 in Carbon County. The inventory states that carvings were left on aspen trees along Wyoming Forest Highway 11 by Spanish-surnamed New Mexicans. This information adds greatly to our understanding of the cultural remnants of New Mexicans and helps us to know the places they have traveled. Wyoming is home to abundant aspen arborglyphs, and archaeologists have listed sites in the State Historic Preservation Office database (WYCRIS). Records show that some are Basque in origin, but many more are related to Hispanics originally from New Mexico and southern Colorado.[26]

For our project, the arborglyphs provided a chance to study yet another manifestation of physical presence of Manitos in Wyoming that could provide a more nuanced history to coincide with oral history interviews, photographs, and literature regarding Manito sheepherders. Although sheepherding in Wyoming is but one of the industries in which New Mexicans have participated, it provides us the opportunity to engage in discussions and research that is culturally relevant and can have larger implications for our current understanding of Wyoming's multiethnic heritage.

Fonseca-Chávez, Herrera, and Lovata set out early in the morning for the Sierra Madre Mountains. When they came to the town of Encampment in southern Wyoming, they stopped at the Grand Encampment Museum to see what they could find out about sheepherding in the area. They came across a couple of books that looked promising but were told by museum workers that they did not have extensive records on sheepherding because the Museum's focus was on the history of cattle ranching. At the time this seemed puzzling, but the FMT team soon came to know more about the famed sheep and cattle wars in the U.S. West.

As they continued on their journey, Fonseca-Chávez was elated to see a man on horseback leading a herd of sheep across the road. They pulled over and engaged in conversation with the sheepherder, a Peruvian on a three-year contract in Wyoming. He only spoke Spanish and, while Fonseca-Chávez chatted with him, Herrera documented the moment with photography and video. The sheepherder, whose name was Walter, was unaware of the larger history of sheepherding in the area. We knew that the days of Manito sheepherding in Wyoming were long gone, but we did not anticipate meeting a new generation of sheepherders who hailed from Peru.

The arborglyphs from Manito sheepherders confirmed the information in the state databases. We located a Manito carving with the date "Julio 1907," which was impressive, considering the life span of an aspen tree is around a hundred years. Some of the trees contained dates, places, and names of Manitos marking the landscape and solidifying their presence in the sheepherding industry from, what we could see, 1907 to 1965. In a special edition on Latinos in Wyoming in *Annals of Wyoming: The Wyoming History Journal*, Fonseca-Chávez documents the presence of Manito sheepherders in Wyoming via oral histories located at the Center for Southwest Research at the University of New Mexico and through poetry originally found in newspapers and reprinted in Anselmo Arellano's 1979 publication, *Los pobladores nuevo mexicanos y su poesía, 1889–1950*.[27] In the same special issue of *Annals of Wyoming*, Lovata writes in detail about the significance of arborglyphs and tree markings in Wyoming and surrounding states. For Lovata, arborglyphs are a form of graffiti that help us to understand more about the people who traveled through distinct spaces.

The FMT documentary *Deciphering the Past: The Arborglyphs of the Sierra Madres*, produced by Herrera, is a visual representation of our trek through the Sierra Madre Mountains in the summer of 2016.[28] As part of the documentary process, Herrera included interviews with Kolleen Kralick, Heritage Program Manager for the U.S. Forest Service (USFS), who notes that the majority of the aspen carvings are from herders who traveled along the sheep drives, though carvings could be found anywhere in the forest. She explains that photography is the most effective means for preserving this cultural heritage, since it is impractical to preserve many trees past their natural lifespan. In another segment of the documentary, Christie Schneider, a USFS silviculturist, discusses the tree management system. Herrera's video footage shows active forest management through the removal of trees with evidence of bark beetle and blue fungus damage. According to Schneider, aspens are very susceptible to damage because of their thin bark.

Documenting the presence of Manito sheepherders is an important effort that serves to cement Manito presence in Wyoming, which likely began with the nineteenth-century sheepherders. Toward the end of the documentary, the camera pans over a fallen aspen with a carving of a naked woman. Lovata confirmed that the tree was, indeed, old and likely carved by Manitos. Herrera secured permission from the U.S. Forest Service to remove the tree and did so by snowshoeing more than three miles to drag the tree out of the snowy forest. After a six-month stay in a friend's garage in Laramie, Herrera retrieved the tree and met Lovata in Denver to transport it to Albuquerque, New Mexico, where it made its debut at a public exhibition titled "Migration" in spring 2018 at the Sanitary Tortilla Factory Gallery.

The culminating effort of our research and community engagement in Wyoming was a gallery exhibit at the University of Wyoming American Heritage Center (AHC) in fall 2017. The FMT team worked with then-University Archivist Irlanda Jacinto and former AHC Director Bridget Burke to coordinate an exhibit that would showcase the many contributions of Manitos to the Wyoming landscape. The AHC website states that the exhibit "document[s], for the first time, the many contributions that Manitos have had on the Western United States."[29] The exhibit included archival documents, photography, a heritage quilt on loan from Annie Vigil Mejorado, the two documentaries we have discussed in this chapter, and an additional documentary produced by the FMT team about a family's migration to Wyoming expressed through song and oral history. On opening night, the entire FMT team gathered in Laramie for a public presentation that was met with excitement and gratitude from the very Manito communities about whose stories we felt so passionate. At this presentation, Mary Louise Sánchez, a Manita currently residing in Colorado, shared the news of her then-forthcoming book, *The Wind*

Called My Name. It was published in 2018 and is one of the only books about Manitos in Wyoming.[30] Later, as members of the public toured the exhibit, they noticed familiar faces and shared stories with other Manitos who also had come to see their histories/stories displayed that evening. As part of our agreement with the AHC, the exhibit is available as a traveling exhibit that any community center, museum, or gathering space may request.

The FMT project, at its core, is about community. Our work has been supported by numerous sources including the University of Wyoming Faculty Grant in Aid, the University of Wyoming Social Justice Research Center, the Wyoming Institute for Humanities Research, and the Wyoming Cultural Trust Fund. The University of New Mexico's Center for Regional Studies (CRS) and the Southwest Hispanic Research Institute (SHRI) have also provided research grants to help further the documentation of Manito culture and history. Beyond institutional support, communities have been receptive to our work, participating every day in the celebration and preservation of their *querencias* in New Mexico and beyond. In countless ways, they strive to serve their communities, uphold cultural traditions, participate in activist movements to improve their neighborhoods, and instill in their children the value of maintaining a sense of place and peoplehood through the values that *querencia* embodies.

We continue to explore Manito migration and diaspora. In 2019, Martínez defended her dissertation, "Living the Manito Trail: Maintaining Self, Culture, and Community." Focusing on her own family's migration to Wyoming and, ultimately, back to New Mexico, Martínez conducts an in-depth analysis of Manito migration, diaspora, and *querencia* from the mid-nineteenth century to the present. Fonseca-Chávez is embarking on new explorations of *querencia* and homeland in eastern Arizona and western New Mexico, where her maternal grandmother's family settled in the late 1800s.

In December 2018, Levi Romero, Vanessa Fonseca-Chávez, and Trisha Martínez met with Estevan Rael-Galvez and Mimi Roberts, Project Director and Project Manager, respectively, for the Manitos Community Memory Project,[31] a new endeavor that aims to create digital *resolana* spaces for Manitos in northern New Mexico and southern Colorado. In typical Nuevomexicano fashion, we gathered over breakfast at a restaurant in Albuquerque's South Valley and talked about where we were from, who we knew, and shared memories of our own families. As we ate our *chicharrones*, *huevos*, and *papas* with healthy servings of *chile rojo* and tortillas, there was a profound sense of *familia* and *comunidad* that moved us to discuss how we could work together to document Manito histories and stories.

The Following the Manito Trail project and the Manitos Community Memory Project are but two examples of ventures that create necessary spaces for underdocumented communities to celebrate their legacies. The various aspects and collective endeavors of this work remind future generations of the paths their *antepasados* took to create and maintain homes in Nuevo México and wherever the Manito trail led them. Though we have merely scratched the surface of the many places Manitos migrated, we are confident the stories of their *querencia* will continue to resonate over space and time.

CHAPTER 7

"Working on the Dark Side"

Public Land Management and Tribal Relations

YVETTE TOWERSAP TUELL

The public dissemination of local and regional history is not always on the radar of Western public land managers, nor is sharing tribal history. Economic and political issues often are prioritized, even as managers strive to serve the public interest in a balancing act among competing interests, uses, and attitudes toward the value of natural resources. As a result, "history" often collapses into "precedent" and is understood as the minimum legal requirements under federal cultural resource laws. When this happens, the significance of regional and local history is not recognized, and the value of local knowledge is not realized. However, when federal land managers use the full range of tools available in the regulatory toolbox provided by federal heritage laws to include Native American history, a new perspective emerges. This chapter seeks to enrich the discussion of public land management by providing a case study that can aid land managers to better incorporate Native history and local knowledge into their policy decisions. It provides an example of how land managers can use their discretion in implementation, in accordance with the federal trust responsibility to tribes, to utilize an alternative land use decision-making model. By recognizing and consulting with federally recognized tribes, as required by federal statutes, executive orders, and internal agency guidelines, one field office of the Bureau of Land Management (BLM) has tackled new issues that can set precedent for other western land managers and tribes.

Managers in the Idaho BLM Burley Field Office (BFO) focused on their federal trust responsibilities to ensure that their management of cultural and natural resources protects the unique values, perspectives, and rights of federally recognized tribes. To do so, they embarked on a series of government-to-government consultations with two tribes, the Shoshone-Bannock Tribes (SBT) and the Shoshone-Paiute Tribes, to develop tribal nominations for two proposed traditional cultural properties (TCP).

Recognizing the potential difficulties of non-Native archeologists in this work, the BLM hired the author to help draft the nominations and assist in tribal consultation. The experience of a tribal member working for a federal agency can be challenging, rewarding, and uncomfortable. So much so that "the dark side" had become a term that Shoshone-Bannock Tribal employees use to refer to tribal members working for federal agencies who are unable to express personal opinions under the constraints of federal trust responsibility and who are sometimes forced to make decisions at odds with their own personal ideology.[1] This chapter identifies the variety of issues encountered during my employment with the BLM, including gathering individual, family, and tribal information; effectively using the cloak of confidentiality and sensitivity; working with tribal individuals and consulting with tribal governments; understanding the difference between member knowledge and the authority of tribal officials; and understanding the limitation on federal employees expressing personal opinions. This chapter also offers suggestions on how to conduct effective tribal consultation and the challenges of managing the "double-edged sword" that is inherent when protecting tribal cultural values versus educating the public.

During the summer of 2014, as a graduate student, I served an internship as an archeological technician with the Bureau of Land Management, in the Burley Field Office, in south-central Idaho. This is a geographic area that I was very familiar with from my previous job as Environmental Coordinator for the Shoshone-Bannock Tribes. In that role, I had served two terms on the Resource Advisory Council (RAC) representing the Tribes. My previous education and experience in coordinating with federal land management agencies was also beneficial in this archeological technician position. I was able to offer guidance to the BLM on various National Environmental Policy Act (NEPA) projects, Archeological Resource Protection Act (ARPA) issues, and general policy advice for government-to-government consultation with tribes. I had extensive knowledge of the consultation history of these projects, as I had authored several response letters on behalf of the Shoshone-Bannock Tribes, identified and mitigated issues, coordinated site visits, and set up formal government-to-government meetings with the Fort Hall Business Council. While the BLM was eager to have my skills and abilities available, as a Shoshone-Bannock tribal member, I had to learn what it meant to work as a federal employee and negotiate my way through divergent tribal expectations and the realities of federal employment.

The National Historic Preservation Act (NHPA) governs historic properties that are listed or eligible for the National Register of Historic Places. Historic properties can be individual sites, historic districts, buildings, structures, and objects that are significant according to criteria identified in federal regulations. To provide basic guidance for Native American traditional cultural properties, the NPS issued National Register Bulletin 38, which provides assistance for the identification, documentation, and evaluation of potential TCPs. Bulletin 38 also recognizes the need to work with Native American tribes and communities for TCPs and other Native American landscapes that are eligible for listing on the National Register. The two potential TCPs within the boundaries of the BFO included the existing Cedar Fields Archeological District (CFAD), which was established in 1999 on the western banks of the Snake River near American Falls, and a combined TCP and archeological district within the City of Rocks National Preserve and Castle Rocks State Park near the Idaho-Utah border.

Of course, in the case of the City of Rocks/Castle Rocks TCP, the challenges involved in coordinating landowners, tribes, tribal members, and the public was more complex than originally projected. Due to the fact that TCPs are broadly defined yet specific to individual tribes and groups, there is no clearly defined process for TCP evaluation and approval. One of the first issues these TCP designations raised was procedural. In the 2013 discussions about the City of Rocks/Castle Rocks TCP, the following were initiated. The Keeper of the National Register agreed to meet with the BLM, the Shoshone-Bannock Tribes, the Shoshone-Paiute Tribes, and the Idaho State Historic Preservation Office to provide guidance. Even so, there were questions about the process of designating a TCP on mixed ownership lands. The Castle Rocks State Park and City of Rocks National Reserve are co-managed by the National Park Service and Idaho Parks and Recreation, but adjacent BLM and U.S. Forest Service lands were expected to be included in the proposed TCP, leading to complicated federal and state land management relationships with the tribes. Who was to be the lead agency? Who was to develop the draft TCP? What role would the state agencies—the Idaho State Historic Preservation Office and the Idaho Parks and Recreation—have in federal consultation?

How would tribal consultation occur with two distinct sovereigns? Who was to conduct the informant interviews? How would the information be secured and safe from public exploitation? What determined the physical boundaries of the TCP? What was the difference between an archeological district and a TCP? In the end, the BLM, of their own volition, took the lead and started drafting a TCP, simply notifying the other federal and state agencies of the process to be followed. As questions arose, the BLM addressed them on a point-by-point basis, rather than allow the entire process to be stymied by rhetoric and artificial barriers.

Many of the challenges with the Castle Rocks/City of Rocks TCP were similar to those experienced with the designation of the CFAD twenty-five years earlier. The process of formal consultation with the tribes and Bureau of Reclamation (BOR) had been heated and controversial. The CFAD, comanaged by BLM and the Snake River Area Office of the BOR, was initially nominated as both a district and a TCP. The TCP recommendation stemmed from a confidential ethnographic study initiated by BOR as a result of the archaeological investigations. Based on the information provided by Shoshone-Bannock informants, the BOR Regional Director acknowledged the significance of the area in a formal directive. Unfortunately, the area encompassing the CFAD had seen over thirty years of consultation and conflict among the BLM, BOR, and the Shoshone-Bannock Tribes.[2] In the early 1990s, public land managers for the BLM and BOR had to address fiery and emotional conflicts between Off-Highway Vehicle (OHV) users and the Shoshone-Bannock Tribes, which sought protection of tribal rights and resources.[3] The OHV users, through the Blue Ribbon Coalition, fought hard for continued access to public lands, regardless of archeological sites and treaty resource issues. Tensions were heightened when tribal staff and elected officials received death threats from local OHV users; police had to be present at public meetings held in American Falls and Pocatello. The tribal members said they were unable to express their feelings at the earlier meeting because of the hostility exhibited by some of the OHV-ers at the prospect of giving up an area they claimed to have been using for at least twenty-five years.[4]

Tribal requests to protect cultural resources were clearly stated at a later public meeting in Fort Hall with the BOR managers. "Leave our sacred land alone," was the overriding message at that hearing. Tribal Land Use Commissioner Hobby Hevewah said Indians have a responsibility, handed down from generation to generation, to protect their sacred sites and graves. "But we can do nothing," he said. "No matter how many times we speak up, we can do nothing. You ask why haven't we spoken up. We do speak up, but nothing happens." Shoshone-Bannock Land Use Department Director Genevieve Edmo said she didn't see why it should be so difficult for the BOR to uphold its trust responsibility to the tribes. "If it was us down there, it wouldn't take you long to tell us to get out," she said.[5]

Regardless of the heated opposition, the BOR and BLM designated the majority—but not all—of the CFAD lands closed to OHV use. Yet the 1990s-era fear and lack of trust has colored much of the tribal-federal relationship to the present time. Since 1999, the BLM and BOR have made little effort to protect the cultural sites within the CFAD, nor were there any efforts to enforce the OHV closure.[6] There are over 200 documented archeological sites within the CFAD. However, the management boundaries between the two agencies were indistinct because no fences or signs designated land ownership. Public recreationalists often did not know whose land they were on as they continued to drive the unauthorized trails. The BLM and BOR contracted law enforcement with the Power County Sheriff's Office, yet the federal agencies failed to give county deputies authority to issue citations. This lax enforcement resulted in continued illegal OHV use for decades, and a succession of BLM land managers paid scant attention to the CFAD. Meanwhile, the BOR and the BLM district archeologist failed to develop a cultural resource management plan to guide land managers.

Finally, in 2012, new federal managers addressed this negligence, taking their responsibilities as trustees to the tribes more seriously and implementing a variety of efforts to work with the tribes. More regular and consistent consultation occurred between the technical staff and policy makers of the Shoshone-Bannock and Shoshone-Paiute Tribes, establishing a more productive government-to-government relationship.

The BLM recognized that clear management of the CFAD was required under Section 110 of the NHPA, and any effects of federal undertakings inside the CFAD must be evaluated under Section 106. In order for the BLM to effectively manage the CFAD, changes to the Cassia Resource Management Plan required NEPA analysis. Although the BFO initially prepared an environmental assessment, managers opted for a full-blown environmental impact statement due to the adverse impacts from OHV use and sport climbing as well as the high levels of public response.[7] One of the tasks required of me was to review the 800-plus public comments received. One main theme of the comments identified the need for public education on regional tribal history. Another thread accused the BLM of ignoring the will of the public and catering only to a special user group, the Indians. In response, the BLM sought to develop an educational campaign.

My assigned task was to review and revise the draft TCP nomination for both the CFAD and the proposed Castle Rocks/City of Rocks properties, working in coordination with two tribes (and later, three[8]) to develop an interpretation of tribal values and perspectives for a draft nomination.

When the BFO and BOR recognized federal obligations associated with historic preservation and proposed changes to protect the CFAD by limiting recreational uses, suggesting use of the TCP designation, the tribes had to reconsider their views of the TCP. Until recently, the tribes have been reluctant to use TCPs or archeological districts as a tool to protect cultural sites and sacred landscapes. There are only two archeological districts in southern Idaho, and only one is designated TCP on behalf of the Shoshone-Bannock Tribes. The tribes had long opposed any federal designation that would extend unique federal management protections for tribal cultural activities in any one place, viewing it as creating artificial cultural or historical boundaries. All lands within the tribes' traditional homelands were important, and they did not want to see their rights limited to specially designated areas.

It fell to me to offer the BFO manager and assistant manager recommendations for tribal government meetings. As a federal agency, the BLM has an obligation to conduct government-to-government consultation with affected tribes, per executive order and federal regulations. I transcribed the September 25, 2013, meeting of the BLM, the National Park Service (which sent representatives from both the Seattle and Washington, D.C., offices), the Idaho State Historic Preservation Officer, Idaho State Park and Recreation manager of Castle Rocks State Park, the Shoshone-Paiute Tribes, and the Shoshone-Bannock Tribes. Transcribing the meeting was an excellent entry into the entire TCP discourse. Although I was familiar with the project, this meeting took place after I had left my tribal employment, so I was unaware of the exact content of the meeting until I listened to the audio tapes. The BLM was excited to finally get a written account of this important meeting, documenting the comments and commitments made by federal and state agencies.

As a former tribal employee who developed several tribal consultation protocols with federal agencies, I was able to offer useful guidance to the BLM staffers and managers on a variety of topics, including best management practices. One was how to develop presentations to tribal leadership for formal meetings. Due to my familiarity with almost all of the items on the agenda, I advised on how to discuss sensitive issues, such as proposing an archeological excavation/data recovery project for a mitigation land parcel adjacent to the CFAD. Because excavations destroy all or a portion of a site and remove the physical components of tribal ties to the land, the tribes generally oppose them except under threat of total site destruction. The BLM had secured a $15,000 grant for the tribes to help train tribal members in archeological methods, using data recovery procedures, as well as other natural resource projects. I was worried that the tribes would view this grant as a compromise for protecting sites, or that the BLM would be viewed as being insensitive to tribal views of data recovery. Fortunately, the BLM managers deemphasized the data recovery aspect and instead shifted the funding toward a broader range of other natural resource projects. Although the grant was not expended due to bureaucratic challenges, the BLM managers were better prepared for meeting with the tribal staff and Council and actually received praise for their efforts to secure grant funding on behalf of the tribes.

While federal land managers are required to consult with affected Indian tribes, over the years the BLM BFO has had a spotty and inconsistent relationship with them, ranging from paternalism to collaboration. One of the main points of contention has been confidentiality and security of federal records pertaining to cultural sites.[9] The BLM has to be cautious when managing tribally sensitive information, especially as it relates to tribal archeological sites, maps that disclose the locations of sites, and confidential ethnographic studies. But when public landownership is checkerboarded with other federal, state, and private lands, despite all the efforts of one vigilant BLM land manager, other inattentive and lax land managers raise the stakes for all federal land managers.

In this regard, a 2010 incident illustrated the need for increased federal security efforts. During a public meeting for proposed closure to rock climbing at the CFAD, two tribal employees attending the meeting noticed that a non-Indian recreationalist had in his immediate possession a copy of the Confidential Ethnographic Report, including site location maps. They recognized the cover of the report, which clearly was identified as "Confidential and Official Use Only." This individual was also a local Forest Service employee who was later terminated for having unauthorized possession of this document.

After the BLM realized that a security lapse had occurred, the BFO manager immediately conducted an internet search and found additional copies available for sale on the Amazon website. He immediately purchased all copies available from a bookstore in Boise. The tribes presented a scathing letter requesting full investigation of the accused individual and sought accountability of federal agencies responsible for the management of cultural sites and information. Further investigation revealed lax security on the part of Forest Service, BLM, and BOR staff alike. Many had failed to properly secure confidential maps, reports, and pictures in their offices. Suddenly, BLM managers became very aware of the need to ensure the safety and security of these reports. Upon my employment, I was instructed to be very cautious in what I was writing on computers and to lock away all reports and maps in secured cabinets, even when taking a break or going for lunch. The extent of the BLM's newfound commitment to confidentially was impressive.

One of my primary duties was to work directly with tribal members willing to offer cultural information to support either the Castle Rocks/ City of Rocks TCP or the reinstatement of the CFAD TCP. To my surprise, not one tribal member was hesitant to share sensitive, personal information, and its quality was detailed and frank. In fact, I had to constantly caution members that I only needed sufficient evidence to support a TCP—not to write a book! Two main meetings were held, one with the family descendants of Chief Pocatello, who used the southern Snake River territory as their aboriginal lands, and another with local residents. Both meetings were productive and revealed key family-held information that was useful to explaining tribal historical significance.

In general, I found that some Indian families claimed specific traditional "neighborhoods" and used that area as their family's home base. Just as importantly, the people explained why tribal history was absent in the historical record. As informants shared confidential stories, it became apparent that the information came from a deliberately closed world—it was offered now to protect that world. People shared stories that had previously been told only within families. For example, at one of the family meetings, one octogenarian stated that she was taught to not trust white people, and for decades it was difficult for Indian kids to go to school and interact with the non-Indian world.

> As Indians were going to school, they were told that the Indians were terrible, that Indians were savages. So Indians would go to school learn about how bad Indians were, then they would go home that night, and be Indians. It was difficult, Indian children

> struggled with the white man's education. There was two different worlds, the Indian family and the "taibo" world.[10] And that is where we grew in, right in between.[11]

Following this statement, this same elder went on to passionately and loudly explain why she was always reluctant to say anything to white people, whether federal government representatives, school, or anyone:

> As a young lady, she was told not to say anything. White people will ask, "What do you eat, where do you go, what do you have?" The old people said, "Don't tell them, because they will turn on you. They will find out what you know, and they will take it away from you. Then when you tell them, you are not Indian anymore."[12]

This was the first time I had heard this message, and it was shockingly clear. It illustrated the tradition of long-held silence and mistrust and explains why there is so little information and direct quotes from many Native people in this area.[13] The emphasis on silence equates to an absence of voice, further emphasized at other local meetings.

In late August 2015, tribal residents revealed several things: first, how willing they were to talk openly to me. Over a dozen people attended the meeting, and it was a challenge to capture all their stories. Again, due to concerns of public disclosure through the Freedom of Information Act, I had to caution community members regarding the purposes of these interviews and how this information was to be used, although some information could be shared to the public. Regardless of such cautions, I had a tribal elder enthusiastically tapping me on the shoulder, wanting to tell me a story about a rock monster near the Snake River, along with other people's personal stories. Throughout these interviews, I worked directly with the tribal staff, who captured sensitive information at the governmental level to help protect cultural information. I took only information specific to support establishment of a TCP.

The elders reiterated again, however, their reluctance to talk to white people, since Indians were scared and fearful of what whites can take away. Silence was their way of retaining a sense of identity and Indianness. Without that information, white people could not know what to take from the Indians. This also explains why local history books do not have many Indian informants. After the land has been taken away, Indian stories are what remains and should not be given away. The elders also emphasized their shared, intrinsic relationship to the lands, the animals, water, and the need to give this history to Indians, especially the younger generations.[14]

Another theme made evident at local meetings was the direct communication and relationship between Indian women and animals, and how tribal people still believe these interactions continue. The ladies shared the story of the meadowlark and how the meadowlark sings and harasses Indian women in the morning. One elder reported her experiences as a young girl with her grandmother.

> She [her grandmother] was blind. I would take her to the outhouse. And there was this crazy bird always singing, and one day she asked me, "Did you comb your hair? That bird is making fun of you. That meadowlark. He is making fun of you."[15]

This exemplifies how tribal members believe their actions connect directly to animals and how animals view and communicate with Indians. It was apparent that these beliefs are not historical in nature but continue to be held by the people.

While it was exciting to hear the amazing stories and information offered, for the BLM's TCP purposes it was vital to have a member with tribal and cultural understanding, experience, and training in tribal consultation, the ability to process and discern what information should be made public, and what should remain in tribal confidence. The challenge at hand was to craft a reasonable solution after seeing and understanding both perspectives, the need to physically protect the area from inadvertent recreational damage by applying federal historic preservation laws, and the need to protect tribal cultural knowledge and respect the confidentiality of tribal informants. Being in the middle of this situation was difficult.

In developing the nomination for the Castle Rocks/City of Rocks TCP, it became apparent that the extensive historical record of overland emigrants' travels through the City of Rocks area and the creation of Euro-American narratives fails to include any Native history. The public history interpretation presented at the City of Rocks included very little on Native American use or even our presence in the area before the emigrant influx. It was as if the Native Americans did not even exist there. Nor was there much consultation occurring between the different land managers and the tribes. For these two reasons, I spent that summer working mostly on the City of Rocks area in order to fill the gaps with tribal history.

As I started working with the BLM and considering the historical lack of willingness to share tribal information, a major question was why the tribes were now supporting use of the TCP designation. Indian people have always known of their traditions tied to these places, and in fact, we already see how these traditions are in danger and how have tribal traditions tied to specific places have disappeared. Upon questioning of tribal elders, the importance of place still rings strong. Yet, given the reticence to reveal such ties in the public sphere, local and regional history generally fails to record Indian narratives, and Indian voices seem silent.[16]

Similarly, non-Natives rarely see the actions or understand the rationale of Native people in history. This was also reflected in the interviews, when tribal members stated that they will generally avoid white people when tribal members go to the City of Rocks area. When they are gathering plants, they turn away and find another location if there are non-Indians in the area. Ceremonial and religious activities are only conducted in solitude, well away from outsiders. Indian men stated they still go hunting for rabbits, rock chucks, and big game, but they reported numerous incidents in recent years of accusations by white ranchers and farmers who reported Indians allegedly stealing or vandalizing their farm equipment. Due to historical distrust of the federal government and its agencies, Indian prefer to exercise their inherent, treaty, religious, and ceremonial rights away from the eyes and pens of non-Indians. Considering there has been over 150 years of suspicion by white people, government officials, and historians toward Indians, it is understandable why Indians would be hesitant to talk to them.

Although federal managers are more knowledgeable of the Native histories of the area, this historical education must now be shared with the public. Public recreationalists do not understand why Indians do not support their activities, believing that their activities are noninvasive, nondestructive, and appreciative of the natural beauty. They do not understand that the rocks themselves are considered tribal resources and are tied to stories and songs. Due to the use of climbing bolts, Indian people are of the opinion that sport climbing is especially destructive. In many popular sport climbing areas, bolted routes may cover the majority of a rock face. Without restraint or management, this form of recreation can result in extensive defacement of sensitive areas. And yet, rock climbing groups, including the Access Fund, are not hesitant to fight climbing closures by filing lawsuits and rallying national organizational support. This makes creating more historical interpretative programs a necessary task, to educate the local and regional public regarding Native American perspectives, history, and rights retained by the tribes as a part of public land management. Yet one of the primary challenges will be to create tribally acceptable public history campaigns that overcome the tribal fear of sharing their history.

Overall, the biggest challenge I had of being "on the dark side," and working for "the feds" was that I had to speak differently and not on behalf of my tribe or even for other tribes. I had to speak objectively. I had to limit my suggestions to the constraints, the regulations, and federal laws that the BLM worked under. It was difficult not to suggest options for the tribes because I no longer worked for them. In work discussions with the BLM, it was difficult to carefully express my personal opinion as a tribal member to staff, but I believe it helped the BLM management's consideration of how to approach the tribes. I further believe that it helped provide cultural context for working with them to better understand tribal perspective.

Working for an agency that has the responsibility to manage off-reservation trust resources was daunting but important. And debating the need for public education on history and cultural resource protection, I understand the double-edged sword, with risks and benefits, of determining public land management, especially in tribal consultations. Education in tribal history is always beneficial, but determining how much information should be released to the public—at the risk of compromising tribal confidentiality—must be done carefully, respectfully, and in full transparency.

My experience working on the dark side was not just upholding the civil service obligations that all federal employees must, but it also meant reconciling my personal teachings and tribal beliefs at the workplace. Navigating the private voices of tribal historical and contemporary narratives alongside the public engagement requirements of a federal agency was challenging but necessary. Native voices introduce differing perspectives where public land managers often overlook tribal rights.

In sum, federal lands make up the majority of the southern Idaho landscape. Although land managers must constantly juggle competing land use objectives, including recreation, grazing, mining, and logging, it is important to balance these demands with historic preservation regulations and federal obligations to consult with tribes—especially if historic preservation goes hand in hand with protecting tribal resources and sensitive landscapes. Tribal dialogue and interaction can enrich the public land dialogue and provide a multilayered conversation on public land management. Despite the extremely politicized nature of federal lands management, it is important to recognize the millennia-long occupation of the southern Idaho landscape. It is diverse, historically complex, and noisy.

CHAPTER 8

The Adjudication of Three Tribes' Water Rights

E. RICHARD HART

Some fifty years ago I began work at the American West Center. I thought at the time that it was pretty neat to be doing research in a library to pay for my education, rather than laying asphalt for the Utah State Road Commission. The work I did at the American West Center, and the training I received there, led to a career doing historical expert testimony in tribal litigation. Historical work for tribes is a highly valuable kind of public history that not only can benefit tribes but non-Native people and communities as well.

Floyd A. O'Neil, in particular, provided me direction in my work, verbally berating me for anything substandard and not berating me for something of standard or above quality. Floyd introduced me to working with tribes and tribal history. I learned that history is alive and important to tribes as they seek self-determination under the long processes established by the United States. I have continued to consult with Floyd, and with others at the American West Center (including Pat Albers, Greg Smoak, and others) ever since I left in 1974.

The first version of this essay was originally presented at a meeting of the International Water History Association in Delft, Netherlands, in 2015. A later version is included in my book *American Indian History on Trial: Historical Expertise in Tribal Litigation*, published by the University of Utah Press (2018).

Since 1982, I have been involved as an expert witness historian in three tribal reservation water rights adjudications: the Zuni Tribe, the Klamath Tribes, and the Coeur d'Alene Tribe. The water rights adjudications of these three tribes provide examples of some of the reasons why public history is of profound importance to tribes today.

ZUNI

The Zuni Tribe (they call themselves "Ashiwi") originally had exclusive use and occupancy over a territory covering a little under 15 million acres (over 6 million hectares) located across today's states of New Mexico and Arizona. At the time of contact with Europeans (Spain) in the fifteenth century, the Zunis had ten to fifteen villages and cultivated many thousands of acres of corn and other crops.[1]

Zuni territory is semiarid and desert-like, receiving only a little over ten inches of precipitation annually. Because of low precipitation, few springs, and generally scarce water, the Tribe engaged in what has been called floodwater irrigation. They did have some larger ditches, use of springs, and one small river, but whenever it rained they moved about in their fields to direct water using small check-dams and small irrigation ditches. It is no surprise that water is sacred to the Zunis, as it is to many other American tribes. Zunis pray constantly for rain. When they pray, they "plant" prayer sticks—native wood carved, painted, and adorned with bird feathers and designed to attract water.

The sophisticated methods of agricultural production used by the Zunis were a mystery to most of the chroniclers of this period. Zuni irrigation ditches, or *acequias*, were observed from the sixteenth century onward, but these were not extensive. Although the observers could see that most Zuni farming was done without the use of canals (or "irrigation," as they called it), they could not quite understand how a people could be so successful as farmers in such a dry climate. Many made the mistake of saying the Zunis did not "cultivate" their farmlands. Few were close enough observers to see the kinds of floodwater and run-off techniques that were being used, but almost all of them described the vast fields of corn and the gardens of melons, gourds, peppers, beans, onions, garlic, and pumpkins. Many thousands of acres of corn were consistently noted in the Zuni Valley—indeed, it seems most of the valley was under floodwater cultivation during this period. There is much evidence of fields located at the mouths of arroyos, where Zunis spread the water out to water crops. In addition, writers observed the presence of irrigated fields of wheat at the farming villages and extensive orchards in the Zuni valley. Their orchards, mostly peaches, were planted during the Spanish period. The Zunis had an excess of corn and other vegetables to trade in the sixteenth, seventeenth, eighteenth, and nineteenth centuries. In 1583, the Zunis promised the leader of a small military expedition, Antonio de Espejo, that they would plant more crops so that the following year they would have an ample supply for the Spaniards, should the foreigners return. Later, in the second half of the nineteenth century, they sold many thousands of bushels of shelled corn to United States military authorities.

The Zunis were consistently reported to be friendly, healthy, industrious people. They traded corn and sheep from their large flocks (at least 15,000 by 1779). They were hospitable to the United States authorities and helped the military in every way possible. In return, they were promised the right to manage their own resources and freedom of religion. "Abundant" was a word almost overused in descriptions of Zuni trust lands—abundant water, abundant game, abundant timber.

The Zuni Tribe's reservation was established by executive order in 1877, the Winters Doctrine priority date for tribal water rights, and expanded periodically over the next half century. Through action and inaction alike, the United States allowed non-Indians to divert considerable water that had flowed onto the reservation from off the reservation. Also, through action and inaction the United States allowed damages to occur to the reservation, which resulted in the loss of thousands of acres of agricultural land and a dramatic lowering of the water table. In the mid-nineteenth century, reports indicate a total agricultural acreage in the neighborhood of 20,000 acres (8,093 ha). By the early twentieth century, cultivated lands had been reduced to around 1,000 acres (404 ha).

Adjudication of Zuni water rights has been ongoing in courts since the early 1980s. Court actions have taken place in federal and state courts. The reservation's water rights are currently in federal court and negotiated partly under state administration. As mentioned, the Pueblo tribes of New Mexico require specialized legal claims because of the large amount of land they were already cultivating when Europeans arrived, because of the centuries of water use subject to laws of Spain and Mexico, and because of particular decisions of the United States courts, particularly *New Mexico v. Aamodt*.[2]

Some tribal water rights have already been established. Zunis believe that after death they go to reside at Kolhu/wala:wa ("Zuni Heaven" in English). This village of supernatural beings exists under the surface of a small lake about seventy kilometers southwest of their main village and that the water creatures (frogs, tadpoles, fish, etc.) that live in the lake are sacred. The Tribe reached a settlement with the parties involved, which Congress approved, in 2003. This has allowed that small lake to be replenished and the sacred area saved for Zuni religious use.[3]

Since historic documentation shows Zuni cultivation of some 20 thousand acres (nearly 8,100 hectares), a very large claim for actual historic use can be made by the Pueblo. The Tribe can also make a claim under the Practicably Irrigable Acreage standard (PIA), which allocates to tribes the water necessary to irrigate all of the lands feasible to develop and treats their reservation (the heart of their aboriginal territory) as a permanent homeland. Thus, their final water right may be based on a combination of historic claims, claims under the PIA Standard, and claims under a Homeland Standard. Claims under the PIA Standard are complicated by arguments as to what definition should be used regarding what constitutes "irrigation."

KLAMATH

Prior to the establishment of the Klamath (and Modoc) Reservation, and for many years after its establishment, the Klamath Tribes subsisted on an array of natural resources that were found within their aboriginal (and reservation) boundaries, including plants, fish, and animals. Food and material cultural resources were closely associated with their marshes, rivers, and lakes. Thus, their permanent winter villages were all adjacent to these bodies of water.[4] Beginning in the early spring, the Klamath moved through their territory as various fish, plants, and game matured with the seasons. Anthropologist Leslie Spier described their seasonal round. People left winter villages early in the spring for

> favorable fishing stations where there are successive fish runs. Through the summer they move to the prairies to gather edible roots and berries or to the mountain and desert to hunt. During most of this time families are widely scattered and the winter villages quite deserted, but with the ripening of pond lily seeds in the marshes during August and September they again congregate. The pond lilies grow in enormous quantities, the seeds (*wókas*) constituting a staple second only in importance to fish.[5]

The Klamath Tribes' unique culture made intense use of riverine, lake, and marsh plants, animals, and fish. Every aspect of their traditional culture interacted with, depended on, and reflected a reliance on the waters about them. Not only their rich variety of foods but also clothing, lodges, as well as social culture—music, song, stories, games—all were associated with the Klamath Tribes' water resources.[6]

Ethnographic fieldwork began early among the Klamath Tribes. Albert S. Gatschet, a linguist and staff ethnologist with the Bureau of American Ethnology (BAE), began his extensive field work on the Klamath Reservation in the 1870s, when tribal cultural practices were as yet still largely unaffected by reservation life.[7] Gatschet published several studies of the Klamath Tribes' folklore, mythology, and songs in which details demonstrated a close cultural association of the tribes with their waterways and with fish and fishing.[8] In one article, he provided the Klamath creation narrative, which accounted for "all the various kinds of fish that live in the water." The narrative also included mention of stone fish traps and the dam that was constructed at the outlet of Upper Klamath Lake.

> Hereupon he [the creator] also ordered that at Cascade Falls (Linkville) a rock-dam should come into existence; that when the south wind blows, it should drive back the waters, loudly roaring at their rushing down, and that the Indians should then, on the dry river bottom, gather up the fish and feed on them.[9]

Anthropologist Roy L. Carlson, in an article published in *American Anthropologist*, reported that, indeed, sometimes when the wind blew upstream from the Link River, the lake actually backed up and the river ceased to flow. The Klamaths thus could benefit in such circumstances by having the water in the marsh-like areas rather than flowing down the river.[10]

Eventually, Gatschet's work would result in a monumental two-volume work, *The Klamath Indians of Southwestern Oregon*.[11] Gatschet observed that the tribes were secluded in rough country, subject to a harsh climate, stating, "But the soil is productive in edible roots, bulbs, berries, and timber, the limpid waters are full of fish and fowl, and game was plentiful before the white man's rifle made havoc with it." Thus, the country was capable of supplying a considerable number of Indians with food, and they never manifested a desire to migrate or "be removed to a better country."[12]

Especially after the Klamath Tribes were limited to their reservation and unable to use all of their aboriginal territory, their reliance on fish, *wókas*, and other water-related resources greatly increased. The Klamath

Tribes gradually accepted a democratic form of government in the late nineteenth and early twentieth century but in the mid-twentieth century were subjected to one of the worst United States policies toward Native peoples that Congress ever devised. The policy, aptly designated Termination, was adopted by Congress in the 1950s and continued to be applied to tribes until about 1970. As Vine Deloria Jr. and David E. Wilkins describe it,

> Termination was the official policy of the federal government toward a number of Indian tribes from 1953 through the 1960s. It was most clearly enumerated through House concurrent Resolution 108, enacted August 1, 1953 (67 Stat., B132). A "terminated" tribe had its share of federal benefits, programs, and services severed.[13]

The Klamath Tribes were terminated in August 1954, and their reservation was opened to non-Indian settlement.[14] While this dire event devastated the Tribes and took most of their land from them, there was a somewhat unusual development regarding their potential water rights. In 1975, a lawsuit was initiated to determine if the Tribes retained water rights to their reservation under their 1864 treaty, even though the reservation had been terminated. Nearly ten years later, in a case that came to be known as *United States v. Adair*, the courts decided that the Tribes retained hunting and fishing rights within their former reservation boundaries—and by implication water necessary for the fish to survive.[15]

Because the Klamath Tribes were terminated and almost all of their reservation land lost to non-Indians, historical evidence sought in the matter did not relate to the relatively small amount of agriculture engaged in by the Tribes. A PIA Standard could not result in much of a water right because there simply was too little land that could be irrigated. However, the court ruling in *Adair* meant that there had to be sufficient water to sustain the fish upon which the Tribes had subsisted. Most of the historical evidence submitted related to the types and amounts of fish used by the Klamath Tribes around the time of their 1864 treaty. In addition, they had once depended heavily on *wókas*, the water lily found in the 10-thousand-acre (4,046 ha) Klamath Marsh, most of which was drained to provide farmland to non-Indian farmers.

The Klamath Tribes' reservation water matter was litigated in Oregon state court at the same time that the Tribes and the U.S. Department of

Justice attempted to reach a negotiated settlement. The matter was contentious, with open antagonism and hostility among some of the parties.[16]

In 2004, a negotiated settlement was proposed by officials. In 2010, a "final" settlement was proposed. In 2011, the Oregon court issued decisions related to historical arguments, supporting the Tribes' fishing claims for in-stream flow to conserve and restore salmon runs to the Klamath River Basin and its tributaries. The settlement was supported by the Tribes, who recommended congressional ratification. The settlement is meant to provide increased stream flows into Klamath Lake, better water quality, and improved fish habitat in the Upper Klamath Basin. Dam removal is to begin within seven years, which should improve fish species recovery in the system.

COEUR D'ALENE

The Coeur d'Alene Tribe's aboriginal territory encompassed more than 4 million acres (over 1.6 million ha). At its heart was Lake Coeur d'Alene, fed by the Coeur d'Alene and St. Joe Rivers. Schitsu'umsh ("those who were found here") is the Coeur d'Alene name for themselves in their own language. Before the first decade of the nineteenth century had passed, French-Canadian trappers had named the Tribe "coeur d'alene" ("heart of an awl," but often translated as "pierced hearts," referring to the Tribe's sharp trading abilities). The Tribe also fiercely protected its territory and defended it against any permanent settlement, though they welcomed trade with Europeans when that became available.[17]

In nearly every aspect of their culture and lives, the Coeur d'Alene depended on their water resources. They fished in their lake and rivers, gathered plants in the surrounding wetlands, traveled by canoe, and recreated on the lake and rivers. Even their hunting practices centered around using waterways to harvest game.

First contact with Europeans came toward the end of the eighteenth century. The Tribe established a valuable trade with the Hudson's Bay Company and came into contact with Jesuit missionaries. Early reports from the Jesuits indicate that many Coeur d'Alene people converted to Catholicism, and a mission was established near Lake Coeur d'Alene in the 1840s. However, there are indications that the Tribe viewed the relationship with the Jesuits as an alliance. The Jesuits worked with them to try and insulate the Tribe from white incursions and later assisted the

Tribe in communicating with U.S. officials when their reservation was established.

In 1846, the United States signed a treaty with Great Britain establishing the 49th parallel as the international boundary to the north of Coeur d'Alene territory. Washington Territory was established in 1853, and efforts began to extinguish tribal aboriginal title in the territory and to place the Indians on reservations. The governor of Washington Territory failed to complete a treaty negotiation with the Coeur d'Alene, and in 1858 a contingent of federal troops entered the Tribe's territory without permission. The Tribe defended its territory, and the troops were soundly defeated. Reports of the battle were published in the national press. In retaliation, the U.S. sent out a much larger military force to exact revenge and establish peace.

Colonel George Wright managed to kill nearly a thousand horses and eventually reached the central Coeur d'Alene villages but only after the Tribe used its own canoes to help the troops cross the water. The resulting "treaty of peace and friendship" was signed. The Coeur d'Alenes indicated they wanted a permanent treaty with the United States that protected their homeland. The net result of the 1858 battle and the Wright treaty was that the U.S. feared war with the Tribe and sought a cession of most of the Tribe's territory without military conflict.

In 1867, the president of the United States signed an executive order setting aside a reservation southwest of Lake Coeur d'Alene, hoping that it would lead to an agreement with the Tribe to cede or sell the remainder of their aboriginal territory. But the Tribe emphatically rejected this reservation because it did not include the Tribe's lakes and rivers and refused to move there, remaining in their villages on Lake Coeur d'Alene.

As non-Indians began to move into the region, it became more and more important to the United States to reach some kind of agreement with the Tribe. In 1873, a commission established by the Interior Department was sent to negotiate and reach an agreement with the Tribe. The 1873 agreement that was negotiated by the Tribe and the commissioners became the basis for the Tribe's reservation and for relations with the United States for the remainder of the nineteenth century.

Under the 1873 agreement, the Tribe received monetary compensation for the portion of aboriginal territory they were to give up and reserved a homeland made up of the heart of that territory consisting of the Lake, its tributaries, and the land around them. The Tribe was astute during the negotiations. The agreement guarantees that water flowing onto the reservation not be diverted to non-Indian land before reaching the reservation. They foresaw the use of water for hydropower (mills) and emphasized that the reservation should be permanent.

Later in 1873, the president signed an executive order establishing the Coeur d'Alene Reservation with exactly the boundaries demanded by the Tribe. In subsequent years, Congress ratified this executive order as being fully effective prior to the time that the State of Idaho was carved out of Washington Territory. During subsequent years, though the 1873 agreement was itself never ratified, the United States complied with almost all of its provisions.

The Coeur d'Alene Tribe is now engaged in an effort to settle its reservation water rights. The State of Idaho, the United States, the Tribe, and a number of non-Indian water rights claimants in the Coeur d'Alene and Spokane River Basin have agreed to attempt to reach a negotiated settlement. However, some non-Indian claimants have demanded that litigation continue concurrently with the negotiations. As a result, there are dual-track efforts to negotiate and litigate Tribal water right claims.

The basis for Indian water claims is determined by the purposes for which a reservation was created. Three types of reservation claims have been described here: actual historic irrigated acreage, Practicably Irrigable Acreage (PIA), and a Homeland Standard. The Coeur d'Alene have a potential claim under each standard.

The Coeur d'Alene did have some irrigated agricultural fields at the time that the United States signed the 1846 treaty with Great Britain. But those fields probably totaled 30 to 40 acres (12–16 ha). It is obvious that a water-right claim for a reservation that originally had 590,000 acres (almost 239,000 ha) within its boundaries cannot be entirely based on a claim for historic fields that totaled only 40 acres.

After the establishment of the reservation, with the assistance of the Jesuit priests, the Tribe did begin to cultivate larger tracts of crops. In fact, by the early twentieth century they had become some of the most successful farmers in the region. It has been argued that the reason the United States established some reservations was to help convert the Indians into farmers. Its actions in this case demonstrate that this was obviously an objective. Once the Tribe became successful as farmers, the United States "allotted" the reservation, opening up most of the reservation to non-Indians and allowing non-Indians to acquire farmland already in production by tribal members. Today, the Tribe has been reacquiring much of that land and has tribal farms with a total of more than 6,000 acres (2,428 ha).

The Coeur d'Alene Reservation is located in the Pacific Northwest. Some crops in this region, such as winter wheat, are grown with the use of rainfall and, although they require considerable cultivation, may not require much irrigation. In addition, climate change is now dramatically altering the timing and amount of moisture that falls in the region. Models predict less winter snowfall, more spring rainfall, and possibly much less available water in summer. Taking into account these factors, the PIA Standard has the potential to form the basis for an inequitable water right for the Tribe.

The Homeland Standard, however, fits both the former and current objectives of the United States and the Tribe. The reservation was set aside as a permanent homeland for the Tribe, which emphasized this objective over and over in its negotiations in the latter half of the nineteenth century. The United States made it clear that it intended the reservation as a permanent homeland, and the United States Congress ratified that decision and agreement. A Homeland Standard can and should include water rights for hydropower, both for today and the future, for agriculture, for both present and future personal consumptive use, for fish and wildlife, and for all other uses seen and unforeseen by the Tribe.

Historical evidence in this water rights matter has focused on the efforts of the United States and the Tribe to establish a permanent homeland. In addition, historic evidence of all types of use by the Tribe in aboriginal times, the nineteenth century, and the early twentieth century has been documented. All of this voluminous documentary evidence supports the Tribe's claim to their reservation water under the Homeland Standard.

TYPES OF HISTORICAL EVIDENCE IN INDIAN WATER RIGHTS ADJUDICATIONS

Historical evidence presented in Indian water rights adjudications can be located in many public, private, and obscure locations. Primary evidence is almost always more important in courts of law. First-hand historical accounts usually sway judges more than second-hand accounts—as they should.

Government relations with tribes are documented in the records of United States departments and agencies. The records of Indian agents are generally found in Record Group 75 in the National Archives in Washington, D. C. Regional National Archives repositories, such as the one in Seattle, have microfilm copies of most of this material. Other record groups in the National Archives contain those of the Department of the Interior, Department of War (now Defense), and Secretary of State. Some National Archives records can be found online. For instance, the annual reports of the Commissioner of Indian Affairs and the findings of the Indian Claims Commission are available online for download.

The congressional "Serial Set" contains the official publications of Congress. All major state libraries in the United States should have the serial set. The serial set will include all official reports about tribes that were published by the United States. Treaties and agreements with tribes were usually accompanied by a series of reports documenting the negotiations.

Important special collections on tribes are found in many university libraries. Yale's Beinecke Rare Book and Manuscript Library and the University of California's Bancroft Library are examples of the best repositories. Private repositories with excellent collections include the Huntington Library. Given that historical research for Indian water rights adjudications can be expensive and time-consuming, it is important that the results of that research and those court cases be preserved for the benefit of the tribes and the general public. My own collection from cases I have been involved in is housed in the excellent Special Collections repository of the Marriott Library at the University of Utah.

Sometimes primary sources are difficult to interpret or to translate. (For instance, documents related to the history of the Zuni Tribe in the sixteenth through nineteenth centuries were often written in Spanish, sometimes with confusing rubrics). Published primary accounts thus can become very important. The University of New Mexico, for instance, has published many important translations of those works.

Secondary sources can frequently provide access to important bibliographic materials that can assist the work of a research historian. The Smithsonian Institution has published such an important work in its multivolume *Handbook of North American Indians* (which we must hope will someday be completed). The multivolume includes both historical and athropological material, with good beginning bibliographies for most North American tribes.

Interdisciplinary work is very often crucial to understanding water history with tribes. In the Zuni water adjudication, I consulted professional publications in many disciplines, including ethnohistory, palynology, geomorphology, dendrochronology, dendroclimatology, anthropology, and, of course, cartography.

One of the most important tasks in creating expert testimony is to locate primary sources relevant to the particular tribe and to legal matter at issue. To include the bibliographies (or exhibit lists) associated with each of these matters in this chapter would be quite simply far too voluminous. Fortunately, it is relatively easy to make digital copies of these records available. I have posted online bibliographies of materials cited in my work on the adjudication of the Zuni, Coeur d'Alene, and Klamath water cases. In addition, I have posted my actual testimony in Klamath cases and the court decisions. This can give the interested reader an idea of how the court used historical materials, for what purpose, and what the outcome relative to the historical materials was to the Klamath Tribes. The website, which was originally created for access by members of the International Water History Association, is erhiwhadocs.com.

CHAPTER 9

"This Is Our Home; This Is Our Land"

Memory, Visual Sovereignty, and Museum Exhibition on the Klamath River Basin

BRITTANI R. ORONA

Public history can be a powerful tool with which to highlight the difficult histories of marginalized groups affected by human rights violations and ecological disaster. In the United States, state-sponsored memorialization fails to tell full, true, and meaningful stories of the effects of settler-colonialism, genocide, and ecocide. By perpetuating settler-colonial narratives, such memorialization negates the histories of Indigenous peoples and other marginalized groups. Yet, Indigenous people around the world use public history methods as well as collective memory studies and visual sovereignty to develop Indigenous operated museums, exhibitions, and cultural centers to tell an all-inclusive decolonial narrative.

This chapter evaluates concepts of "history as activism" through memory, visual sovereignty, and the examination of two exhibitions related to the Klamath River dam removal efforts in northwestern California: *River as Home* and *Stories of the River, Stories of the People: Memory on the Klamath River Basin*. For California Indians, environmental history and activism are intertwined with human rights, public history, and collective memory. We will investigate the memories, perceptions, and documentation by California Indian activists and scholars who have interpreted their history outside academia. Further, the chapter evaluates how exhibition and memory influence contemporary California Indian and environmental justice activism.

Traditional life for the Tribes of northwestern California changed drastically when Europeans invaded the territories of the Hupa, Yurok, Karuk, and Tolowa peoples. White miners, settlers, businessmen, and soldiers overwhelmed California traditional territories, forcing Native peoples to contend with them for land and natural resources. The Tribes of the North Coast, along with most California Indian Tribes, faced genocide, government-forced assimilation, and the attempted destruction of their culture.

The Tribes attempted to maintain traditional knowledge in secret, sharing practices and passing that knowledge to younger generations. Cultural traditions including jewelry making, basket weaving, and ceremonial dances did not disappear during colonization but were forced underground. In the new introduction to Lucy Thompson's 1916 *To the American Indian: Reminiscences of a Yurok Woman*, Julian Lang (Karuk) writes of the destructive influence of settlers: "From 1849 until 1900 attacks against the Yuroks and Karuk people by the miners and settlers had disrupted the World Renewal ceremonies many times. After 1900, Indian ceremonies were being outlawed in some cases, and even when not outlawed were strongly discouraged."[1] And despite the best efforts of Tribal members, certain ceremonies, such as the Fish Dam Ceremony, have not been performed since colonization.[2]

Ceremonies and traditional stories are often linked to water, from the Klamath River Basin, the Pacific Ocean, or smaller bodies. Ceremonies such as the World Renewal Dance or Fix the Earth Dance, which encompasses the White Deerskin and Jump Dance, follow a path that takes dancers and viewers from dance site to dance site, often along the water's edge. Included in the World Renewal ceremonies are the Boat Dances, performed on the water to ensure that the rivers maintain health, continue to flow, and provide salmon, eel, and trout to the Hupa, Yurok, and Karuk. To the Karuk, Hupa, and Yurok peoples, the river is not merely a river; it is a living being, subject to its own will, upon whom the Tribes depend for spiritual and physical health. The Klamath River Basin, in particular, forms an important nexus in their culture and livelihood.

Thus, with the manipulation of the natural waterways of the Klamath River Basin, North Coast Indians experienced deep cultural damage. The first irrigation ditch in the Basin was constructed in 1882 in White Lake, Oregon, to provide water for new farms in arid southern Oregon. Subsequently, private interests began to irrigate thousands of acres in order to transform the arid land into profitable agricultural lands.[3] From 1903 to 1962, a series of dams were built on the Upper Klamath River in Oregon and California. In the early twentieth century, the U.S. government took over private irrigation efforts and began the Klamath Reclamation

Project. The project was designed to irrigate 100,000 acres in Oregon and to generate power for Northern California and Southern Oregon.[4] These dams wreaked havoc on the tributaries of the Lower Klamath, and over the decades water quality deteriorated.

The period of dam building in the twentieth century coincided with a time in which the Tribes in the Lower Klamath tributaries had no federal recognition and very little legal recourse. Water was diverted to southern Oregon farmers and agricultural centers, creating dangerous conditions for the wildlife that depended on the rivers of the Lower Klamath Basin. With low water from diversion on the Upper Klamath, conditions on the Lower Klamath River were disastrous. Salmon and other fish species could not adequately spawn with the construction of the dams. If the water and fish were not healthy, Tribal communities could not "fix the world" and maintain balance within their communities. The fish that did survive were subjected to deadly warm-water conditions, conditions that threatened the physical and cultural life of the Native people who depended on the natural world around them.

Yet damming is not the only reason for decline in the Basin's fish population; introduced species, diseases, and new plant life also contribute to relative decline. Moreover, commercial fishing and overfishing on the Klamath and its tributaries have led to the decline in salmon, lamprey, trout, and sturgeon populations. State and federal water policies continue to have detrimental effects on the Lower Klamath River tributaries and remain the biggest blockade to spawning salmon. The fight to preserve the integrity of the rivers is a struggle over natural and cultural resources. The Native population of the Lower Klamath Rivers, including the Hupa, Yurok, and Karuk peoples, argues that the fish in the tributaries are a large part of their cultural heritage and the loss of those fish equals the loss of that culture. As Karuk activist Leaf Hillman notes, "It's all around, it's the trees, it's the water, it's the fish, it's the deer—this is our home, this is our land—we're Indian people, we believe in these things, we have these values, and it does mean something, and it is important. And we do have something to say about it, and we can do something about it."[5]

Modern Native people, in areas as remote as the Hupa, Yurok, and Karuk country, still rely on the abundance of natural resources to provide sustenance and continued health for families and individuals. With the loss of salmon habitat and logging practices that have made acorns and other foods scarce, they often rely on a diet high in saturated fats, foregoing a traditional healthy diet in favor of foods that cause diabetes, weight gain, and vitamin deficiencies.[6] In addition to the physical benefits of salmon consumption, Tribal members believe that the relationship between salmon and the river is central to cultural life and practices for their communities. As feminist and Hupa/Yurok/Karuk scholar Cutcha Risling Baldy commented, the importance of salmon is not merely physical but spiritual and cultural as well. "You go out and fish because it's your responsibility to sort of maintain that balance because you're interconnected with that fish because it becomes a part of you and takes care of you from the inside."[7]

The battle over the watershed's future heated up in the 1990s. Southern Oregon farmers argued that releasing more water for the Lower Klamath tributaries would endanger their livelihoods.[8] The situation between Oregon farmers and the Tribes of the lower tributaries came to a head in 1997. That year, the coho salmon received federal protection under the Endangered Species Act.[9] Protection would require greater releases from the Klamath dams to maintain minimum in-stream flows for salmon spawning. In 2001, this meant that 1,400 Klamath Reclamation Project farmers would not get irrigation water because of the water restrictions placed on the dams. The farmers practiced civil disobedience by opening irrigation canals and demanding more water. "In March 2002, Agriculture Secretary Ann Veneman and Secretary of the Interior Gale Norton flew to Klamath Falls to open the valve into the main diversion canal and assure farmers they would have the water they needed."[10] Inevitably, in September 2002, the lower tributaries of the Klamath River witnessed a salmon die-off characterized as one of the largest in U.S. history.

Although there is debate over exactly why the fish died, there had been warmer and lower water levels in previous years, and the sequence of events in the salmon die-off of 2002 was clear. The salmon swam upriver toward Requa, California, then retreated because of warm water conditions. They then tried to swim upriver again and, either because of warm water, disease, or both, 80,000 salmon expired along the banks of the Klamath River tributaries.[11] Fallout from the die-off was immediate. Oregon farmers, Tribes, environmentalists, and scientists blamed one another for the disaster. Almost universally, PacifiCorp, the company that owned the hydroelectric plants, came under scrutiny from all parties. Grassroots activism on the part of farmers, environmentalists, and fishing groups began in earnest. It was, however, the Klamath River Basin Tribes that pushed activism the hardest.

Activists calling themselves the Klamath Justice Coalition traveled to Scotland to protest outside the headquarters of Scottish Power, the company that then owned the Klamath River dams. When Scottish Power sold the dams to PacifiCorp, owned by Warren Buffet's Berkshire Hathaway, Native activists traveled to Portland and Omaha, Nebraska, to demonstrate outside of company meetings and to educate shareholders on issues arising from the Klamath River tributaries.[12] The Klamath Justice Coalition would spend eight years crashing shareholder meetings, compiling scientific evidence through their various state natural resources departments, and running a media-intensive effort through websites, exhibitions, films, and print to raise awareness about the health of the Klamath River Basin. The final effort turned to litigation. The Tribes sued PacifiCorp and agencies, including the Bureau of Reclamation, for failure to uphold existing environmental laws such as the Endangered Species Act. Craig Tucker recalled, "So between the grassroots action, the science and the litigation—all that put a lot of pressure on PacifiCorp and the agencies to seek a resolution for the problem."[13] The Klamath Restoration Agreements, signed on January 7, 2010, became that resolution.

The Agreements are comprised of two parts, the Klamath Basin Restoration Agreement and the Klamath Basin Hydroelectric Settlement Agreement. Accordingly, four dams, Iron Gate, Copco 1, Copco 2, and Boyce, are slated for removal by 2020. While the Yurok and the Karuk tribes have both signed off on the Klamath Restoration Agreements, the Hupa have not, nor do they do concur with the dam removal process laid out in the agreements. The Hoopa Valley Tribe (Hupa) raised concern that the removal of the four dams will not bring water flow to a sufficient level needed to sustain the salmon population.

The Tribes of Northern California, specifically the Hupa, Yurok, and Karuk, have participated for generations in nonviolent protests to protect their lands and home. These efforts produced collective memory projects that highlight the history of the Klamath River Basin. Native people have been fighting against environmental injustice and environmental racism since Columbus arrived in 1492. Through 500 years of forced assimilation, murder, genocide, and land removal, Indigenous people from all parts of the Americas have contended with government and private interests coopting, abusing, and mismanaging land.

Many modern environmental problems, such as mercury contamination from abandoned mines, are the result of settler-colonialism and its horrific affects over Indigenous lands and bodies. Northern California in the areas surrounding the modern-day counties of Trinity, Humboldt, Del Norte, and Siskiyou have all felt the effects of ecological colonialism.

Settler-colonialism is "a structure, not an event," and depends on the continued constriction of Indigenous people and their displacement.[14] Settler-colonialism also depends on coercive control over labor as part of environmental resource grabs. Such domination and normativity further depend on the acceptance of continued subjection of Indigenous people around the world. Decolonization, as defined by Maori scholar Linda T. Smith, can be viewed through the "social movement of Indigenous peoples."[15] These social movements involve coalition building toward land rights, sovereignty, and language, cultural, human, and civil rights. Smith argues that these actions helped to build a worldwide decolonial movement. "It involves a revitalization and reformulation of culture and tradition, an increased participation in and articulate rejection of Western institutions, a focus on strategic relations and alliances with non-Indigenous groups."[16]

In *Indigenous and Decolonizing Studies in Education: Mapping the Long Way*, Smith and education scholars Eve Tuck and K. Wayne Yang argue that one cannot separate Indigenous people from land, water, or the environment. Very simply, one cannot have decolonial movements without acknowledging Indigenous first rights to land and the relationship that Native people have to it.[17] All of the different "justice" movements that developed out of the broader environmental movement, to include climate and conservation, cannot be valid without Indigenous presence as leaders within these movements. Often, Indigenous people are relegated to sideline players in mainstream environmental causes, asked to give land acknowledgments that verge on tokenization.

Klamath Justice Coalition activists use different public history and multimedia formats and methods to detail the ongoing ecological struggles on the Klamath Basin. Collective memory is important to advocacy efforts for the Klamath River tribes, as well as the struggle to uplift ongoing human rights on the Basin. The interpretation of Tribal groups in museums and other mediums, such as film or photography, demonstrates how "memory communities" and "memory palaces" define the culture of Tribal communities. As Historian Peter Burke notes: "Historians are concerned or should be concerned with memory as a historical phenomenon, with what might be called the social history of remembering."[18] He acknowledges that social organization and different media can affect memories differently, depending on the group of people. We may connect Burke's example to collective memory on the Klamath River Basin. Out of the activism detailed above, Tribes of the Klamath River Basin produced fine art, film, oral history, theater, performances, and archival materials serving to memorialize the history of dam-removal efforts for generations to come. Further, Tribal members produced museum exhibitions telling the history of the Klamath River as it is represented in both past and present. Through museum exhibits, performance, and written record, the Tribes of the northwestern coast perpetuate their own history of the Klamath River Basin, challenging mainstream perceptions of Native people.

Much of the art and literature produced on the Klamath River come from an intertwined sense of belonging that is both decolonization and a lived experience. For example, Yurok/Karuk poet Shaunna Oteka McCovey's collection *The Smokehouse Boys* highlights the challenges and joys of being a Karuk/Yurok (or more broadly northwestern California) Indian grappling with tradition, modernization, and colonization. In her poem "Religious Freedom?" McCovey questions the government's right to determine what land is sacred, what land is not, and the effect that determination might have on Yurok, Karuk, and Tolowa people.

> The supreme law of the land is this:
> if sacred lands lie
> within government lands,
> they are no longer sacred
> and in government's hands
> *Lyng* emits injudicious disgraces
> Our religion means nothing
> In the stern, blank faces
> Of the court and their exceptional ruse,
> We Indians, they opine, are but sad fools.
> So what is a poor Yurok, Karuk, or Tolowa to do?
> Find a comfortable place at the end of the pew.[19]

Another literary example comes from playwright and theater scholar Theresa May. The play *Salmon is Everything* takes the Klamath River salmon die-off of 2002 and creates a performance piece that speaks to its devastation. May, herself a non-Native, became interested in the project when she noted that few discussions on the Klamath River involved the Hupa, Yurok, or Karuk, the tribes most affected by the fish kill. "I began to think about the voices in the larger story that were not being heard, and how I might use my position of power and privilege as an academic and an artist to help amplify those voices."[20] She worked with several Indigenous artists, including Kathleen McCovey and Suzanne Burcell, to create a play that spoke to the importance of salmon to the Upriver (Karuk/Yurok) and Downriver (Hupa) Tribes. This play, through performance and literature, honors the past worlds of the Klamath River Basin while also imagining a future where salmon are protected and thriving. May's collaboration with Indigenous artists and advocates creates a future where they can discuss the past and create their own realities through performance. The character of Rose describes the feelings of both hope and loss after the fish die-off.

> We felt that it was our responsibility to take care of them, because they took care of us. Now, we struggle with wanting to do something, but feeling helpless. I don't believe this means it is lost. It is an opportunity to bring back something that has done since time before time. We need to once again take care of the Salmon physically and spiritually. This is the time, for their survival and ours.[21]

May demonstrates that Native voice cannot be truly incorporated without actively working, interviewing, and being in strong partnership with Tribal community members. Creating Indigenous futures through multimedia projects is part of acknowledging our own worlds: past, present, and future.

Museum and Indigenous Studies scholar Amy Lonetree assesses the trauma that Native American communities experience with museums and their efforts to represent a history that is inclusive, accurate, and reliable.[22] "Museums can be very painful sites for Native peoples," she argues, "as they are intimately tied to the colonization process." The efforts today by tribal communities to become involved in developing exhibitions points to the "recognition that controlling the representation of their cultures is linked to the larger movements of self-determination and cultural sovereignty."[23] Decolonization of Native American history and culture within museums serves to extend remembrance that has not always been present within institutional confines. Native American groups, including the Hupa, Yurok, and Karuk, have led a sustained effort to decolonize museums by including not only historical or anthropological methods but also by privileging the Native American voice in exhibitions. The inclusion of the Native voice permits multilinear or multivocal storytelling in museums and cultural institutions.

An example of multilinear storytelling is found at the Mille Lac Museum in Minnesota. The Mille Lac Band of Ojibwe Indians joined with the Minnesota Historical Society to create a museum that features the ideals and culture of the Ojibwe using western curatorial and museum practices. These practices include creating a tribal "hybrid" museum. Amy Lonetree writes, "Native communities have constructed a collective public memory and history through the medium of tribal museums—or, in this case, a 'hybrid' tribal Museum. In doing so, Native communities have attempted to take control of the public's perception of their past."[24]

The example of the Mille Lacs Museum complements the exhibit *River as Home* at the Morris Graves Museum of Art in Eureka, California. The exhibit ran from February 2, 2013, to March 24, 2013, and featured sixty native artists working in different mediums such as sculpture, painting, interpretive panels, and basketry. The Graves Museum, along with a group of North Coast Native artists, created an exhibit relaying the art of the Hupa, Yurok, Karuk, Wiyot, Tolowa, and Tseungwe peoples. The exhibit was predominately an art effort with very little historical context, as the artists hoped it would primarily speak to the feeling of the Basin using visual sovereignty to convey their message.

English scholar Michelle Raheja defines the term "visual sovereignty" as "a way of reimagining Native-centered articulations of self-representation and autonomy that engage the powerful ideologies of mass media."[25] In Raheja's view, filmmakers, museum curators, and artists deploy community knowledge through new media technologies that frame and render Native American intellectual and cultural paradigms. That is, Indigenous individuals and communities take new media, such as film production, theater, and museum curation, and assert their own forms of sovereignty and self-representation through these art forms. Like many methodologies, this is based in settler-colonial technology and practices but is employed to reframe the histories of Indigenous people to create a better-understood past and a broader future.

In the *River as Home*, the North Coast artists illuminated the history that they did not personally live but that continues to affect them. They interpreted not only the artistic history of the Basin but also its traumatic memories. Most of the artists did not go to the government-funded boarding school on the Hoopa Valley Indian Reservation, which closed prior to 1960, but much of the Native art featured harkens back to that multigenerational trauma. Nor did many remember a time before dams afflicted the Klamath River Basin, yet much of the art exhibit interpreted the river before dam construction. The artists "remembered" because the memory of a healthy ecosystem had been passed down to them through elders, media, and traditions. By displaying artwork that showed the river as a healthy and thriving ecosystem, they recreated and celebrated the living river. This memorial to the Klamath River and its tributaries through visual sovereignty speaks to both the devastating reality of the watershed's current state and the cultural memory of the rivers as life sustainers.

By including traditional and contemporary forms of basketry, the artists decolonized the settler narratives surrounding Basin culture. Basketry is a continued, lived practice for Tribal members. As Native American Studies scholar Vanessa Esquivido writes, basketry is both a methodology and a source of history. Weaving a basket takes time, dedication, and effort. In the eyes of other Indigenous weavers, such baskets tell histories through twining, markings, and materials.[26] In this way, Native artists were able to interpret the memory of the Klamath River Basin through their own perspectives and cultural ideals. The basketry display did not have any context or didactic panels but rather displayed the baskets as methodology separate from western ways of knowledge. By demystifying basketry and not interpreting the skills involved in creating them, the Yurok/Karuk/Hupa artist and basket weaver Kateri Masten defined basketry as a way of knowing that was not privy to outsiders. This created inclusivity not easily interpreted by outsiders. In a broad contextual sense, the exhibit provided insight into the culture of the North Coast and the memories and meanings associated with the Klamath River system.

In *River as Home*, the viewer was forced to animate a story that he or she may not have understood fully. By not interpreting artworks through panels and text, the participating artists defined memory rather than history and demonstrated inclusive feeling only found from full cultural understanding. The generations of Indigenous people affected by colonization on the North Coast have carried those memories—orally, traditionally, and through art works to teach subsequent generations of their collective past. By forcing the viewer to "fill in the blanks," the exhibit artists forced viewers to question their knowledge of and relationship to the Basin.

Historically, museums have served to perpetuate a master colonial narrative, excluding Indigenous people from their own narratives. The history and memory of culture that was apparent to Native Americans—because they had lived it—was absent from large institutional museums because the Native voice had been silenced. Education scholars Eve Tuck and Rubén A. Gaztambide-Fernández argue that settler-colonial histories engage in "projects of replacement," which replace Indigenous people with settlers who erase them from the land and in effect make settlers the new, "true" Native people.[27] Narratives that are not defined or are not acknowledged cannot be adequately and fairly interpreted.

Social Historian Peter Burke rightly notes, "It is often said that history is written by the victors. It might also be that the victors forget history. They can afford to forget, while losers are unable to accept what happened and are condemned to brood over it. . . ."[28] He acknowledges that victors forget traumatic events that did not occur to them because they "won" and, ultimately, are separated from the hardships of those who "lost." The "winners" do not dwell on the hardships of the "losers" because they are distant from it; whereas those who lost culture, land, and rights are left to pick up the pieces of life shattered. In this sense, trauma is passed down through generations to create a social and collective memory that harkens to not only victimization but also self-determination and cultural sovereignty.

Repression of traumatic history seen in large institutions such as the National Museum of the American Indian and the California State Indian Museum, which make no mention of the devastating effects of colonization, is the effort of the state to censor and protect hegemonic histories. With regard to the National Museum of the American Indian, Amy Lonetree argues, "The museum's silences around the tragedies that took place were, again, not an oversight but intentional, a conscious choice." Founding director Richard West defends this choice by saying that the period of tragedy is only a small portion of our time in the Americas: "Here's what I want everyone to understand. As much and as important as that period of history is . . . it is at best only about 5 percent of the period we have been in this hemisphere. We do not want to make the National Museum of the American Indian into an 'Indian Holocaust Museum.'"[29]

Individual Native groups, by repurposing museums to decolonize these state memories, are perpetuating a collective historical understanding that is not privileged in institutional spaces. Small exhibits, such as *River as Home* at the Morris Graves and *Stories of the River, Stories of the People* at the California State University, Sacramento (CSUS), Anthropology Museum, discussed below, define the Klamath River Basin as a site of cultural and traumatic memories but also relay the importance of Indigenous self-determination. Museum exhibitions, for large institutions such as the Smithsonian's National Museum of the American Indian as well as small tribal and regional museums have redefined their efforts to tell an all-inclusive story and privilege a voice that has long been silenced.

In the Fall of 2013, with the support of the CSUS Anthropology Museum, the author curated an exhibition titled *Stories of the River, Stories of the People: Memory on the Klamath River Basin*. The author/curator's intention was to highlight Native American voice using Western forms of interpretation such as video, photography, textual panels, oral history, and painting above other modes. The majority of participants involved in its development were from the Klamath River Basin Tribes. For example, Hupa, Yurok, and Karuk artists painted scenes of the river system using acrylic paint, and Native participants took photographs of modern Hupa, Yurok, and Karuk traditions. *Stories of the River* attempted to decolonize old forms of interpretation by using those methods to tell the history of the Klamath River through Native, multilinear perspectives.

In an effort to decolonize memories and histories, small exhibitions such as *Stories of the River* rely on the experiences of Indigenous people, who provide context with editorial authority, and museum professionals, who install the exhibit. Here, Native participants detailed their histories to the curator, a member of the Hoopa Valley Tribe (Hupa), who then determined how to interpret that information using museum methods. The curator and participants worked back and forth on oral histories, context, and object selection to create an exhibit that illuminated the Native voice and kept it accessible to non-Natives, relaying the struggles of the Hupa, Yurok, and Karuk to remove dams that affect their cultural resources, health, livelihood, and culture. Using Lonetree's thesis, the curator continuously addressed the effects of colonization and how the Tribal communities of Hupa, Yurok, and Karuk people worked to decolonize their homelands through environmental activism. Different sections of the exhibit explored the importance of art, activism, and tradition in the memory of the three Tribes. The Tribes used these three methods to combat the hegemonic narrative, which privileges water diversion to the farmlands that surround the Klamath River Basin.

Rather than ignore Native worldviews and traditions, *Stories of the River* aimed to tell the story of the Klamath River with tradition and worldview deeply embedded in the exhibit. To add spatial context, three photographs of the Hupa, Karuk, and Yurok, by Edward Curtis, were included. The Curtis photographs depict two conflicting worldviews in the exhibit: that of Native informants who carried on their culture and tradition but lived in a modern world, and that of Curtis, who believed that Native people were "vanishing" and thus acted as a kind of salvage ethnographer. His photographs were then juxtaposed with modern Tribal members working, living, and fishing on the Klamath. This was meant to directly negate Curtis and other salvage ethnographers who believed they were capturing a "vanishing" culture. By including both colonial and Native perspectives and using Western means of interpretation, cultural institutions can thus enable visitors to absorb new understanding.

The Hupa, Yurok, and Karuk in the *Stories of the River* exhibit also used their voices to privilege their history. Jean O'Brien's work on Indigenous history and methodology is foundational in understanding the ongoing struggles of Native perspective in mainstream history. O'Brien argues that the discipline of history is rooted so deeply in national narratives that analysis and interpretation of other experiences is impossible. Imperial mastery overshadows the history of Indigenous people to great effect—United States history does not account for the complexity of Indigenous cultures or the continued political nature of Native history. Simply, Indigenous Studies cannot have *culture* in the absence of *politics*—*Stories of the River* clearly favored Native perspectives on water rights, taking a strong political stance for dam removal. Native history, through different forms of documentation that do not fit the norm of "mainstream" archives or records, is critical to an engagement in Native American and Indigenous Studies.[30] Portraying inclusive and nuanced histories in museums allows a more full-bodied understanding of collective history outside of written source materials.

Photography, art, oral history, and cultural artifacts are all critical to telling Native American stories through our own worldview. This is because American history continues to ignore the full, complex, and devastated history of Indigenous people. Indigenous scholars have taken upon themselves to demystify these histories. Creating an exhibit around the trauma of colonization helps non-Native visitors relate to history they may not understand or have never engaged with—history that has been removed in favor of settler-colonial narratives. The history of Native people, as presented in exhibits such as *Stories of the River* and *River as Home,* is tied to colonization, genocide, and politics. The experts of these Native histories and cultures are not historians or anthropologists but rather people who are still affected by colonization. It would be impossible to adequately interpret the history of the Klamath River Basin without their knowledge and shared experiences. Native people in *Stories of the River* relinquished control to a curator—albeit a Native one—to accurately interpret their histories.

In both the *Stories of the River* and the *River as Home* exhibits, Native people were represented by regional Native art. Using different forms of interpretation that relate to Western understanding—oil on canvas, printmaking, Polaroids, etc.—the artists interpreted their histories in ways that non-Natives could "understand." Lyn Risling's paintings *are* the history of the Hupa, Yurok, and Karuk people, demonstrating dances, interpreting cultural dress, and harkening back to traditional stories. Her work demonstrates that Native history uses many methodologies beyond the realm of written sources. Risling's paintings are also her individual interpretations of the culture she was raised in. While her art represents many ideals held by her people, her paintings are also subjective to her own individual experiences—forming an archive of both herself and her Tribes.

The artists of *Stories of the River, Stories of the People* similarly require the viewer to question their knowledge and memory of water usage, the history of reclamation, and the meaning of water to Indigenous communities. Artists Julian Lang (Karuk, Wiyot, Shasta), Lyn Risling (Hupa/Yurok/Karuk), Brittany Britton (Hupa), and Annilea Hillman (Yurok) not only ask the viewer to integrate themselves into the struggles of the Klamath River system itself but forthrightly question the importance of the dams. They asked the viewer to "remember" the dams, not merely in their usage of electricity and water storage but as an ongoing human rights violation for the Tribes on the Klamath River Basin. Take, for example, Annilea Hillman's work "No Amount of Stalling Will Stop the Dams from Falling." The painting is relatively simple: a piece of plywood painted bright yellow with the title painted in blood red. Around the words, however, there is painted a red fist clutching a bomb. The painting is at once a threat and a call to action. The Tribes and activists on the Klamath River will do whatever it takes to protect and restore their traditional homelands.

The effects of colonization, as devastating as they have been for Karuk, Hupa, and Yurok people, refocus and repurpose the way in which the three Tribes collectively and individually remember the Klamath River Basin. For thousands of years before white encroachment, the Basin supported cultural and traditional livelihood. As colonization took effect, the Klamath River Basin became a typical battleground between colonizers and colonized. It has only been within the last ten years, since the salmon die-off of 2002, that North Coast tribal communities have worked to interpret the history and memory of the Basin to outsiders. By relaying the memory of the Klamath River Basin, the Tribes hope to garner not only sympathy but also support for the wider Indigenous environmental justice movement.

While Native American voices were ignored in museum spaces without consultation or engagement for decades, interpretations through oral histories, objects, photographs, and acrylic paintings can create contact zones between Native and non-Native visitors. Non-Native visitors absorb information in a way they can easily understand, and Native participants can share their culture with a wider audience. Ultimately, the battle for the Klamath River has taken place not only through picket lines and grassroots activism but also through museum exhibitions and public memory.

CHAPTER 10

Placemaking in Public

Building a Native American Studies Program on the Indigenous Columbia Plateau

LAURIE ARNOLD

In 2013, I joined Gonzaga University as the inaugural director of the Native American Studies program. I had many goals for the program (all of which I characterize as still being in progress), but centering the program in place and reinforcing the presence of Native American people today were among my most important priorities. The program is built upon a foundation of tribal political and cultural sovereignty, and we utilize multivocal tribal narratives from the Columbia Plateau to demonstrate each.[1]

Native American and American Indian Studies programs are informed by varied theoretical and methodological approaches. Some scholars consider interdisciplinarity a limitation because it de-centers Native priorities and perspectives, but I argue that interdisciplinary work can and does center Native voices.[2] I witness this success at several institutions including my own. My program must rely on an interdisciplinary approach because I hold the only faculty appointment in Native American Studies (NTAS), and this cooperation enhances rather than proscribes our work.

As we designed strategies for creating, embedding, and growing an academic program in an institution that had never hosted such a program, I looked to the American West Center (AWC) at the University of Utah and its public history practices as a paradigm. While our program is in its infancy compared to the AWC, I am pleased to note we are making progress toward engagement with public history and digital humanities. I hope this work will lead to more direct partnership with tribes in the model of the AWC. I see enormous potential for future projects that will enrich our students and our region and that will allow NTAS to more fully achieve the Four Rs of Native American/Indigenous-centered values: relationship (also characterized as respect), responsibility, reciprocity, and redistribution (also characterized as relevance).[3]

BACKGROUND

Gonzaga resides on the ancestral homelands of the Spokane Tribe of Indians in the Columbia Plateau region, in view of one of the most historically significant fishing sites in the north American west, the Spokane Falls. The Indigenous Columbia Plateau fostered Native peoples for at least nine millennia prior to European, Canadian, or American immigration to the region; this place was and remains the Indigenous Columbia Plateau.

In 1880, Father Joseph Cataldo, a Jesuit priest and Superior of the Rocky Mountain Missions, imagined a college that would serve the Native American boys being educated at Jesuit missions throughout the region—an educational home that would allow them to continue their intellectual development. By the time the college opened in 1887, however, Father James Rebmann, the institution's first president, barred the door to prevent Native boys from entering the building and enrolling in the college.

Despite being planned as an institution for local Native students, Gonzaga operated for 125 years without a Native American Studies program. In the years preceding the program's launch, a few faculty members including Dr. Jessica Maucione and Dr. Ann Ostendorf, plus a couple of administrators, including then-Dean Robert Prusch and Academic Vice President Patricia Killen, collaborated to design the program. The design supported an open-field search to allow any hire to bring his or her vision to building a program; it was flexible enough to accommodate interdisciplinary collaboration within the College of Arts and Sciences; and it recognized that the director must have dedicated time for administration/program development in addition to teaching.

Gonzaga celebrated its 125th anniversary during the year that the Native American Studies program was approved, and those intervening decades brought great change to the Plateau. Residents of Spokane, particularly recent arrivals, often characterize this place as "white." In fact, five federally recognized tribes are located within a few hours' drive of Spokane, and the region is home to as many as forty distinct bands of Indians, depending on how one counts bands included as part of confederations.

Spokane has a significant urban Native population and is home to Native peoples from more than 300 tribes.[4]

Given these historical contexts—Indigenous, Native, Jesuit, non-Native—and a contemporary era informed by dynamic regional tribal cultural, political, and economic sovereignty, how can an academic program most effectively serve the Indigenous Plateau, students, tribes, publics, and institutions? I have only begun to answer these questions and am aware that we may never have definitive answers. But so far, public history assignments, public-facing scholarship, and partnerships with institutions across the region have provided a good start.

DIGITAL AND PUBLIC HISTORY IN THE CLASSROOM

Ojibwe scholar David Treuer observed that when we understand American Indians, we understand America. Historian Colin Calloway has argued that Indians shaped the nascent identity of colonists as they shed their old skins in the process of becoming "American." The authors of *You Can't Teach United States History without American Indians* certainly agree—we cannot understand ourselves as Americans unless we know Native American histories, lives, and people.[5]

Gonzaga is a predominantly white institution, and students generally arrive in class with almost no foundation in Native American history or meaningful awareness about contemporary Native peoples. The Native American Studies courses are electives that serve the university core, and the courses typically fill to capacity. The number of students who enroll in the minor is small, however, so most students who enroll in the courses might only take one Native American topics course. To reflect the dynamism of contemporary Native experiences and tribal priorities, as well as to orient the courses in both history and place, colleagues and I have created a variety of public history and digital history assignments.

During the last six years, 1,000 students have enrolled in Native American Studies courses, a significant number considering Gonzaga's typical class size is twenty-five. Faculty teaching in the program have utilized public history and digital humanities assignments as one aspect of their pedagogies, and one-quarter of NTAS students have completed public history or digital humanities projects. Gonzaga does not have a public history major or minor, and while there is a public history course, the assignments described here were offered in Native American Studies and Religious Studies courses, thus their disciplinary orientation is from those fields of study.

Public history interpretation makes the past visible to broad audiences, and digital humanities expand that reach into the virtual realm. These assignments offer great ways to demonstrate both relevance and responsibility being practiced in our classrooms. Even when we must rely on content created by colonial actors (whether priests or newspaper reporters or business leaders), our assignments require students to frame their analysis from Native perspectives whenever possible—and it usually is possible. For example, traders sometimes complained that Indians were unreasonable when they would not allow them to come ashore from the Columbia River without first offering tribute. Instead of reinforcing this narrative, a student might discuss the importance of gift-giving in establishing relationships, especially when visiting territories outside one's home, and the student's interpretation could include images of objects typically given as gifts or images of exchanges reproduced by painters of the era.

One fall, in Introduction to Native American Studies, students completed an archival research project in the Foley Library archives. At that time, the Jesuit Oregon Province Archives (JOPA) were housed there, though in March 2019 the Province transferred the materials to St. Louis University, rendering the materials inaccessible to us. The collections featured Plateau tribal language dictionaries created by Jesuits as they learned Native languages in order to more effectively convert Plateau peoples to Catholicism. The collections also held a wealth of documents such as mission school records, genealogies, correspondence, and Jesuit diaries full of daily observances that created part of the historical record of the Indigenous Plateau.

In the assignment, students were "hired" as historical consultants by one of four Montana tribes to survey the Foley materials and to report on primary and secondary source materials relating to their assigned tribe. At the conclusion of this assignment, with the students' permission, I sent the final reports to each of the tribes the students researched. As a direct result of the students' Blackfeet Tribe report, an administrator from Blackfeet Community College visited Gonzaga months later and conducted further research in the Foley Library and JOPA archives. This was an ideal outcome for the project, and it demonstrated to students that history isn't just a foreign country—it has relevance for us all today. In the case of student projects, historical research and historical documents produced very specific value to tribes, and student work demonstrated both respect and reciprocity.

Dr. Emily Clark in the religious studies department at Gonzaga also used the JOPA collections to create a digital humanities project with students in her Native American Religions course. Students curated twenty exhibits built from historic photographs of Jesuits and Native peoples of the Plateau and Alaska. These exhibits provided narratives about Plateau spiritual practices, Catholic ceremonies and conversion efforts, Native children attending Catholic boarding schools, and Jesuit records of tribal languages. The exhibits made Native lives and histories visible. Equally significant, people in the photographs can be traced to their living descendants today. This work was tremendously valuable to students in advancing their comprehension of place and of Native peoples as real people, rather than simply historical figures. The images, along with selected exhibits, are available on the Digital Jesuits website, http://as-dh.gonzaga.edu/omeka/.

We have also used digital archives for research and creation of digital projects. In Introduction to Native American Studies, students completed an assignment built from Carlisle Indian Industrial School records combined with Ancestry.com research. Students each began with a list of twenty names found in the Carlisle Indian School Digital Resource Center. Carlisle student files vary in terms of documents associated with each student, but documents often include school enrollment information, student demographic information, alumni responses to Carlisle requests for information on occupations and households since leaving Carlisle, and so on. Students used the Carlisle documents to select a smaller number of Carlisle students to research in the next step of the project, searching for Carlisle alumni and their families in the Ancestry.com database. Since Gonzaga does not have a subscription to Ancestry, students worked with a librarian at the downtown Spokane Public Library to learn that tool. The assignment aimed to demonstrate that "boarding schools" were not simply a concept or event from the past, but that real Native people lived in them (and survived them), as evidenced by family trees that in most cases included descendants living today. Students shared their Carlisle students' stories in classroom presentations and felt affinity for the Carlisle students once they discovered the lives alumni and their children and grandchildren lived.

In other courses, students curated digital exhibits of Native American art and, inspired by the work of Spokane Historical,[6] mapped Indigenous sites and historic sites on the Plateau. In Native American Art and Performance, the exhibits could feature any medium of Native art or performance student curators found compelling and each used both art history and tribal histories as a foundation. Curators researched the artist in context of his or her home communities and cultures, then researched the history of those communities before they could begin to frame the art. Students have created exhibits about Ojibwe birch bark baskets, Plateau basketry, Navajo rugs, Hopi pottery, Coast Salish carving, Alaskan and Maori tattooing, First Nations spoken word, contemporary mural art, contemporary Native music, painters such as Ric Gendron (Colville) and Wendy Red Star (Crow), ancient tools, and so much more. When artists primarily grew up in urban Native communities, students included histories of relocation and oriented their exhibits through those lenses.

The process of researching and curating an exhibit got students past their "I don't know anything about art" anxieties and introduced them to artists and tribes they might not have encountered otherwise. Students conducted exhibit walk-throughs for their peers, and these tours allowed students to identify similarity and difference across art form, artist, and region. This assignment had the broadest geographical reach of any assignment and best represented breadth and diversity in Indian Country.

In the Indians of the Columbia Plateau course, students worked in groups to create maps focusing on one of four subject areas: geographic feature, plant, person/animal, and historic site or publicly known spiritual site (such as Kettle Falls). Each group created twelve entries on their map, and at the end of the project we had a map with more than fifty entries. Students were excited to see where sites overlapped—a salmon at Kettle Falls, which was also a spiritual site and two historic sites (Hudson's Bay Company and St. Paul's Mission). The Colville Confederated Tribe published a place names document and, where possible, groups also included place names written in Nselxcin, the Colville-Okanagan dialect of Salish. More than any other assignment for that course, this one grounded students in the Columbia Plateau as a place and an Indigenous space. Students understood homeland as more than a concept by the end of the project, and, upon reflection, I view it as one of the most effective assignments Native American Studies has offered.

In addition to completing course work, NTAS minors must complete capstone projects, either a research project or an internship. One minor was a history major completing an elementary education certificate. She became so engaged with digital history projects that she completed a hybrid research paper/digital project for her capstone. She wrote about Christine Quintasket (Colville), pen name Mourning Dove, from her early life through her experiences as a mission-school and boarding-school student, and then her career as an author, activist, and public intellectual. The student adapted this research into a web-based course module, for a fourth-grade class, that was broken down into categories including history, biography, traditional medicine, homeland, family, and language.

Two minors completed internships at the Northwest Museum of Arts and Culture (MAC) in Spokane. Their projects consisted of processing boxes from the collections, sorting, and cataloguing, detailed item-level work that gave them deep appreciation for the behind-the-scenes labor that must occur before researchers are able to access materials. In addition to collection processing, students interacted with members of the public doing research and with academic researchers and observed meetings about museum business. One meeting focused on the Native American Graves Protection and Repatriation Act (NAGPRA) items held by the MAC and the museum's implementation of NAGPRA policy. This experience was meaningful to them. Each student separately identified collections of photographs that were ultimately designated as restricted items because the photos included ceremonies, ceremonial objects, and burial sites. Because of their foundation in Native American Studies, particularly because of the topics we discussed in Native American Art and Performance, the students were equipped to bring the photos to the curator's attention and to participate in discussing why access to the photos should be restricted. By the conclusion of their internships, the students were thinking like public historians, weighing approaches to curating the photos and documents they processed, discussing the struggles of interpreting the past for curious but underinformed members of the public, and feeling simultaneously exhilarated and exhausted by how much work there is left to do.

Public history and digital humanities assignments in Native American Studies courses have offered meaningful engagement with Native American lives of the past and the present. We have used more common classroom assignments, as well as papers and tests, but students simply connect more and retain more when creating interpretation with the public in mind. They are more invested in the outcome of projects and more likely to share this hard-won knowledge; several students have included their projects in portfolios when seeking jobs. One student showed her digital art exhibit during a family holiday gathering! As Gonzaga's Digital Humanities (DH) initiative expands, we hope to share student projects through digital or physical gallery space hosted by DH. We know these types of assignments will continue to be important, as Native American Studies enters the next phase of its development and becomes more established in the university.

PUBLIC-FACING SCHOLARSHIP AND COMMUNITY PARTNERS

As I began my work directing Native American Studies at Gonzaga, I recalled Dr. Gregory Smoak's observation about our responsibilities as historians—that it is the job of all historians to make history accessible and meaningful to broad public audiences.[7] In addition to the 1,000 students who enrolled in NTAS courses, NTAS public events on campus drew 1,400 people into conversation about Native American histories, lives, and contemporary priorities. Our program strives to reach beyond our classrooms and campus to engage with publics where we meet them. My colleagues and I give guest lectures in classrooms on and off the Gonzaga campus, as well as public talks locally, regionally, and nationally. These visiting lectures expanded the NTAS program's audience by another 1,000. In sum, 3,400 people engaged with Native American topics specifically as a result of Gonzaga's Native American Studies program. Our work in the program is a jumping-off point, the beginning not the end, for audiences interested in learning more. So much good work is happening within Plateau communities and the Spokane community and other campus communities, and Native American Studies has been fortunate to learn from and share in that work.

For example, in 2014 the Columbia River Treaty (CRT) entered a ten-year period of renegotiation. The CRT is a U.S. State Department-level agreement between the United States and Canada. The Upper Columbia United Tribes (UCUT) has been a common voice for the Plateau and a key leader of conversations about tribal representation in the updated treaty and inclusion of culturally relevant practices such as ecosystem management. UCUT is supported in collaboration by the Coeur d'Alene Tribe of Indians, the Confederated Tribes of the Colville Reservation, the Kalispel Tribe of Indians, the Kootenai Tribe of Idaho, and the Spokane Tribe of Indians.[8]

In the fall of 2013, an old friend and fellow Colville tribal member introduced me to UCUT and to a group planning a Columbia River

Treaty conference at Gonzaga for spring 2014. That group included tribal and First Nations representatives, spiritual leaders from multiple denominations, and colleagues in the philosophy and political science departments. The conference, "One River, Ethics Matter," drew an audience of 120. Since that first year, it has traveled to a different university each year, expanding the conversations and regional engagement with the CRT.

The Columbia River flows more than 1,200 miles from its source in British Columbia to the Pacific Ocean. It is currently clogged with fourteen dams. One of the conference aims has been to illustrate the critical importance of salmon for Columbia Plateau tribes. Salmon, "n̓tyỷtyix" in the Nselxcin dialect of Salish, is a food chief. According to ancestral stories, Salmon was the first to volunteer to give his body to humans to eat when they could not take care of themselves. Prior to colonization, estimates indicate that Indigenous groups along the Columbia River consumed on average two pounds of salmon per person per day—more than 700 pounds per year.[9] Commercial fishing at the mouth of the Columbia affected salmon runs first, but dams have done far more damage. Grand Coulee Dam, until recently the largest concrete dam in the world, ended fish passage and spawning above it. Salmon practically disappeared from Plateau diets after 1940. Members and leaders from the Colville Tribe and other tribes observed the occasion with the "Ceremony of Tears" in June 1940, marking the loss not only of the salmon but also the flooding of Kettle Falls. The falls still exist, but they are now completely submerged. Characterizing this loss as a tragedy is an understatement.[10]

Salmon also disappeared from the Spokane River. The Spokane Falls remain intact and visible, but they are now empty of salmon. Dr. Brook Swanson in Gonzaga's biology department likened the disappearance of salmon after construction of Grand Coulee Dam to someone turning off a faucet. One day, salmon swam in rivers across the Plateau, the next day they were gone.[11]

The loss of salmon is not just "an Indian issue." Salmon is more than food; it is kin, spirituality, and culture. David Treuer (Ojibwe) notes that Native American cultures are important to everyone, or should be: "When we lose cultures, we lose American plurality—the productive and lovely discomfort that true difference brings."[12] In recognition of the CRT's vast importance for our region, NTAS has invited and welcomed UCUT to Gonzaga's classrooms and public spaces.

The Columbia River Treaty is a social justice issue and thus fits squarely within Gonzaga's social justice mission. In fall semester 2015, a student attended a campus event that featured discussions of environmental justice in context of tribal priorities, including the Columbia River Treaty. She reached out to learn more because she was on the environmental justice committee of the Ignatian Solidarity Network, and the Gonzaga student delegation was preparing for the "Ignatian Family Teach-In for Justice," an annual Catholic social justice conference. The students researched several regional environmental issues and, upon learning more about the Columbia River Treaty and discussing the imperatives of tribal representation and cultural context with UCUT partners, brought the Treaty into the Ignatian conference conversation. The Treaty also became one item of advocacy during the students' day of lobbying in Washington, D.C. Neither NTAS nor UCUT requested this advocacy. Rather, the students drew their own conclusions based on Indigenous Plateau homelands and Gonzaga's location—and responsibilities—within them. Welcoming tribal friends, partners, and leaders has been critical to NTAS success. This engagement reinforces the importance of place, place-based knowledge, and Indigenous homelands and also animates the program's practices of respect, reciprocity, relevance, and responsibility.

Beyond the classroom, off-campus events and programming provided great opportunities for growth. As we developed NTAS curriculum and established the program, colleagues at other institutions invited us to discuss program design, curricular approaches, and possibilities for collaboration. At the Pacific Northwest American Studies Association meeting at Whitman College in 2016, my colleagues Dr. Maucione and Dr. Ostendorf and I discussed the process of designing and implementing a Native American Studies program. These discussions grew into a collaboration with Dr. Christopher Leise at Whitman College and resulted in a National Endowment for the Humanities Summer Institute funding application. Dr. Leise and I designed a two-week institute, "The Native American West: A Case Study of the Columbia Plateau," hosted by Whitman College in Walla Walla, Washington, and informed by interdisciplinary content and methods, including archival research, digital humanities, and museum practices. The NEH funded the program and we hosted thirty two- and four-year-college faculty on the Indigenous Plateau, ultimately traversing almost all of it as we visited Tamástslikt Cultural Institute in Pendleton, Oregon, the Columbia Gorge Interpretive Center in The Dalles, Oregon, and the MAC in Spokane.

Dr. Laura Ferguson, Senior Curator of Western History at the High Desert Museum in Bend, Oregon, was one of the Summer Institute participants. Dr. Ferguson had been strategizing approaches to curation of the reinstallation of *By Hand Through Memory,* a permanent exhibition at the museum. The two-week immersion in Columbia Plateau content and discussion provided insight for some of the guiding questions related to the reinstallation. Subsequent to the Summer Institute, Dr. Ferguson won an NEH Exhibition Planning grant award for the project, "Creating Together: Reimagining the High Desert Museum's Exhibition on the Indigenous Columbia Plateau," and four Summer Institute faculty are participating in the planning grant as advisors. Public-facing scholarship led to collaboration with Whitman College that in turn led to an NEH summer institute and now to additional, ongoing institutional relationships across the region. NTAS will continue to contribute to and benefit from such intellectual and interpretive partnerships, which reinforce the importance of institutional kinship across the Plateau.

At the MAC, opportunities for collaboration abound. The MAC's American Indian Collections contain more than 5,000 material culture items. The museum also holds an archive of primary source documents that represent the first-person perspectives of people who lived on the Plateau, including Native and First Nations peoples. NTAS students can continue the work begun by previous interns, and the resulting projects could include curation of digital or physical exhibits, in addition to independent student work. Applying lessons from Amy Lonetree's *Decolonizing Museums,* students and professional partners can build American Indian/Native American interpretations that both face the hard truths of colonization and celebrate the culture, artistry, and persistence of Plateau peoples.[13]

It is exciting to imagine NTAS supporting tribal endeavors to create Plateau-centered interpretation of Plateau art, material culture, and histories. Gonzaga is not alone in striving to do this work, and these collaborations could put us in partnership with the MAC as well as with Eastern Washington University (EWU) and Washington State University (WSU). EWU is planning a new center named for Colville Confederated Tribes' leader Lucy Covington. The center will house her personal papers as well as oral history interviews with leaders throughout Indian Country who shared stories of Covington's influence on their leadership practices.[14] As the center grows, so will the collections, which will eventually support Native-centered research and programming. EWU has a master's program in public history; we can imagine ways Gonzaga NTAS students might collaborate to curate interpretations of interviews and documents with EWU master's students and students studying in the Covington Center. WSU hosts the Plateau Peoples' Web Portal, a digital repository of material cultural items held in a number of museum and library collections. Representatives from eight Plateau tribes selected images of items for inclusion in the portal, and tribal representatives curated the collection. Campus partners include the WSU Center for Digital Scholarship and Curation and Native American Programs. NTAS would like to both learn from the model provided by the tribal/university/digital partnerships and support the work in any way possible.

LOOKING AHEAD

Native American Studies courses at Gonzaga are constructed from multidisciplinary and interdisciplinary content. Faculty who teach in the program employ the cultural and methodological values of the Four Rs. Public history and digital humanities may not represent common methodologies for American Indian Studies/Native American Studies programs, but NTAS at Gonzaga Indigenizes those practices when we employ them to advance Native American and tribal narratives. We will be able to more fully engage with tribes and Native peoples as partners in interpretation, an ideal the program strives to attain, as these assignments become more pervasive across the program, and as NTAS becomes more intentional in outreach to tribes and tribal organizations such as UCUT and the Salish School of Spokane.

Public history allows NTAS to demonstrate relevance in explicit ways: interpretation, research, and collaborative learning to the extent it serves tribal aims. Institutions sometimes have tendencies to make more work for tribes, even when they earnestly want to partner and to share that work. The simple truth is that there is so much to do and not enough people to do it, thus we want to do our collective best as often as we can create opportunities to do so.

The Plateau's public institutions hold remarkable collections we can learn from while we contribute to decolonizing missions underway at various stages in different institutions. Tribes hold material culture pieces and archival materials as well. NTAS students can contribute to processing those materials while also navigating the full circle of respect, responsibility, relevance, and reciprocity. Even if a fully decolonized, state-funded museum is not possible in the near term, student practices certainly can be, as can tribal museum practices. The MAC and the High Desert Museum are committed to advancing this work but may need more support from tribal leaders and scholars as they pursue it.

When I think about historians modeling partnerships built on democratized public history practices—that is, recognizing experts without academic credentials—and authority that truly is shared between public/academic professionals and tribal people,[15] I recall the work Dr. Katrine Barber and Dr. Donna Sinclair with the Chinook Indian Nation through their appointments at Portland State University.[16] Their work began as part of a larger project, the Center for Columbia River History, with the aim of creating a multidisciplinary website containing interpretation about the Chinook Nation built upon public history praxis while centering Chinook narratives and perspectives. Barber noted that cultural sustainability, defined as "[emphasizing] social foundations . . . those aspects of culture that are carried forward with intergenerational solidarity as key to moving toward a sustainable future," was the core of this work.[17]

In their analysis of the project, Barber and Sinclair discussed the rich experiences the collaboration produced, the difficult conversations inherent to decolonial processes and practices, the fruitful give-and-take with the Chinook community, and the achievement for some PSU faculty and students of being elevated to kinship status, which both enveloped them in welcome and assigned them even greater responsibility to their Chinook family. Many, many lessons reside within this collaboration, and as director of a nascent program I was heartened to see the pragmatic solutions Barber and Sinclair engaged in when funding disappeared before the project's completion: they used their classrooms and their well-trained undergraduate and graduate students to continue the work. Barber noted, "Working with students forced us to carefully articulate our methods, especially those that addressed sovereignty and cultural sustainability. . . . [It] turned into a way to enrich the project with student energy, time, and intellectual insight."[18]

Resources, or lack thereof, are always a challenge for Native American Studies programs. Ours is no different. However, Barber and Sinclair demonstrate an upside to forced frugality. That upside represented growth for their students, their public history program, and their own intellectual work. When I consider what PSU and Utah's American West Center have accomplished, I admire and, yes, envy those accomplishments. The scope of oral histories collected through the American West Center is astounding. Those histories serve their communities as well as future generations of students, scholars, and professional practitioners. The best practices that emerged from both PSU and the AWC will inform our approach in Native American Studies at Gonzaga and will extend to our institutional partners across the Plateau. Partnership will be key in serving Native communities and Native-authored and Native-centered interpretation. In creating culturally sustainable interpretation, we need to remember ancestral practices and follow the model of old: when we share our resources, we all live better.

CHAPTER 11

Scholarship, the Public, and the Challenge of Local History

JEDEDIAH ROGERS

In *Hell of a Vision: Regionalism and the Modern American West*, Robert L. Dorman distinguishes between the *nationalist* West, the region known as the American West, and the *localist* West, subregions within the West that "might be as large as the Columbia River Basin or as small as a single pasture." He argues that, however one defines the West and one's association with it, the West is best conceptualized "as a collection of subregions than as a single unified region."[1] Clearly, subregions take many forms, depending on economic metrics, environmental characteristics, cultural identities, and geopolitical boundaries. In a sense, all history is defined by its borders, whether it be a neighborhood, town or city, a state, a region, or a nation—even a business, event, or idea.

The conceptual challenges of Utah history stem from matters of boundaries and definitions. Like other subregions, one might think of Utah in a number of geographical (basin and range, Colorado Plateau, Wasatch Mountains) and cultural contexts. These affiliations rub against the largely uncontested justification of a history based on geopolitical boundaries.[2] The physical boundaries of Utah history as a legitimate field of study are only one side of the coin; more compelling and considerably more contested is the question of what constitutes that history and what it means. The historical enterprise, certainly since the advent of the new social history, is driven in large part by inclusion and diversity, and in Utah, as elsewhere, historians are now pushing into new areas of inquiry and questioning worn narratives. As is well documented, this work occupies contested space, particularly in the local context where history is often a point of pride and the basis of a community's identity.

The contested nature of the content of local history undergirds this chapter, but it is not my principal concern. The challenge concerns not only "the what" but also "the how." Local history is often cast on one side of a choice between the academic and the popular. The distinction is partly one of methodology, approach, and temperament. Academic history is often considered dry and tedious, unappealing and largely unreadable to the general public, too objective to have any relevance to issues that animate a community. And, yet, what often goes unnoticed and underappreciated, even by institutions that support the work of public history, is the extent to which academic history forms a central pillar that informs and connects every other history enterprise.

I use as a case study an institution at the core of history-making in Utah for close to a century, *Utah Historical Quarterly* (*UHQ*). A close look at the journal and its parent organization, the Utah State Historical Society, suggests how a state-produced publication, aspiring to scholarly respectability but also public accessibility, has both reflected and pushed the boundaries of local history. The orientation and content of the journal has changed over the decades, of course, depending on trends within the discipline and the personalities of its editors and administrators. The challenge for local and regional institutions such as *UHQ* is to maintain a tradition and identity while adapting the production of history to today's audience and its needs. Central to this is the role of scholarship in local and state history—a role increasingly questioned by some administrators seemingly less interested in the permanence and durability of history than in its public visibility and engagement. To that end, this chapter reflects on the value and significance of local history, the intersection of scholarship and public history, and the role of a state journal in a shifting public and intellectual landscape. The case here may be applicable to any institution grappling with the tensions of transition and continuity.

Certainly, local history often is, as Anne W. Ackerson of the Museum Association of New York writes, "a rich tapestry of socioeconomic, ethnic, and political variations . . . that are often deeply rooted in a place,"[3] but it is also often a staid affair, beset by "one damn fact after another." This is in many respects by design: if history may be viewed at an elevation, the local has almost no bird's-eye view at all. It occupies the ground level, surrounded by the immediate subjects that it seeks to describe. This is not to say that local history is not sometimes beautifully conceived and presented, only that on par it is so occupied by the immediacy of the people and events of a particular place that it rarely ventures beyond the borders of its community or group. And because history on the local level is often focused on a specific place, community, group, or people, it too often remains disconnected from broader events, movements, and trends that define the historical discipline.[4]

The on-the-ground familiarity of local historians with their subjects is at once useful and limiting. The flood of historical detail generated by local historians can be overwhelming though essential to the important work of historical synthesis. If local historians construct the bricks that contribute to the larger structure (to draw from a history-as-structure metaphor), they offer an essential service. The problem is that local history sometimes operates in its own vacuum. Almost by definition, if not practice, it tends to look inward at the minutiae of a community or event, and rarely does it venture engagement with outside voices. Moreover, it is often bound up in biography, entangled with myth and memory, and sometimes not methodologically rigorous. The historian Peter Novick referred to preprofessional history as "overwhelmingly local and sectional, often in the most narrow and bigoted fashions." To Novik, the move to professionalize history in the late nineteenth century was a move toward nationalizing what had been local and regional, with the intent on making it impartial and objective.[5] Local history was then, and in some respects remains today, an interplay between history and the more popular forms of remembered history, such as folklore and community ritual, in which the past is simplified "into forms that can be memorialized, celebrated, and emotionally appropriated."[6] So, as much as local history may attempt to explain, the result can be simplistic and two dimensional, more concerned with group identity formation and boundary maintenance than historical "fact" or analysis. This should not be surprising; as Wallace Stegner observed, "Any people in a new land may be pardoned for being solicitous about their history: they create it, in a sense, by remembering it."[7]

Upon its organization in 1897, the Utah State Historical Society acted as a form of ritualization through which Utahns—mostly white Mormons proud of their heritage—sought to commemorate their past. The organization of historical societies, like those in other states, corresponded to a general movement of refashioning community and group histories to project a particular image. The historian Gary Topping, in his history of the society at the commemoration of its centennial, referred to "a tendency toward introspection" among Utahns who had experienced "the most fundamental changes imaginable" in the previous half century. The forming of a historical society was an act of memorialization by a people and a society that had transitioned from the pioneer era but hoped to retain a memory of its ancestry.[8] The same impulse gave rise to historical monuments, spearheaded locally by the Daughters of the Utah Pioneers and the Utah Pioneers Trails and Landmark Association, which placed hundreds of them. Combine these with visual representations in other mediums—in monuments, paintings, photographs, buildings, books—and we see the layering of collective memory wherein each representation reinforced the other, offering a particular image of what the past was and what it meant.

Yet these representations are hardly accurate depictions of past events, nor do they offer a cross section of the possible range of events to commemorate. History forgets more than it remembers. However much our commemorations speak to past individuals and events, more than anything they reflect the culture and more precisely the organization, or individual, that placed it. Moreover, monuments are subjective representations, one-sided depictions designed to meet the needs of an individual or group. Often, they are shaped by politics, meaning that more than memorializing the past they address present and future concerns. For instance, memorials that commemorate western settlement tend to adopt perspectives of white settlers with almost no regard for Native inhabitants.[9]

Like monuments, the Society functioned as a sort of club where members might remember and commemorate their own ancestors. It came into being as the public was awakening to the more rigorous scholarship then being taken up by history departments across the country. From the beginning, the organization's founders seemed to have appreciated the role of professional history at the state level through collection of historical manuscripts and documents, the investigation of Native "monuments and remains," and the "interchange of views and criticisms" among historians and the public.[10] The Society occupied this middle ground, keeper of family stories and community lore, yet with aspirations to project history as a social science, worthy of inspection and study. What it represented was an amphibious mix of popular and scholarly history that was reasonably respected by professionals and the public but suffered in rigor and prestige as a state organization isolated in the interior West.

This is best seen through the first generation of *UHQ*, a state publication that diverged from but also came to embrace the trends of the broader historical profession. The professionalization of the journal in the midcentury was in part an organic product of Utah historians—many by then having trained in PhD programs, employing the tools of their profession. But it was also the product of dominant personalities intent on making Utah history relevant to the state and the discipline.[11]

The journal's first issue was published in 1928, a full thirty years after the founding of the Society, its sponsoring organization. In it, Society president Albert Philips issued an appeal to individuals to turn over historical manuscripts, journals, and other records to the care of the state. Even copies would be appreciated, and these documents would be published in a quarterly magazine "to the advantage of the possessors, and for the ready use of all." The central purpose of what the state statute called "a historical magazine" was publishing original source materials.[12] Published documents and essays generally did not carry the trappings of scholarship and, with the exception of a few contributions from Brigham Young University professor William J. Snow, were written by historians with no formal training. Some primary sources, like the memoirs of Alice Parker Isom, were presented without any editorial context at all, and most were hagiographies, characteristic of many local histories.[13] The journal published accounts of Native American groups, the slave trade, frontier violence, exploration, and pioneer settlement patterned after narrative themes that then dominated histories of the American West. Snow's 1941 essay "Robert Gardner: Typical Frontiersman and Early Utah Pioneer" reflects characteristic subject matter and the historical, monolithic perspective. Readers, for example, were expected to know exactly what was meant by "typical frontiersman"—European, white, masculine.[14]

This flavor of history, celebrating in heroic fashion the early years of Utah settlement, would have appealed to many Utahns. Although the publication of primary source documents limited *UHQ*'s reach, the ideology and storytelling undergirding the journal—a brand of triumphal Turnerianism—was history that would have been familiar to a public that had been fed a diet of DUP and LDS church histories. As a matter of scholarship, however, it lagged behind national standards. Up to 1940, according to Topping, Utah historians had published little of note, reflecting the state's rather backwater intellectual climate beset by "a Mormon triumphalism" that produced mostly poorly researched histories unimaginatively executed.[15]

UHQ contributions sometimes suffered from these weaknesses, but its devotion to factual accuracy may be considered a signature offering. Charles Kelly, a renowned student of trails and longtime contributor, was representative of *UHQ* contributors in his "hoof-prints on the ground" approach to history. In an essay on the trader Jedediah Smith, Kelly contended that historians had not "fully appreciated" Smith's crossing of the west desert in 1827, "principally because of the historians' lack of knowledge concerning that section of the west."[16] The celebrated career of Juanita Brooks—courageous author of *The Mountain Meadows Massacre*, published in 1950—began with the Utah State Historical Society, and even though her first publication in *UHQ*, "Indian Relations on the Mormon Frontier," reflected a rather wooden methodology, with a structure that relied on the presentation of one quote or document after another, it was thorough and clearly presented.[17] *UHQ* in these years, and even thereafter, seemed to take up the essential work of accurately documenting a history that had suffered from misinformation and lore. The journal's first editors and contributors considered it a historical corrective to misinformation and inaccuracies. The on-the-ground historical presentation of data, performed by writers like Brooks and Kelly and other careful contributors, was an important service, even though they so often ignored or omitted the broader context or meaning.

The ship was steadied in its first two decades by an assiduous and dedicated staff. The journal's founding editor was J. Cecil Alter, untrained in history but an enthusiast and promoter who kept the publication on life support during the lean years of the Depression. Herbert S. Auerbach followed as editor, even as Alter continued his association with the journal while living outside the state. The challenge was then stringing together enough material to fill *UHQ*'s pages, to say nothing of procuring high-quality essays and documents to publish. Correspondence from society staff reveals the angst of finding enough material and of interpersonal conflicts within an organization of dominant personalities. This was especially so for Marguerite Sinclair, the office manager and only paid employee other than the editor until her resignation in 1949, who confided that Alter and Auerbach "would pile all the heavy editing and responsibility on me and yet give me no authority."[18] Sinclair also had a strained relationship with Joel Ricks, a member of the Board of Control and faculty at Utah Agricultural College in Logan. Both Alter and Ricks were rather strict in demeanor. Despite her absolute essential role in acquisitions, editing, and production, Sinclair never felt, and apparently never was, truly appreciated for her work and talents. The organization and management of the society was patriarchal, with men taking leading places at the helm, while Sinclair was left to grit it out.[19]

These management and personnel issues hampered the development of an organization beset with few resources. The young historian Dale Morgan contended in 1945 that the historical society had made "great strides" in large measure "because of Miss Sinclair's efforts," which the organization's leadership had taken for granted. Now Morgan thought the Board needed to make institutional changes, beginning with a head—or superintendent—of the society to guide the organization at its crossroads. This superintendent would stand over "department heads"—a secretary, archivist, and librarian—overseeing vital functions of the society. As for *UHQ*, he called it the society's "most valuable property," since it was its "one sanctioned avenue of expression." Morgan expressed concern with current arrangement of the editor working "from a distance" and proposed hiring an editor who worked in state, as well as engaging the part-time labor of undergraduate and graduate students at state universities. But his concern principally centered on the journal's purpose and orientation. *UHQ* primarily published long sources of primary documents, itself a useful service but not a serialized publication with research articles, news updates, and bibliographic citations that he thought would aid in "actively building up the Society." He urged the Board to consider how the journal could "promote the interests (1) of the Society, and (2) the cause of history in Utah."[20]

Morgan more than anyone was instrumental in the midcentury years in elevating Utah history as a field of study. Born and raised in Salt Lake City, he cut his teeth on history after college when he secured a job in the Historical Records Survey. Thereafter, he researched and wrote history with remarkable assiduousness—all as a man who had entirely lost his hearing at age fourteen from bacterial meningitis. As others have observed, Morgan had his own limitations as a historian, with an overriding concern for detail over interpretation, but his indefatigable work ethic tracking down and editing primary sources and authoring books and essays infused much-needed vitality into the study of Western American and Utah history.[21] Although never having been trained in graduate studies, Morgan became an accomplished and respected historian and probably most distinguished employee and associate of the Society. From the late 1930s into the early 1950s, as researcher, author, and sometime editor, his fingerprints were all over the journal. Prior to his work, the journal was thinly documented. Citations, he believed, were essential to establish scholarly credibility. "I think this work will stand on its own, even though I understand you do not think we out here in the West are capable of proper and complete footnoting," Sinclair wrote Morgan in 1946, perhaps tongue-in-cheek.[22]

Although sometimes rare, even then, the move to include scholarly notes—and to do so properly and completely—signaled the kind of publication *Utah Historical Quarterly* aimed to be. The problem for Morgan was that maturation came too slowly. In 1950, having already spent several years in the nation's capital, he planned to move to the East Coast where he would secure employment at the Smithsonian. His move was in large measure influenced by his perception of Utah as "an economic and cultural desert," and although he had been considered for the position of director of the society—a role he would have relished—the position was only prospective. Besides, his published and forthcoming work made him a controversial figure in conservative, Mormon Utah—"not culturally innocuous," as he put it.[23]

And yet Morgan continued to believe that the society stood poised to enter a new era of credibility and influence, led by its publication. While Marguerite Sinclair sometimes called the organization her "baby," Morgan thought that it was "no longer anybody's baby but is growing up to maturity."[24] He considered *UHQ* an "instrument" to promote the institution's interests, which went well beyond producing "a handsome volume pertaining to the history of Utah and the West." This meant considering the proper "relationship of members and Society." To Morgan, the journal could be the means by which USHS members and Utah citizens participate in the production and consumption of history (even to the point of possibly having members elect the organization's governing Board of Control). The journal would advertise the happenings of the society, solicit manuscripts and pamphlets for the research library, and otherwise connect readers and members to the larger project of Utah history. In short, the society would be a truly public organization, unlike the LDS Church Historian's Office, which had its own research collection but limited public accessibility and did "not pretend to and [could not] serve the interests of the people of the State as a whole."[25] The journal, he argued, was the vehicle for scholarship *and* public engagement, though it was treated by administrators "as at once a step-child and the only reason for existence that the Society has."[26]

For Morgan, the one served the other. The larger purpose of *UHQ* was to promote the interests of the society, which, as he wrote the new director Russell Mortensen, "is the only institution at present in the State which has the inclination and the potential resources to serve the highest ideals of scholarship, open to all." Utah scholarship, he believed, was ready to assume a new quality and visibility.[27] For Morgan, the society's "proper place in the cultural life" was as "a sort of liaison agency for all institutions and social groups interested in its history, at once a clearing house and a coordinating force. No other institution within the State has either the will, the moral authority, or the legal sanction for such a role, and if the Historical Society does not assume the function, nobody will."[28]

Morgan's words to the new, professionally trained director signaled a new era for the Society. Hired in 1950 and armed with a PhD in history from UCLA, Russ Mortensen gave further academic credibility and brought professional growth to the organization. One of his contributions was to realize the work of Brooks, Morgan, and Sinclair in the 1940s to establish a research library. By the time Mortensen took the society's helm, a small but significant collection of books and manuscripts had been built.[29] On this foundation, he hired a trained librarian and instituted modern library cataloguing, so that the society manuscript and book holdings eventually became "a respectable research facility on Utah, the Mormons, and Western history."[30]

Mortensen's other contribution was to reinvent the *Quarterly* by giving it "a new dress."[31] The first issue to assume this new look appeared in 1958, a photo-filled special issue devoted to "Utah's Parks and Scenic Wonders," followed the next year with the full-color "Valley of the Great Salt Lake." The latter eventually sold upward of 100,000 copies to visitors at the Utah State Capitol and shoppers at stores such as Safeway.[32] Without question, the success of these issues and others that followed, along with the professionalization of the research library and other initiatives, elevated the visibility of the society as a major cultural force in the state.[33]

When looking back, it might be tempting to pine for days when the general public widely read the work of professional historians. What ought not to be forgotten is the uncompromising commitment of Mortensen and subsequent directors of the society to a standard of scholarship. In 1954, Mortensen compared the "literary value" of a journal such as *Western Humanities Review* with the more pedestrian offerings in *UHQ*. In his mind, while the former demanded "a higher literary standard than we can or do," being concerned principally with the "values of art" over "the values of knowledge," the latter offered "more items of lasting, permanent value." Mortensen pointed to a recent piece in the *Review*—"a masterpiece of drival [*sic*], nonsense, trivia, and obfuscation"—to argue that if one had to choose between "art or information," he heavily favored the latter.[34] Of course, the dilemma is that essays and articles devoid of innovation or literary flourish are often also bad history, little more than chronicles designed to convey historical stories and information. This is not to say that some articles do not have the literary value that Mortensen referred to, but these tend to come from writers trained in literature or creative writing, often in the form of memoir. Limited to the geographic borders that dictate its content and talent pool, journal editors haven't always had the luxury afforded by finding someone like Morgan who seamlessly blends rigorous scholarship with literary sensibility.

The journal's status and reputation were also probably compromised, given Utah history's peculiar association with the polemical, devotional nature of Mormon history. Richard Saunders has referred to Utah history prior to the 1960s as "almost an outgrowth of LDS church authority," written as part of a pioneer myth "master narrative," and rooted in the myth and commemoration that characterized local history.[35] In fact, the journal had a dual identity, one closely aligned with Mormon history yet emphasizing western American themes. In the first decades of publication, the documentary histories were often but not exclusively from Mormon pioneers, as reflected by whole issues devoted to the Dominguez and Escalante expedition, the overland migrations of 1846, and the John Wesley Powell surveys.[36]

After midcentury, as history in Utah became more professionalized and specialized, the compartmentalization of the discipline into focused subcategories limited the range of the journal. Previously, a wide range of contributors and readers consumed the pages of *UHQ*. But the founding of other history publications served to funnel the interest of specialists more precisely toward more narrowly defined publications. The result was that while the journal became more professional and scholarly it also began to constrict, as the discipline became cast into silos.[37] Consequently, state history's association became more local than regional. The earlier, more expansive scope of the *Quarterly* perhaps, in part, reflected Morgan's sensibility as a Western and not exclusively Utah historian. Early contributors did not feel circumscribed within the state's geographic boundaries. But increasingly Utah history narrowed as a field. While in some regards Utah history has benefited from increased specialization, it has also suffered from it, as it has been divorced from broader regional history and considered a stepchild of Western history. As fewer academics contributed to more popular history magazines, a divide began to appear between publications considered academic and others catering to a more public audience.

It is this academic-public divide that lies at the heart of what concerns the current caretakers of the journal. As we have seen, *UHQ* always had a commitment to factual history, but not until after midcentury did it solidify its bona fides as a work of scholarship. The academic quality of articles varied, as they often do in publications, but neither at midcentury nor presently has the publication wavered from its commitment to establish a place at the academic table. At the same time, the journal has always occupied a public role as an outlet for local and state histories that, in the words of the current editorial policy, "appeal to scholars as well as lay readers" and "present a compelling narrative written in clear prose."[38]

Still, looking back nearly a century, the journal's *raison d'être* has been historical research and scholarship. The durability of the publication's commitment is remarkable, given that state journals at other institutions have either folded or changed to a magazine format without the trappings of scholarship. Now, with several decades of declining subscription numbers, and membership revenue not enough to cover production and printing costs, the journal's reason for being is increasingly being questioned. Concerns about funding have prompted a general discussion among the *UHQ* editors, administrators at the Utah Division of State History and Department of Cultural and Community Engagement, the Board of State History, and the wider historical community about the value of scholarly publication and the foundational purposes of the journal.

These specific concerns are underscored by broader trends related to who consumes history, what type of history, and how. Those who continue subscribing to scholarly journals clearly value the scholarship, but the amorphous "public" prefers narrative over analysis, color photos over the printed word, and free content over paid subscriptions. Current members of the Utah State Historical Society, according to a December 2019 survey, generally support the approach and offerings of the journal. They see the value of the evidence-based, footnoted research. But among some, the journal has not struck the right balance between academic and popular interest. One respondent wrote, "I think the quarterly is getting very academic. I would like to see more general articles and more about the contributions minority groups have made to the history of Utah. I know of individuals who have left the organization because of lack of popular interest articles."[39]

This is one response, but without question the average lay reader would prefer narrative-driven, popular-interest articles over the more specialized research articles that often appear in the journal. *UHQ* has attempted, and continues to attempt, a balance of the two, and in fact our article awards distinguish between scholarly and general-interest essays. Yet, on the whole, as coeditor I can say that we have indeed, quite consciously, attempted to swim in academic waters. I see our work as a continuation of the tradition advanced by Morgan and others of his generation, as well as a strategic choice that recognizes the bedrock importance of scholarship to local and state organizations.

The first point to make here is that, to remain viable and relevant, *UHQ* needs the "buy-in" of the academic and professional communities. The journal relies on submissions of scholars and academics, and its scholarly orientation is intended, in part, to attract the work of historians, many of whom need a line on a CV and publication credit for academic tenure. We are incentivized to continue the longstanding model of relying on the free labor of contributors who produce history, since we hardly have the funds to pay authors for their work. Although we consider how history is consumed, our principle concern is with its *production*, and much of our time is spent "infiltrating" the universities and connecting with academics who supply much of the content that we publish. This effort is about much more than finding material to publish; it is about cultivating the field of Utah Studies, particularly among students who will become its leading practitioners.

For sixty years, the *Quarterly*'s readership has ranged somewhere between 1,000 and 4,000 members, but these numbers belie the real interest in Utah history and the reach of the historical society. Today, this is partly reflected by citations and references to the journal found in books and other publications and by traffic accessing digital content beyond the analog. In 2019, Google Scholar provided over 3,000 citations of *UHQ* in the humanities, science, business, and case law. A scan of influential books or articles in Utah history reveals a reliance on material found in the journal. Institutional subscriptions from Utah libraries and public schools, as well as academic libraries in and outside the state, provide a reach beyond our individual subscriptions. For over ten years, journal back issues, along with other society publications, have been available through our website.[40] The reach is expanding with a recent publishing partnership with the University of Illinois Press. This consolidates production under one roof and makes available back issues to JSTOR, a platform that will help *UHQ* offerings to swim in swift academic waters rather than remain pooled, untapped by readers and scholars. This and other digital content on our website and on the popular site *Utah History to Go*, much of it derived from scholarship originally published in *UHQ*, continue to engage the public.

Still, in the face of declining membership and revenue, it is tempting for some to dismiss academic work in favor of more popular forms of history (in magazines, social media, and other platforms) that reach a broader audience. In the case of *UHQ*, which relies largely on membership revenue for production, printing, and distribution costs, current administrators have proposed a fundamental rehaul of the journal.[41] Might Utah be better served with a high-gloss, color-photo publication that offers shorter popular-interest articles? Put more generally, what is the value of scholarship to the public, particularly for an organization reliant on state funds and beholden to the public?

With the prospect of a watered-down publication designed for greater mass appeal, dozens of historians are defending an institution that, although no longer the "one sanctioned avenue of expression," as Morgan believed it was in 1950, they regard as indispensable. In written statements and at a special meeting of the Board of State History on July 2, 2020, historians spoke of scholarship foundational to every other history initiative in the state, academic and public—books and articles, blogs, exhibits, musicals, lesson plans, markers, news articles, documentaries, magazines. A fixation on content that is more appealing to the general reader may be missing the picture: the scholarship in the journal is permanent and durable, and the research found therein is bedrock to any serious history endeavor. Rather than watering down the journal, we should embrace and support what it is doing for the field of Utah history and look to other products for even wider public engagement.

It is therefore shortsighted to tether the *value* of the publication to the society's membership numbers and to readership trends. Scholarship may appeal to a general public, but not necessarily. As John Alley argues, "Attaining a broad audience without compromising scholarship is a worthy goal, . . . but there are inevitable tight limits on how wide an audience one can reach while maintaining the peer-reviewed validity and quality of scholarly work. Prioritizing accessibility risks pandering and compromised scholarship."[42]

For these reasons, it seems important to maintain the core identity of *UHQ* as a place for well-researched stories and analysis. The journal editors have made efforts to add high-quality filler content, such as photo galleries and shorter think-piece essays. Attempts have also been made to include public content that has contemporary resonance and that takes a broader, regional approach.[43] Both have been achieved in recent special issues on the Great Salt Lake and public lands in the modern West, published in the winter 2019 and spring 2020 issues, respectively. The health of the lake, when seen in the context of saltwater bodies worldwide, is a matter of concern, and we designed the special issue to bring awareness to problems confronting it. The subject of public lands is also compelling: the special issue seeks to contextualize political debates and tell broader, untold histories of public lands.

At the same time, the editors remain devoted to telling good local history and providing a platform for local historians and authors. The journal continues to solicit and publish what may be considered traditional subjects of Utah history, but contributors are urged to bring broader meaning, sophistication, and complexity to the stories they tell. *UHQ* seeks to publish manuscripts that have contemporary relevance, create spaces for dialogue, and commemorate publicly significant events. Although as a state agency the society must be cautious in how it approaches and treats matters of public policy, it is committed to defending its methods and processes, insisting that history and its practitioners have something to contribute to public dialogue. The goal is to interact with experts in other disciplines and to break out of the silos that so often beset local and state history. Hopefully, this will help to inch the society closer to Dale Morgan's midcentury vision of an organization that better engages the public in real and meaningful ways.

Utah Studies has not fully coalesced as a self-conscious subfield, one that attracts scholars and graduate students. This may be in part due to the insularity of Utah history—and Mormon history—which Jared Farmer compares to the history of the Great Basin, in that it pools and finds no outlet to the larger historical community.[44] Another challenge is that, despite the blooming of Mormon Studies, and numerous "amateur" and independent historians working on topics related to Utah Studies, the field does not have a critical mass of scholars and historians moving the conversation forward in deliberate and creative ways. Although one certainly recognizes patterns in essays published in *UHQ*, and in some cases one can see how scholarship builds on the work done before, it is rarely self-consciously reflective. Seeing Utah history as that which, for the most part, occurs within the state boundaries has limited the field. This is an intractable problem, given that *UHQ* relies on the state's political governing officials for funding, but this does not excuse the inaction of Utah historians when it comes to explaining their relevance and significance in some larger sense.

All this is to say the journal has suffered from a dual, and perhaps tortured, identity. It is a journal that yearns for scholarly respectability while retaining its long tradition as a publication that the people can relate to. Also ambiguous is whether the journal occupies the space of local or regional history—or some nebulous middle ground between the two. What seems clear is that carving history into these bite-sized chunks—in particular, into divisions that correspond to political boundaries—is not only narrowing but untenable. If history is borderless, then even the term "Utah history" betrays the nature of the discipline. The recent statement on the inside front cover of *UHQ* reflects a move to see Utah history in a more expansive, regional context.

And so *Utah Historical Quarterly*, and perhaps other state journals, would do well to think expansively of its content. At its best, according to the folklorist Austin Fife, writing in its pages, local history reaches beyond the immediate locale, until it is "integrated wholesomely, logically, and beneficially, with the ever-expanding realms of history which ultimately encompass the story of the world and of man. This balance between the particular and universal—however impossible to achieve—is what the historian, or any historian, must constantly strive to realize."[45] As *UHQ* has shown, the balance between the academic and the popular is indeed difficult to achieve. Above all, the guiding principle must be to maintain scholarly standards, which in no way dismisses a commitment to broader audiences and to the public good. It illustrates, rather, a commitment to increase the reputation of local history as a worthy enterprise. The *UHQ* may not be all things to all people, but it occupies a critical place in that important endeavor—in the critical work of publicly engaged history.

CHAPTER 12

Building Bridges

STEPHEN ARON AND VIRGINIA SCHARFF

In this chapter, we explore the challenges to historians working to build bridges from the academy into diverse public arenas. Over the last two decades, our efforts have focused principally in two areas. First, we engaged with the Autry Museum, where we were tasked with bringing the best scholars and the best scholarship to the museum's exhibitions, publications, and programs. Second, we joined an initiative of the American Historical Association (AHA) that aims to broaden the training of doctoral students to prepare them for a wide range of careers beyond the professoriate. Both of these enterprises produced important results. Yet were we to assign a grade to our bridge building, it would have to be an "incomplete."

Our formal association with the Autry Museum dates to 2002. That year, what had been the Gene Autry Museum of Western Heritage and then the Autry Museum of Western History was rechristened as the Autry National Center, with the Autry Institute for the Study of the American West (the Institute) established as the Center's research entity. Stephen Aron assumed the position as the Institute's first executive director, a half-time appointment that allowed him to continue, on the other half, as a professor of history at the University of California, Los Angeles (UCLA). Shortly after, Virginia Scharff, a professor of history at the University of New Mexico (UNM), came on board as the Autry's Women of the West Chair. In collaboration with one another and with curators, conservators, educators, fundraisers, program managers, theater producers, and trustees at the Autry, we engaged scholars in a variety of disciplines and from around the world in the work of the Center. Guided by the Autry's unifying concept—that the diversity of the Western past and present is best viewed through the lens of "convergence"—we collectively developed and contributed to a record of exhibitions, publications, and programs about which we are justifiably proud. But for all that was accomplished by the Institute, its demise in 2014 demonstrated that bridge-building can be a precarious endeavor.

Our second bridge-building project launched in 2014, when the Andrew W. Mellon Foundation awarded the American Historical Association a $1.5 million grant to promote "career diversity" for PhDs in history. The AHA selected the history departments at UCLA and the University of New Mexico as two of four pilot programs (along with Columbia University and the University of Chicago). Aron, as chair of the UCLA History Department, and Scharff, as Associate Provost for Faculty Development at UNM, took leading roles in shaping the initiative at their respective universities. Working collaboratively with colleagues and students, we generated curricular innovations and promoted shifts in long-held ways of thinking about the purposes and possibilities of doctoral education. Still, at this writing, the bridges that have been constructed from the university to nonacademic careers remain on fragile foundations.

From its inception, plans for the Gene Autry Museum of Western Heritage included a commitment to "developing a major research center to further its mission" as a museum. Space was set aside for a reading room, book stacks, and a film vault. Like the museum to which it was attached, the library would concentrate "on acquiring holdings that add to our understanding of the role myth and legend have played in the creation of [popular] notion[s] of 'the Old West.'" At the same time, the museum's founders amplified their broader concerns by seeking out materials that document "the history of women and minorities, and other aspects of western history that cast particularly strong light upon stereotypical icons and notions." In partial fulfilment of these goals, the Autry purchased for $2,500,000 a 35,000-volume collection of western Americana from bookseller Fred Rosenstock.[1]

It took some time to get the research facility up and running. When the museum opened in 1988, the hope was to begin admitting researchers to the library by 1992. The demands of processing the vast Rosenstock acquisition, however, fully occupied staff and pushed the opening date back to 1995. In June of that year, the Autry convened a multiday symposium to celebrate the library's availability to researchers and to explore the state of scholarship on the imagined West. That theme spotlighted the strengths of the Autry's collections and served to distinguish its library from other research centers. As Martin Ridge, then the director of research at the Huntington Library, observed, the Autry's research focus filled a significant niche. While the Huntington had "unrivaled" holdings in Western Americana, "the image of the cowboy is not something we do." In the same vein, Kevin Mulroy, director of the Autry Library, described his as "a very different kind of library." Where the Huntington "will be pulling out rare books," the Autry librarians will "be pulling out a tourist brochure or a movie poster."[2]

Through the late 1990s, Mulroy's goal was to make the Autry "the major center for the study of the invented West." That involved continuing to collect books, manuscripts, and ephemera related to the West of the imagination. It also necessitated that the Autry's Research Center "become *access driven*" in order to build "a stronger presence outside the museum." To enlarge its public face and increase the Research Center's visibility in the scholarly community, Mulroy and John Gray (who had become President of the Autry in 1999) formed an advisory committee for the library, which Aron joined in 2000.[3]

Gray's visionary leadership drove big changes at the Autry in the first years of the new century. Mulroy's departure in 2002 for a position at the University of Southern California library led to Aron's appointment as executive director of the newly established Autry Institute for the Study of the American West. A merger between the Autry and the Women of the West Museum in Denver created an endowment for a western women's history scholar-curatorship, which became two positions: a curatorial appointment taken up by Carolyn Brucken, and the Women of the West Chair that Scharff assumed. An even bigger merger between the Autry and the Southwest Museum of the American Indian, the oldest museum in Los Angeles with its nearly unrivaled collections of Native American arts and artifacts and the equally impressive holdings of its Braun Research Library, gave birth to the Autry National Center. The press quickly dubbed this a union between "cowboys and Indians."[4]

Within the structure of the Autry National Center, the Institute for the Study of the American West drew on the libraries of the two museums, while also acting as a conduit to scholars in the academy. In his initial report to the Board of Trustees of the Autry National Center in September 2002, Aron defined "the mission of the Autry Institute" as "to broaden the connections between the Autry and academia, to promote new and better scholarship on the American West, and to ensure that the museum's exhibitions and programs are informed by the best of that scholarship." In bringing university-based scholars into the work of the Autry, the Institute sought to cross the divide that had long separated the academy from the museum and academic history from public history. Those links began with Aron's home university, UCLA, which, as part of Aron's now split appointment, committed $25,000 per year for three years. This was matched by the Autry to support graduate students researching the museum collections and working in various roles for the Autry National Center.[5]

The ambitions for connections to the academy and with the public went well beyond UCLA. At a time when several universities were also establishing or expanding their centers devoted to the study of the American West, the Institute differentiated itself by stressing research with a public outcome. That is, while other Western history centers promoted original and innovative scholarship as an end in itself, the Institute encouraged research that generated programs, publications, and exhibitions as a means to enhance public understanding of the history of the American West. Following a well-established model, the Autry Institute created a modest fellowship program to support research in the collections of the Autry National Center. More resources, however, were devoted to engaging scholars working on the projects and initiatives of the Autry, which led also to fruitful collaborations with other university-based research entities including Stanford's Bill Lane Center, Yale's Lamar Center, the USC-Huntington Institute for California and the West, Southern Methodist University's Clements Center, and the University of New Mexico's Center for the Southwest.

The Autry Western History Workshop was one innovative manifestation of the Institute's bridge building. Initiated in 2002 and convened by Aron, these monthly gatherings at the Autry departed from both academic and museum conventions in several key ways, while bringing together some of the best of both worlds. Where museums often brought scholars in to give lectures about their publications, Aron conceived the Autry's gatherings as workshops discussing precirculated works in progress. As the Autry Workshop developed through the years, it became a unique public seminar bringing together faculty, graduate students, and museum professionals from around southern California with docents and Western history "buffs" to participate in the process of scholarship (as opposed to simply learning about the product of research through lectures). Engaging with such a mixed, sometimes cantankerous group pushed presenters, usually academy-based historians, out of their scholarly comfort zones and helped them learn how to communicate with a much wider audience.

Convergence, a magazine that the Autry National Center launched in 2004 with Aron as its editor, featured similar acts of translation. The name of the magazine traced to what had emerged as the organizing concept of the Autry National Center. "Convergence," each issue of the magazine proclaimed, "is a way of seeing the large, evolving story of the American West as an interwoven tapestry of cultures and peoples, and a way of understanding how their stories are connected to one another and to us." Individual articles and themed issues amplified this perspective on the western past and present. And, as with the Western History Workshop, *Convergence* magazine provided a venue for academics to write for a far larger readership than any scholarly journals reached.[6]

As Women of the West Chair, Scharff participated in the Workshop, wrote for *Convergence*, and took part in numerous educational and scholarly programs at the Autry. She also served, with Brucken, as cocurator of two major exhibitions, *Home Lands: How Women Made the West* (2010) and *Empire and Liberty: The Civil War and the West* (2015), as well as coauthor and editor of the companion volumes accompanying the exhibitions. As works of historical interpretation, the two exhibitions represented attempts to build bridges between fields of scholarly specialization: women's, Western, and environmental history in the case of *Home Lands*; and the histories of slavery, freedom, and American expansion for *Empire and Liberty*.

Most history professors do their scholarly work in solitude, direct their publications at specialized audiences, and confine their thinking to the two-dimensional space of written text. Working closely with Brucken (a PhD in American Studies with an MA in Museum Studies) and Aron as dynamic thinking partners, Scharff not only convened groups of scholarly advisors but perhaps more importantly learned to rely on the expertise of diverse museum professionals; to work in concert with those experts to use objects, text, and three-dimensional space to interpret history; to confront the challenges and pleasures of securing and displaying historical artifacts from the Autry collections and on loan from other institutions; and to translate research into visual and textual terms that would appeal to the broadest public, from school-age children to distinguished professors.

As professionals bridging the gaps between our areas of expertise in the service of a common task, we became a kind of human embodiment of the Autry ideals of convergence and collaboration.[7]

The Autry's ambitions, however, ran up against budgetary and political challenges. Badly damaged in the 1994 Northridge earthquake, the Southwest Museum's historic structure on Mount Washington needed retrofitting and other system upgrades. Its priceless collections of Indian arts and artifacts were jammed together in rooms that lacked adequate climate and pest control. Water damage and vermin infestations jeopardized hundreds of thousands of objects. Safeguarding the building and conserving the collections consumed millions of dollars. At the same time, the Autry's plans to expand its facility at Griffith Park—to provide proper storage space for the Southwest's collections and to expand gallery space, as well as to construct a building to house the combined libraries of the Southwest and serve as a home for the Institute—faced determined opposition from a cadre of neighborhood activists in Mount Washington. Mounting expenses soon cut into the Autry's operating budget. Reductions in staff and programming affected all of the museum's activities, including those of the Institute.

The Great Recession brought further retrenchment. Stalemated at City Hall, the Autry's Board of Trustees pulled the plug on the Griffith Park expansion in 2009. A year later, John Gray departed. The following year, Aron returned to a full-time appointment at UCLA, though he maintained a connection to the Autry as Chair of Western History at the Institute. Meanwhile, after 2014, Scharff transitioned from being Women of the West Chair to Senior Scholar at the Autry, taking on a role at once more limited and broader than her original charge.[8]

Leadership of the Institute passed to David Burton, an experienced museum professional, who had helped to shepherd the Autry's acclaimed Native Voices Theater Company. Burton reenvisioned an Institute that would "extend its focus beyond . . . history" to embrace a range of "academic and artistic disciplines, cultural lifeways, science and technology, politics, public policy, and the social fabric of everyday life." That expansion of subject matter and approach, Burton wrote optimistically, would position the Institute to "make sense of the fabric of the West" in "a time characterized by a mash up of ideas, styles, cultural identity, interpersonal and global relationships."[9]

Burton's bold ideas were never implemented. In the face of budgetary pressures, Gray's successor, Dan Finley, prioritized activities that more immediately enhanced the Autry's bottom line. *Convergence* magazine first reduced its schedule and then published its last issue in 2011. In 2012, Finley gave way to W. Richard West Jr. In his previous stint as founding director of the National Museum of the American Indian (NMAI), West had established himself as a leader who challenged museum orthodoxies. At NMAI, that translated into exhibitions and programs that privileged native voices and visions and, in critic Edward Rothstein's words, that "advocate[d] not just for artifacts, but also for the living cultures that created them." At the Autry, by contrast, West embraced the ethos of convergence. But his attentions and the Autry's fundraising were diverted to completing a separate storage facility to house the combined collections of the Autry and Southwest Museums, a project to which the Autry's board had committed when it scuttled plans for expansion at Griffith Park. In 2014, with budget cutting again necessary, West decided to eliminate the Institute, aborting Burton's proposals for it.[10]

The decline and demise of the Institute did not doom bridge building. Although West disputed the wisdom of a stand-apart Institute, under his tenure the Autry maintained a commitment to complementary partnerships with academics and their institutions. In 2013, the UCLA-Autry collaboration produced "Jews in the Los Angeles Mosaic." This project grew out of a seminar that Aron had cotaught with David Myers, then the director of the UCLA Center for Jewish Studies (CJS). Curated by Aron's former student, Karen Wilson, the exhibition and its companion volume (which Wilson edited) drew on the collections of the Autry and digital mapping undertaken by CJS. In 2014, the Autry partnered with Occidental College to undertake a joint search for a scholar of Native American cultures. That resulted in the hiring of Nancy Marie Mithlo as professor of art and art history at Occidental and as Chair of American Indian Studies at the Autry. Finally, in 2015, Scharff and Brucken collaborated on "Empire and Liberty." A series of symposia cosponsored by the Autry and the Clements Center for Southwest Studies informed the exhibition and gave rise to a volume of essays that supplemented the collection edited by Scharff.[11]

In recent years, West, with the support of the Autry Board of Trustees, particularly its chair, David Cartwright, have involved scholars in many aspects of the museum's work and built out networks. Scharff, in particular, has spearheaded efforts on several fronts. "Dress Codes," an exhibition slated to open in the spring of 2020, but pushed back a year because of the COVID-19 pandemic, adds another chapter to the productive collaboration between Scharff and Brucken. In 2020, Aron partnered with Autry curator Tyree Boyd-Pates and obtained a grant from the UCLA History Department's Luskin Center for History and Policy to further the reach of the Autry's "Collecting Community History Initiative: The West during COVID-19 and Black Lives Matter."

Still, at the time when this chapter was originally written, Aron and Scharff imagined they were writing mostly a history of their engagement with the Autry. Mithlo had left her joint position with the Autry and Occidental for an appointment at UCLA. Aron believed his bridge-building efforts would likely be directed elsewhere. Scharff continued as an occasional advisor on programs and exhibitions, but she was no longer developing Autry projects of her own.

In 2014, the year that the Autry formally closed its Institute, the American Historical Association officially opened its initiative to build bridges from doctoral education to careers beyond the professoriate with three-year pilot projects at Columbia University, the University of Chicago, the University of California–Los Angeles, and the University of New Mexico. By then, the initiative had been many years in the making. In the view of many observers of graduate training, it was already many years overdue. And yet, the experiences of the pilot projects show that, for many in the academy, the initiative still represents a bridge too far.

Certainly, by the time Anthony Grafton and James Grossman published "No More Plan B" in October 2011, the issue they were addressing—the difference between the number of PhDs earned in history each year and the number of available tenure-track positions—was no secret. The Great Recession enlarged the gap between candidates and openings, but talk about the "crisis" in the academic job market dated back forty years. For decades, historians and fellow humanities scholars and social scientists had lamented the situation, without doing much of anything to address it. Those responsible for doctoral training preferred to bury their heads in the sand rather than change the ways they prepared students. The institutions where they taught often buried the evidence by keeping very incomplete records about graduate placement. In effect, department websites embraced graduates who secured tenure-track appointments, while they erased those who did not. But Grafton and Grossman, respectively President and the Executive Director of the American Historical Association, determined to shine a light on the practices and purposes of doctoral education. Although they subtitled their article "A Very Modest

Proposal for Graduate Programs in History," their manifesto raised a profound challenge to academic business as usual.[12]

In the piece, Grafton and Grossman highlighted "a curious irony" about doctoral training in history. On the one hand, the study of history had been enlivened in recent decades by an array of new approaches and technologies. On the other, the "breadth and range, this openness to new ways of thinking and working, somehow disappear when we consider our students' careers." Instead of telling students that "there are many ways to be a historian" and "many ways to apply what you've learned to a career," mentors ignore "the facts of academic employment" and push "talented scholars into narrow channels."[13]

As its authors hoped, "No More Plan B" inspired a fresh round of conversations. And more than talk, the essay sparked actions. The AHA began gathering hard information about the employment outcomes for history PhDs. It reached out to PhDs employed outside the academy and convened focus groups with them and their employers. From these discussions came understandings about career opportunities and the skills required to succeed beyond the professoriate. In particular, the conversations called attention to the need for graduate training that taught students to communicate in a variety of media to a variety of audiences; to collaborate with people with diverse backgrounds, training, and perspectives; to develop quantitative and digital literacy; and to acquire the intellectual self-confidence that would enable them to adapt their skills to a range of situations. Armed with these insights and partnered with the four pilot institutions, the AHA made its successful application to the Mellon Foundation.[14]

At the University of New Mexico, the career diversity initiative proved to be something of an exercise in recovery of suppressed institutional memory. At the project's outset, a few faculty voiced reservations about the initiative, worrying that preparing students for diverse careers diluted the mission of the PhD program as a training ground for professors. Others expressed concerns about how they themselves could teach skills they had not learned. A large core of faculty seized the possibilities of the program, though they, too, wondered how the department would get there. Scharff, working closely with department chair Melissa Bokovoy, began the process by putting together a faculty-student team and by appointing Jennifer McPherson as the project's Graduate Coordinator (a position funded by the Mellon grant). Together, Scharff, Bokovoy, McPherson, and the larger team then set out to develop internships, create new and reconfigured course assignments and objectives, and plan workshops, programs, conferences, and outreach to alumni and others.

After a first attempt at a special "Mellon seminar" produced mixed results, Assistant Professor David Prior, an avid proponent of the initiative (and a former staffer at the *Journal of American History*) conjured up a useful tool for curriculum change. Prior argued that the department did not need a separate course to teach "career diversity" skills. Instead, it needed an inventory of skills people already taught in their seminars, which aligned with the program's objectives. Prior called this tactic "Mellonizing the seminar," an innovation that helped to change the conversation. By suggesting how existing seminars could be "Mellonized," the initiative took deeper root, transforming departmental curriculum and culture. To be sure, not everyone got fully onboard, but the "coalition of the willing" began to expand, one colleague, one event, one class at a time. Moreover, Bokovoy took the opportunity to launch a rethinking of UNM's MA program, aimed at using what had been learned through the AHA's doctoral initiative to promote career-building connections and skills throughout UNM's graduate (and eventually undergraduate) programs.

The UNM team also soon realized what should have been obvious from the start. Because UNM lacks the prestige of more elite programs, history faculty at UNM have long worked to connect students with professional opportunities outside the academy, in museums and archives, historical societies and libraries, government agencies and nonprofits. UNM alumni, indeed, were the department's greatest asset. By the third year of our project, Scharff and the UNM team focused on creating an alumni network that would serve both former and current UNM PhD students in a variety of ways. Over a joyful and fruitful weekend "alumni retreat," UNM launched what is intended to be a sustainable network built on alumni commitment and satisfaction.

Perhaps most importantly, Scharff came to see that the need for "career diversity" was a consequence of student diversity. The academic career market assumes that students will possess unlimited individual mobility and hold a desire for a tenure-track job above all other things. But that's not the case for many, if not most, students at UNM or many other public universities, who have needs and desires connected to other people (partners, children, parents, and community) and reasonable ideas about where they do or don't want to live. For some of those students, staying near home takes precedence over seeking the coveted tenure-track job. But they still want to be historians and still see the PhD as a valuable intellectual and professional asset. For them, the bridges between the academy and the public are already built. Our job is to see how to help them traverse the spans more fluidly and happily.

At UCLA, the Career Diversity Initiative had financial advantages not available at UNM, but the project encountered cultural hurdles that were in many respects higher. On the plus side, the UCLA History Department's fundraising has enabled its endowment to grow over the last two decades from around 1 million dollars to close to 50 million. That support put the graduate program on a much sounder financial footing, which, along with a shrinking of the program, made admission exponentially more selective. Boasting impeccable academic pedigrees, entering students, like their peers at elite universities, expected that their accomplishments would lead them to tenure-track employment. To a considerable extent, department faculty reinforced those expectations, or at least, as Grafton and Grossman pointed out, "nourish[ed]" their students' presumption that a tenure-track faculty appointment is the true measure of success in graduate education. The result, on the minus side, has been the entrenchment of a departmental culture impervious to changes in the service of career diversity.

As at UNM, the reaction of UCLA faculty to the grant from the Mellon Foundation included a mix of indifference and resistance. The coalition of the willing, as a percentage of the faculty, was smaller at UCLA than at UNM. Indicative of resistance was the response from some faculty to Aron's presentation to incoming students of the employment statistics for UCLA History PhDs. More than one colleague wondered why Aron wished to "demoralize" the students. Subsequently, leaders of the History Graduate Student Association reported to Aron that some advisors discouraged their students from participating in career diversity programs, while other students only attended because they felt pressure from the chair.

Seeking better understanding of student views of the Career Diversity Initiative, Aron held a series of illuminating discussions with graduate student representatives. From them, he learned that students accepted the numbers but believed that their only chance to beat the odds was to focus single-mindedly on pursuit of a tenure-track appointment. From this perspective, the skills and experiences that expanded career horizons were seen as a diversion that curtailed professorial possibilities. Aron also discovered an ironic outcome of the department's success in fundraising, which had allowed it to provide multiyear guaranteed support for all admitted students. In the past, UCLA students had scrambled to find adequate funding. That meant seeking out opportunities and gaining experiences at a range of entities on and off campus. Under the new system, however, students had less reason to be so enterprising. Indeed, their fellowships and teaching assistantships worked against entrepreneurship by prohibiting students from taking "outside" employment.

In spite of opposition and apathy, the Career Diversity Initiative at UCLA made headway during its three-year pilot phase. Key was the hiring of Karen Wilson, fresh off her stint as curator for the Autry's "Jews in the Los Angeles Mosaic" exhibition, as the department's Graduate Career Officer. (Like McPherson's position at UNM, Wilson's was funded by the Mellon Foundation grant.) Once in place, Wilson began advising students about preparing for a variety of careers and connecting them to history PhDs working in museums, media, government, and corporations. Wilson also developed a graduate seminar, "The Many Professions of History," which she cotaught with Aron in 2016 and again in 2017. "The Many Professions" course featured assigned readings and viewings that covered debates about the role of historians in contemporary society, emerging ways of presenting and teaching history, and past and future uses of history. Wilson and Aron also explicitly designed the course to put the key skills identified by the Career Diversity Initiative into practice through collaborative projects that the students undertook. Pre- and post-course student self-assessments showed that the course fulfilled its major aims. Seventy percent of the students rated two or more of their competencies in key skill areas higher at the end of the course than at the beginning. Half the students changed their stated career goals.[15]

The sample size, however, was small. Only eight students enrolled in the first iteration of the course and six in its second. Although these numbers eclipsed those in many graduate seminars, they attested to the limited reach of the Career Diversity Initiative at UCLA. And unlike the University of New Mexico, the UCLA History Department had introduced no "Mellonized" seminars to complement and augment "The Many Professions" course. For the majority of students and faculty in the History Department at UCLA, after three years of piloting, doctoral training remained a track to the tenure track, not a fan that opened to a range of career option.

The expiration of the first phase of the Mellon grant leaves pilot sites with the problem of how to sustain and extend the bridges that have been built. At the University of New Mexico, Melissa Bokovoy led a team of four humanities departments (History, American Studies, English, and Linguistics) along with UNM's Office of Graduate Studies in securing a National Endowment for the Humanities (NEH) "Next Generation PhD" planning grant. During the 2016–2017 academic year, each department sponsored an afternoon-long seminar to disseminate the lessons of the AHA-Mellon project across disciplines—in effect, to "Mellonize" the humanities at UNM. UNM intended to apply for a larger implementation grant, with a focus on developing a permanent career-service infrastructure for graduate students in humanities disciplines, but the NEH canceled the program. Meanwhile, Bokovoy and others at UNM and at Central New Mexico Community College (CNM) began to build a new bridge. They directed their efforts toward funding to create a pipeline between CNM and the university to support students interested in studying the humanities. They were successful in winning a grant from the Mellon Foundation and continue to pursue that endeavor.

At UCLA, the way forward took a fortuitous turn when the History Department received a $5,000,000 gift in 2017 that established and endowed the Luskin Center for History and Policy. With a mission to bring historical information and perspectives to bear on a range of policy questions and to prepare historians to play more active roles in the public sphere, the Center gives the career diversity initiative a new focus and new funds. These resources should encourage more graduate students to pursue training in applied history and to position themselves for employment in the policy realm.

As we look back on these years of work to bring our collective expertise as historians to varied dimensions of public life, we are proud of what we've achieved. Working together with colleagues both inside and outside the academy, we have developed a host of ideas and initiatives, put potentially important programs in place, established networks, finished projects, and begun the work of changing academic culture. But we have yet to establish firm foundations on which to build permanent bridges. We are keenly conscious of the need for more work, more allies, and more efforts to continue building a record of achievement. Coalitions of the willing are essential, but they are not sufficient. Universities and colleges, professional associations, and institutions like the Autry will need to seek deeper, fully institutionalized collaborations, sustained with continuous commitment of people, time, and resources.

This, however, is not just a time to look back. To date, our grade for this long-term group project, we admit, remains "incomplete." But there is every reason to persist, and no reason to let up now. There's a lot at stake, for our colleagues, our students, and for the universe of public discourse that reminds us every day how much history matters. We simply can't afford to fail, and, as every college student knows, an incomplete left to languish too long converts not to an A, but to an F.

To that end, we look forward to the next chapter of collaborations, with the Autry returning again to the center of our future web. In 2021, Aron will retire from UCLA and become President and CEO of the Autry Museum of the American West. Scharff, now retired from the University of New Mexico, has in recent years been drawn into a widening array of Autry projects and looks forward to continuing that work with renewed enthusiasm. In the face of a still-raging pandemic, political and economic strife and uncertainty, and warning signs for both universities and cultural institutions of all kinds, we remind ourselves that amid troubled waters, we must still seek to build bridges.

Notes

INTRODUCTION

1. "Western Lands, Western Voices: The American West Center at Fifty" took place September 19–21, 2014.
2. Leighton M. Quarles, Cassandra L. Clark, Floyd A. O'Neil, and Gregory E. Smoak, "The American West Center, University of Utah," *Journal of the West* 52 (Fall 2013):91–94.
3. Robert Kelley, "Public History: Its Origins, Nature, and Prospects," *The Public Historian* 1 (Fall 1978):16.
4. *History@Work* (blog), National Council on Public History, accessed December 29, 2020, https://ncph.org/history-at-work/.
5. Michael Frisch, *A Shared Authority: Essays on the Craft and Meaning of Oral and Public History* (Albany: SUNY Press, 1990), xii.
6. See the roundtable discussion, "Public History as Reflective Practice," *The Public Historian* 28 (Winter 2006):9–74.
7. David Glassberg, *Sense of History: The Place of the Past in American Life* (Amherst: University of Massachusetts Press, 2001).
8. Michael Bradshaw, *Regions and Regionalism in the United States* (Jackson: University of Mississippi Press, 1988), 3–11.
9. James Oliver Horton and Lois E. Horton, eds., *Slavery and Public History: The Tough Stuff of American Memory* (Chapel Hill: University of North Carolina Press, 2006).
10. For examples see Olivia Williams Black, "The 150-Year War: The Struggle to Create and Control Civil War Memory at Fort Sumter National Monument," *Public Historian* 38 (November 2016):149–66; Tiya Miles, *Tales from the Haunted South: Dark Tourism and Memories of Slavery from the Civil War Era* (Chapel Hill: University of North Carolina Press, 2015).
11. "Federal Land Ownership: Overview and Data," Congressional Research Service, updated February 21, 2020, https://crsreports.congress.gov.

CHAPTER 2

1. Sean Hannity, "Nevada Rancher Threatens 'Range War' against the Federal Government," *Hannity*, April 9, 2014.
2. Ibid.
3. Ken Cole, "Cliven Bundy Has No Claim to Federal Land and Grazing," *Wildlife News*, April 14, 2014; Michael Bastasch, "Environmentalists Pushed Bundy Ranch Standoff over Endangered Tortoises," *Daily Caller*, April 21, 2014; Paul Rauber, "John Muir on Cliven Bundy," *Sierra: The National Magazine of the Sierra Club*, May 6, 2014.
4. Leisl Carr Childers, *The Size of the Risk: Histories of Multiple Use in the Great Basin* (Norman: University of Oklahoma Press, 2015), 7, 64.
5. Kent Blansett, "The New Manifest Destiny: A Brief Political History of the Idle No More Movement," *BlogWest: Thoughtful Conversation about the American West*, BlogWest.org, October 28, 2013.
6. Leisl Carr Childers, "Understanding Cliven Bundy," *BlogWest: Thoughtful Conversation about the American West*, BlogWest.org, April 21, 2014.
7. Ibid.
8. Comments Section, Leisl Carr Childers, "Understanding Cliven Bundy," *BlogWest: Thoughtful Conversation about the American West*, BlogWest.org, April 21, 2014.
9. Ann Little, "Being Cliven Bundy," *Historiann*, April 26, 2014; Comments Section, Carr Childers, "Understanding Cliven Bundy," *BlogWest.*
10. Nancy Langston, "In Oregon, Myth Mixes with Anger," *New York Times*, January 6, 2016.
11. "Who Should Control the West?," *New York Times*, January 7, 2016.
12. Tah-Nehisi Coates, "What it Means to Be a Public Intellectual," *Atlantic*, January 8, 2014.
13. John Issett and Duncan Jackson, "What Does it Mean to Be a Public Intellectual?," Higher Education Academy, March 2013.
14. Adam Sowards, "Reckoning with History: Interior's Legacy of Bad Behavior," *High Country News*, January 3, 2018.
15. Issett and Jackson, "What Does It Mean to Be a Public Intellectual?," 5.
16. Leisl Carr Childers, "The Angry West: Understanding the Sagebrush Rebellion in Rural Nevada," in *Bridging the Distance: Common Issues of the Rural West*, edited by David B. Danbom (Salt Lake City: University of Utah Press, 2015), 213–38. The article produced was Tay Wiles and Brooke Warren, "Federal-lands Ranching: A Half-Century of Decline," *High Country News*, June 13, 2016.
17. The article produced was Leah Sottile, "A Year Ago, Armed Occupiers Seized a Wildlife Refuge in Harney County. This Oregonian Was Ready to Join," *Portland Monthly*, February 23, 2017.
18. Comments Section, Leisl Carr Childers, "Understanding Cliven Bundy," *BlogWest: Thoughtful Conversation about the American West*, BlogWest.org, April 21, 2014.

19. "American Patriot: Inside the Armed Uprising against the Federal Government," *Frontline*, PBS, May 16, 2017.
20. Leisl Carr Childers to Abby Ellis, email, December 22, 2016.
21. "American Patriot," *Frontline*. The version of my statement that appears in the episode is from the second interview, though the question was asked at both interviews.
22. Abby Ellis and Leisl Carr Childers, text message exchange, March 28, 2017.
23. "American Patriot," *Frontline*, May 16, 2017.
24. Abby Ellis to Leisl Carr Childers, email, May 6, 2017; Leisl Carr Childers to Abby Ellis, May 6, 2017. This email exchange was under the heading "Cliven's fees."
25. Abby Ellis to Leisl Carr Childers, email, May 6, 2017; Leisl Carr Childers to Abby Ellis, email, May 6, 2017. This email exchange was under the heading "Fact check Q."
26. "American Patriot," *Frontline*, PBS, May 16, 2017.
27. Abby Ellis, Twitter, December 26, 2017.
28. Stephen Ross, Response to Post "In 'American Patriot,' FRONTLINE investigates how the Bundy family's fight against the government has invigorated armed militias across America. Starts May 16 on PBS," *Frontline* Facebook feed, May 14, 2017.
29. Robert Kelley, "Public History: Its Origins, Nature, and Prospects," *The Public Historian* 1, no. 1 (October 1978):16.
30. Barbara J. Howe and Emory L. Kemp, eds., *Public History: An Introduction* (Malabar, FL: Krieger Publishing, 1988), 2.
31. Thomas Cauvin, *Public History: A Textbook of Practice* (New York: Routledge, 2016), 13.
32. Joe Rassenfos to Patricia Limerick, Sarah S. Elkind, Peter S. Onuf, and Leisl Carr Childers, email, November 15, 2017.
33. "WGA, Leading Western Policy Organizations Share 'Principles to Clarify and Strengthen the State-Federal Relationship,'" Western Governors' Association website.
34. Western Governors' Association, "Policy Resolution 2017-01: Building a Stronger State-Federal Relationship," Western Governors' Association website.
35. Ibid.
36. Patricia Limerick to Peter S. Onuf, Leisl Carr Childers, and Sarah S. Elkind, email, November 20, 2017.
37. Western Governors' Association, "Policy Resolution 2017-01: Building a Stronger State-Federal Relationship," quoted in Patricia Limerick to Peter S. Onuf, Leisl Carr Childers, and Sarah S. Elkind, email, November 20, 2017.
38. Benjamin F. Shambaugh, "Applied History," in *Proceedings of the Mississippi Valley Historical Association for the Year 1908–1909*, edited by Benjamin F. Shambaugh (Cedar Rapids, IA: Torch Press, 1910), 2:137.

39. Rebecca Conard, *Benjamin Shambaugh and the Intellectual Foundations of Public History* (Iowa City: University of Iowa Press, 2002), 4.
40. Benjamin F. Shambaugh, "Editor's Introduction," *Applied History* (Iowa City: State Historical Society of Iowa, 1912), vol. 1:viii.
41. Shambaugh, "Applied History," 139; Conard, *Benjamin Shambaugh*, 33–34.
42. "First National Symposium on Public History: A Report," *The Public Historian* 2, no. 1 (October 1979):9–10.
43. Cauvin, *Public History*, 13–14.
44. Patty Limerick, "Why Denver?—A Habitat for Historians," *Perspectives on History*, September 2016.
45. Ian Frazier, "A Historian of the American West Shares Her Insights," *New Yorker*, May 8, 2017.
46. Western Governors' Association, "WGA Winter Meeting Day 2: Autonomous vehicles, keynotes by Secretary Chao and NFL's Bidwill, evolving state-federal relationship dominate," https://westgov.org/news/article/winter-meeting-autonomous-vehicles-secretary-chao-michael-bidwill.
47. Western Governors' Association, "WGA Winter Meeting Day 2."
48. Jean-Pierre Morin, "Historical Thinking and the Place of History in Public Policy Development," *History@Work: The NCPH Blog*, February 24, 2017.
49. Richard White, "Are Public History and Public Intellectuals in Danger of Becoming Oxymorons," *OAH Newsletter*, November 2006, 3.
50. Jack Holl, "Cultures in Conflict: An Argument against 'Common Ground' between Practicing Professional Historians and Academics," *The Public Historian* 30, no. 2 (May 2008):47.
51. Ibid., 48–49.
52. Ibid., 47–48.
53. Ibid., 49.
54. Richard White, Keynote Address, "Western Lands, Western Voices: The American West Center at Fifty," September 19, 2014, Salt Lake City, Utah, YouTube, https://www.youtube.com/watch?v=90KnXv1mOQw.
55. Terence O'Donnell, "Pitfalls along the Path of Public History," *The Public Historian* 4, no. 1 (January 1982):65–72; Thomas Cauvin, *Public History: A Textbook of Practice* (New York: Routledge, 2016), 251. Many historians have written similar criticisms, but I find O'Donnell's to be particularly scathing.
56. Hal K. Rothman, "Hal Rothman Has a Message for Outgoing Interior Secretary Gale Norton: Keep Your Mitts Out of Our Kitty," *Las Vegas Sun*, April 2, 2006.
57. Gregory E. Smoak, "Joint Working Group on Evaluating Public History Scholarship," *Perspectives on History*, September 2008.

CHAPTER 3

1. Hal Rothman, "Do We Really Need the Rural West?," *High Country News*, April 24, 2000.

2. Char Miller and Marc Cioc, "Interview: Hal Rothman," *Environmental History* 12, no. 1 (January 2007):145.
3. Hal Rothman, "The New Old West," *Denver Post*, October 5, 2006.
4. Mette Flynt, "Devil's Bargains in a New Century: The Legacy of Hal Rothman," *BlogWest.org*, https://blogwest.org/2017/03/29/devils-bargains-in-a-new-century-the-legacy-of-hal-rothman/.
5. "Hal Rothman (1957–2007)," *Las Vegas Sun*, February 27, 2007.
6. C. L. Higham et. al., "Western Provocateur: Living with Hal Rothman—A Roundtable Discussion," (roundtable, 48th Annual Western History Association Conference, Salt Lake City, Utah, October 24, 2008); Miller and Cioc "Interview."
7. Hal Rothman, *Navajo National Monument: A Place and Its People: An Administrative History* (Santa Fe, NM: Southwest Regional Office, Division of History, 1991); Rothman, *Managing the Sacred and the Secular: An Administrative History of Pipestone National Monument*, coauthor Daniel J. Holder (Henderson, NV: Hal K. Rothman and Associates, 1992); Daniel J. Holder and Hal K. Rothman, *The Post on the Marmaton: An Historical Resource Study of Fort Scott National Historic Site* (Omaha, NE: U.S. Dept. of the Interior, National Park Service, Midwest Regional Office, 2001); Rothman, *The Park That Makes Its Own Weather: An Administrative History of Golden Gate National Recreation Area* (San Francisco: Golden Gate National Recreation Area, 2002); Rothman, *To Ride Alone in a Forever Unpossessed Country: An Administrative History of Death Valley National Park* (Death Valley, CA: National Park Service, 2005).
8. Hal Rothman, *Preserving Different Pasts: The American National Monuments* (Urbana, IL: University of Illinois Press, 1989).
9. Don Hibbard, "Review of *Preserving Different Pasts: The American National Monuments*," *Winterthur Portfolio* 25, no. 1 (Spring 1990):96; Michael Schene, "Review of *Preserving Different Pasts: The American National Monuments*," *The Public Historian* 12, no. 1 (Winter 1990):90.
10. Hal Rothman, "'A Regular Ding-Dong Fight': Agency Culture and Evolution in the NPS-USFS Dispute, 1916–1937." *Western Historical Quarterly* 20, no. 2 (May 1989):141–161.
11. Hal Rothman, *On Rims and Ridges: The Los Alamos Area since 1880* (Lincoln: University of Nebraska Press, 1992), 2.
12. Miller and Cioc, "Interview," 141.
13. John Opie, interview by Lisa Mighetto, March 13, 2008, http://aseh.net/about-aseh/copy_of_oral-histories-with-aseh-founders/John%20Opie.pdf.
14. Hal Rothman, "A Decade in the Saddle: Confessions of a Recalcitrant Editor," *Environmental History* 7, no. 1 (January 2002):9.
15. Interview with Char Miller by author, March 17, 2017; Char Miller, "The Greening of Gifford Pinchot," *Environmental History Review* 16, no. 3 (Autumn 1992):1–20.

16. Interview with Robert Gottlieb by author, March 15, 2017.
17. Interview with Dan Flores by author, March 19, 2017.
18. Miller, "The Greening of Gifford Pinchot"; Dan Flores, "Place: An Argument for Bioregional History," *Environmental History Review* 18, no. 4 (Winter 1994):1–18.
19. Interview with Steven Anderson by author, February 20, 2017.
20. William Cronon, "The Trouble with Wilderness: Or, Getting Back to the Wrong Nature," *Environmental History* 1, no. 1 (January 1996):7–28; Samuel Hays, "Comment: The Trouble with Wilderness," *Environmental History* 1, no. 1 (January 1996):29–32; Michael Cohen, "Comment: Resistance to Wilderness," *Environmental History* 1, no. 1 (January 1996):33–42; Thomas Dunlap, "Comment: But What Did You Go Out into the Wilderness to See?" *Environmental History* 1, no. 1 (January 1996):43–46.
21. Alan Taylor, "Unnatural Inequalities: Social and Environmental Histories," *Environmental History* 1, no. 4 (October 1996):16.
22. Rothman, "A Decade in the Saddle," 12.
23. Ibid., 9.
24. Ibid., 20.
25. Elliot West, "A Longer, Grimmer, but More Interesting Story," in *Trails: Toward a New Western History*, eds. Patricia Nelson Limerick, Clyde Milner, and Charles E. Rankin (Lawrence: University Press of Kansas, 1991), 103–111.
26. Patricia Nelson Limerick, *Legacy of Conquest: The Unbroken Past of the American West* (New York: Norton, 1987); Richard White, *"It's Your Misfortune and None of My Own": A New History of the American West* (Norman: University of Oklahoma Press, 1991); Frederick Jackson Turner and John Mack Faragher, "The Significance of the Frontier in American History: (1893)" in *Rereading Frederick Jackson Turner: "The Significance of the Frontier in American History" and Other Essays* (New Haven: Yale University Press, 1994), 21–60.
27. John Mack Faragher and Clyde Milner, "The Frontier Trail: Rethinking Turner and Reimagining the American West," *American Historical Review* 98, no. 1 (February 1993):106–17.
28. Gerald D. Nash, "Point of View: One Hundred Years of Western History," *Journal of the West* 32 (January 1993):3–4; William Savage Jr., "The New Western History: Youngest Whore on the Block," *AB Bookman's Weekly* 4 (October 1993):1244.
29. Larry McMurtry, "How the West Was Won or Lost," *New Republic*, October 22, 1990, 22–28.
30. Jordan Bonfante, "Boom Time in the Rockies," *Time*, September 6, 1998, 20–27; William Travis, *New Geographies of the American West: Land Use and the Changing Patterns of Place* (Washington, D.C.: Island Press, 2007), 25.

31. Patricia Limerick, interview by David Burns, *KNPR's State of Nevada*, April 16, 2007, https://knpr.org/knpr/2007-04/remembering-hal-rothman-ii.
32. William Kittredge, ed., *The Last Best Place: A Montana Anthology* (Seattle: University of Washington Press, 2000).
33. Mike Davis, "House of Cards," *Sierra Magazine*, November–December 1995, 41.
34. Claire Noland, *Los Angeles Times*, March 1, 2007.
35. Eugene Moehring, *Resort City in the Sunbelt: Las Vegas, 1930–2000*, 2nd ed. (Reno: University of Nevada Press, 2016), 268.
36. Ed Marston, "Unlikely Reformer: Can Sinful Las Vegas Help Change the West?" *High Country News*, April 3, 1995.
37. Eugene Moehring, *The University of Nevada, Las Vegas: A History* (Reno: University of Nevada Press, 2007), 124–142.
38. Hal Rothman, *Devil's Bargains: Tourism in the Twentieth-Century American West* (Lawrence: University Press of Kansas, 1998), 10–11.
39. Earl Pomeroy, *In Search of the Golden West: The Tourist in Western America* (New York: Knopf, 1957). On framing the national experience, see John Sears, *Sacred Places: American Tourist Attractions in the Nineteenth Century* (New York: Oxford University Press, 1989); Cindy Aron, *Working at Play: A History of Vacations in the United States* (New York: Oxford University Press, 2001); Marguerite Shaffer, *See America First: Tourism and National Identity, 1880–1940* (Washington, D.C.: Smithsonian Institution, 2001); David Wrobel and Patrick Long, eds., *Seeing and Being Seen: Tourism in the American West* (Lawrence: University Press of Kansas, 2001); Annie Gilbert-Coleman, *Ski Style: Sport and Culture in the Rockies* (Lawrence: University Press of Kansas, 2004); Connie Chiang, *Shaping the Shoreline: Fisheries and Tourism on the Monterey Coast* (Seattle: University of Washington Press, 2011); Lawrence Culver, *The Frontier of Leisure: Southern California and the Shaping of Modern America* (New York: Oxford University Press, 2012); and William Philpott, *Vacationland: Tourism and the Environment in the Colorado High Country* (Seattle: University of Washington Press, 2014).
40. Henry Williamson, "With the Devil's Bargain of Tourism, Winners are Few," *Winter Park Manifest*, September 22, 1999, 6.
41. Paul Sutter, "Sutter on Rothman's Devil's Bargains: Tourism in the Twentieth-Century West," *H-Environment*, https://networks.h-net.org/node/19397/reviews/20392/sutter-rothman-devils-bargains-tourism-twentieth-century-american-west.
42. Rothman, *The New Urban Park: Golden Gate National Recreation Area and Civic Environmentalism* (Lawrence: University Press of Kansas, 2004), 201.
43. Rothman, *Devil's Bargains*, 7.
44. Hal Rothman, "Colony, Capital, and Casino: Money in the Real Las Vegas," in *Grit Beneath the Glitter: Tales from the Real Las Vegas,* eds. Hal

Rothman and Mike Davis (Berkeley: University of California Press, 2002), 308.

45. Hal Rothman, *Neon Metropolis: How Las Vegas Started the Twenty-First Century* (New York: Routledge, 2003), 89.
46. "Vegas Finds a Sure Thing," interview by Jonathan Mann, CNN, May 12, 2002.
47. William deBuys, foreword to *Playing the Odds: Las Vegas and the Modern West*," by Hal Rothman, ed. Lincoln Bramwell (Albuquerque: University of New Mexico Press, 2007), xiv.
48. Miller and Cioc, "Interview," 145.
49. Rothman, *Devil's Bargains*, 423.
50. William Philpott, interview with the author, April 6, 2017.
51. David Sproul, interview with the author, March 26, 2017.
52. Hal Rothman, "Colloquium in American History: The 20th-Century American West and the World," University of Nevada, Las Vegas (2005).
53. "'I'm Not Brave': History Professor Hal Rothman on his Career his ALS Diagnosis and His Future," *UNLV Magazine* (Summer 2006):32.
54. Char Miller, ed., *Between Ruin and Restoration: An Environmental History of Israel* (Pittsburgh: University of Pittsburgh Press, 2013).
55. "'I'm Not Brave,'" 30.
56. 153 Cong. Rec. S2593 (daily ed. March 5, 2007) (statement of Senator Harry Reid).
57. Miller and Cioc, "Interview," 145.

CHAPTER 4

1. Robert Manning, Rolf Diamant, Nora Mitchell, and David Harmon, eds., *A Thinking Person's Guide to America's National Parks* (New York: George Braziller, 2016), 11.
2. This essay takes the West to be a geographic portion of the United States, as conceptualized by Patricia Limerick and Richard White, comprising eleven states, and follows Joseph E. Taylor et al. and the Stanford Spatial History Project in the same. The Park Service is a significant landholder in its own right. NPS administers more than a million acres in each of eight different Western states and over 51 million in Alaska. East of the Rockies, only Florida, with just over two million acres, compares to these eight Western states in terms of NPS landownership. For a breakdown of federal agency land by state, see http://www.propertyrightsresearch.org/2004/articles6/state_by_state_government_land_o.htm.
3. For a quick illustration of the point, note the cover of Lary M. Dilsaver's excellent and freshly reissued compendium, *America's National Park Service: The Critical Documents* (Lanham, MD: Rowman and Littlefield, 2016). The cover of this truly pan-NPS volume ignores the East entirely and features a group of photos displaying Devil's Tower National Monument in

Wyoming, California's Joshua Tree National Park, and Olympic National Park in Washington—all classic examples of Western land preservation and monumental scenery designation. Why not also use a picture of the equally photogenic Fort McHenry National Monument and Historic Shrine in Maryland or Lowell National Historic Park in Massachusetts?

4. E. Richard Hart, *Parks in the West and American Culture* (Sun Valley, ID: Institute of the American West, 1984), 3.
5. David Harmon, "Sense of Place," in *A Thinking Person's Guide*, eds. Manning et al., 21–30, 21.
6. See, for example, Mark David Spence, *Dispossessing the Wilderness: Indian Removal and the Making of the National Parks*, rev. ed. (New York: Oxford University Press, 1999); Robert Keller, *American Indians and National Parks* (Tucson: University of Arizona Press, 1999); and Daniel E. Coslett and Manish Chalana, "National Parks for New Audiences: Diversifying Interpretation for Enhanced Contemporary Relevance," *The Public Historian* 38, no. 4 (November 2016):101–128.
7. Ari Kelman, review of *Imperiled Promise: The State of History in the National Park Service*, by Anne Mitchell Whisnant, Marla R. Miller, Gary B. Nash, and David Thelen (Bloomington, IN: Organization of American Historians, 2011), *Journal of American History* 100, no. 3 (December 2013):767–770.
8. National Park Service Organic Act, 16 U.S.C. 1., 1916.
9. Since the 1920s, the Park Service has been tied to academic institutions, particularly the University of California, Berkeley, which veritably dominated NPS scientific thinking for decades through such powerhouses as Joseph Grinnell and George Melendez Wright. For a comprehensive look at the Berkeley connection, see Richard West Sellars, *Preserving Nature in the National Parks: A History* (New Haven: Yale University Press, 1997; 2009).
10. Interview with Robert M. Utley, October 5, 2012, Everett L. Cooley Oral History Project, Accn 814, Box 70, Folder 4, Interview 677, Special Collections and Archives, University of Utah, J. Willard Marriott Library, Salt Lake City, Utah.
11. Whisnant et al., *Imperiled Promise*, 20.
12. An Act to set apart a certain Tract of Land lying near the Head-waters of the Yellowstone River as a public Park, U.S. Statutes at Large, vol. 17 (1871–1872), ch. 24, pp. 32–33, Cong. Globe, 42 Cong. 2nd Sess., 1 (January 30, 1872) [S. 392].
13. Distinguished national park historians Alfred Runte and Richard West Sellars have argued from completely opposite sides of this spectrum. Runte asserted in the 1970s that only "worthless lands" had received or would keep national park status. Sellars retorted that not only was Runte's definition of national parks ridiculously narrow, but his thesis was essentially groundless and overlooked the tremendous power of the tourist economy in particular. For a summation of the two viewpoints, see "The National

Parks: A Forum on the 'Worthless Lands' Thesis," *Journal of Forest History* 27, no. 3 (July 1983).

14. Dwight Pitcaithley, "Being Born Western and the Challenges of Public History, in *Preserving Western History*, edited by Andrew Gulliford (Albuquerque: University of New Mexico Press, 2005), 389–395, 392.
15. Ibid., 392–393.
16. William E. Brown, "Western Parks and American Character," in *Parks in the West and American Culture* (Sun Valley, ID: Institute of the American West, 1984), 13.
17. A. S. Leopold, S. A. Cain, C. M. Cottam, I. N. Gabrielson, and T. L. Kimball, *Wildlife Management in the National Parks* (Washington, D.C., U.S. Department of the Interior, National Park Service: Government Printing Office, March 4, 1963), http://npshistory.com/publications/leopold_report.pdf.
18. "'Skinheads' Group Moves in Near Zion Park." *Deseret News*, October 1, 1992.
19. The full quote: "Everybody needs beauty as well as bread, places to play in and pray in, where nature may heal and give strength to body and soul alike," John Muir, *The Yosemite* (New York: Century, 1912), 56.
20. Spence, *Dispossessing the Wilderness*.
21. Zion National Monument, Utah. By the President of the United States of America. A Proclamation. No. 1435—Mar. 18, 1918—40 Stat. 1760.
22. Dena S. Markoff, *An Administrative History: Decision-Making That Shaped Zion National Park, 1909 to 1981* (Springdale, UT, and Arvada, CO: Zion Natural History Association and Western Heritage Conservation, July 1982), 6.
23. Jack Burns, interview with Leighton Quarles, August 18, 2017.
24. David Graber, "Maintaining Biodiversity," in *A Thinking Person's Guide to America's National Parks*, eds. Manning et al., 68–79, 79.
25. Morgan Sherwood, "The End of American Wilderness," *Environmental Review* 9 (1985):197–209.
26. National Park Service, "Bryce Point," https://www.nps.gov/brca/planyourvisit/brycepoint.htm. Bryce's laconic dismissal of his eponymous canyon's beauties has become such a catchphrase that TripAdvisor and National Geographic both quote it.
27. George A. Hicks, 1864, quoted in Andrew Karl Larson, *The Red Hills of November: A Pioneer Biography of Utah's Cotton Town* (Salt Lake City: Deseret News Press, 1957).
28. Wallace Stegner, *Mormon Country* (New York: Duell, Sloan and Pearce, 1942; repr., Lincoln: University of Nebraska Press, 1970), 45.
29. Quoted by Eileen Smith-Cavros, "Zion Pioneers and Spirituality in the Land of Zion," in *A Zion Canyon Reader*, edited by Nathan Waite and Reid Neilson (Salt Lake City: University of Utah Press, 2014), 237–244, 239.

30. Admittedly, Snow's clinical statement was a far cry from the awestruck rhapsodizing of Clarence Dutton or Grove Karl Gilbert. Dixie State University Special Collections, Leo Alva Snow Papers, 1870–1962, MC 03, Box 3(of 6), Folder 14 (MC03 Series III-A-Contract #304 Survey Field Notes, 1908 June 8–1911 August 4).
31. "Redford Burned in Effigy for Opposing Power Plant," *New York Times*, April 19, 1976.
32. *National Park Service Administrative History: A Guide*, U.S. Department of the Interior, National Park Service, 2004, 7.
33. Whisnant et al., *Imperiled Promise*, 57.
34. Ibid., 55.
35. Julissa Treviño, "These Were America's Most-Visited National Parks in 2017," *Smithsonian Magazine*, March 2, 2018, https://www.smithsonianmag.com/smart-news/these-were-americas-most-popular-national-parks-2017-180968320/.
36. National Park Service, Park History Program, Park Histories, https://www.nps.gov/parkhistory/parkhistories.htm.
37. Whisnant et al., *Imperiled Promise*, 67.
38. "How's The Park Service Administration Doing?," *Yosemite News*, May 1, 2001, http://www.yosemitenews.com/administration.html; Markoff, "An Administrative History."
39. National Park Service, State of the Park Report for Zion National Park, Cultural Resources, June 19, 2017, https://www.nps.gov/stateoftheparks/zion/culturalresources/culturalresources.cfm.
40. Robert C. Heyder, interview with Leighton Quarles, February 10 2017, 8, Everett L. Cooley Oral History Collection, Marriott Library, University of Utah, Salt Lake City.
41. U.S. Department of the Interior, Budget Justifications and Performance Information, Fiscal Year 2018, https://www.nps.gov/aboutus/upload/FY-2018-NPS-Greenbook.pdf.
42. Hal Bernton, "Jury Acquits Leaders of Malheur Wildlife-Refuge Standoff," *Seattle Times*, October 27, 2016, https://www.seattletimes.com/seattle-news/crime/verdict-near-in-malheur-wildlife-refuge-standoff-trial/.
43. Kirk Siegler, "Utah Sheriffs Threaten to Arrest Rangers If They Try to Close Public Lands," NPR, May 31, 2016, http://www.npr.org/2016/05/31/480100279/utah-sheriff-threatens-to-arrest-rangers-if-they-try-to-close-public-lands.
44. John Maounis, in *A Thinking Person's Guide*, eds. Manning, et al., 177.

CHAPTER 5

1. For Lake City history, see Carolyn Wright and Clarence Wright, *Tiny Hinsdale of the Silvery San Juan* (Lake City: Western Reflections, 2012); and

P. David Smith, *The Story of Lake City, Colorado and Its Surrounding Areas* (Lake City: Western Reflections, 2016).

2. For histories of summer tourism in Colorado, see William Philpott, *Vacationland: Tourism and Environment in the Colorado High Country* (Seattle: University of Washington Press, 2013); Melanie Shellenbarger, *High Country Summers: The Early Second Homes of Colorado, 1880–1940* (Tucson: University of Arizona Press, 2012); and Peter Blodgett, "Welcome to Wonderland: Promoting Tourism in the Rocky Mountain West, 1920–1960" (PhD diss., Yale University, 2007).
3. For general histories of tourism in the American West, see Hal Rothman, *Devil's Bargains: Tourism in the Twentieth-Century American West* (Lawrence: University Press of Kansas, 1998); and David Wrobel and Patrick Long, eds., *Seeing and Being Seen: Tourism in the American West* (Lawrence: University Press of Kansas, 2001).
4. For literature on an evolving sense of place, see Yi-Fu Tuan, *Topophilia: A Study of Environmental Perception, Attitudes, and Values* (New York: Columbia University Press, 1990); Joseph Amato, *Rethinking Home: A Case for Writing Local History* (Berkeley: University of California Press, 2002); and David Glassberg, *Sense of History: The Place of the Past in American Life* (Amherst: University of Massachusetts Press, 2001).
5. For analysis of the relationships between local history, public history, and tourism, see Martha Norkunas, *The Politics of Public Memory: Tourism, History, and Ethnicity in Monterey, California* (Albany: State University of New York Press, 1993); David Lowenthal, *The Past Is a Foreign Country—Revisited* (Cambridge: Cambridge University Press, 2016); Mike Wallace, *Mickey Mouse History: The Politics of Public Memory* (Philadelphia: Temple University Press, 1996); Patricia Mooney-Melvin, "Harnessing the Romance of the Past: Preservation, Tourism, and History," *The Public Historian* 13, no. 2 (Spring 1991):35–48; Wilton Corkern, "Heritage Tourism: Where Public and History Don't Always Meet," *American Studies International* 42, no. 2/3 (June–October 2004): 7–16; Nikolas Glover, "Co-produced Histories: Mapping the Uses and Narratives of History in the Tourist Age," *The Public Historian* 30, no. 1 (February 2008):105–124; and David Kyvig, *Nearby History: Exploring the Past Around You* (Lanham, MD: Roman and Littlefield, 2010).
6. Carol Kammen, *On Doing Local History* (Lanham, MD: Rowman and Littlefield, 2014), 153–156.
7. Grant Houston, interview by Mette Flynt, July 9, 2017, Lake City, CO; "Historical Museum to Open July 4th," *Silver World*, June 30, 1978, 11.
8. Houston, interview.
9. *Hinsdale County Historical Society Newsletter*, Summer 1998, Hinsdale County Historical Society, Lake City, CO.
10. Chay Rees Runnels, email to author, July 12, 2017.

11. Steve Priest, interview by Mette Flynt, June 29, 2017, Lake City, CO; Houston, interview.
12. Adolph Assenheimer, interview by Mette Flynt, June 27, 2017, Lake City, Colorado. I define "seasonal residents" as individuals who are tourists but who have more permanent ties to the community, whether as seasonal workers, volunteers, or residents.
13. Ibid.; "Caboose Restoration, Helen's Garden Celebrated at Museum Dedication Saturday," *Silver World*, August 4, 2006, 1, 7–8, 13; "August's Lake City History Month Offers a Variety of Special Events," *Silver World*, July 31, 2009, 3.
14. Gregory E. Smoak, "Beyond the Academy: Making the New Western History Matter in Local Communities," *The Public Historian* 31 (November 2009):86–89.
15. Kammen, *On Doing Local History*, 123–124.
16. Jodi Linsey, "Museum's 'Scarlet Belles' Drama Gives Glimpse of Town's Bluff Street Women," *Silver World*, August 1, 2014, 5.
17. Houston, interview.
18. Carol Perry to Linda Iiams, March 9, 2004, Hinsdale County Historical Society; Leslie Vogel to Grant Houston, August 29, 2003, Hinsdale County Historical Society; "Historical Society on Prowl for Pioneer Food Recipes," *Silver World*, January 8, 2004, 1, 7.
19. "Cookbook Publication Progressing," *Hinsdale County Historical Society Newsletter*, Summer 2004; "Memorable Cooks Recipe Tasting," Hinsdale County Historical Society, Lake City, CO; Kammen, *On Doing Local History*, 56–57.
20. "History-Inspired Garden Planned at Museum," *Silver World*, September 2, 2005, 5.
21. "Step into History . . ." Hinsdale County Historical Society, Lake City, CO.
22. "August's Lake City History," 3.
23. "Historical Society Ghost Tour Sat. Eve., July 1," *Silver World*, June 30, 1995, 1.
24. Tiya Miles, *Tales from the Haunted South: Dark Tourism and Memories of Slavery from the Civil War Era* (Chapel Hill: University of North Carolina Press, 2015), 11, 98, 112–114, 117.
25. Ibid.; Alena Pirok, "Goodwin's Ghosts: Colonial Williamsburg's Uncanny Legacy," *The Public Historian* 41, no. 3 (August 2019):9–30.
26. HCHS, "Volunteers Key to Society Projects," n.d.
27. Priest, interview.
28. Houston, interview.
29. "Register May Become a Reality," *Lake City Pioneer*, April 28, 1977, 1.
30. "Historic Planning Committee Report," *Lake City Pioneer*, July 7, 1977, 4.
31. Angela Hollingsworth, interview by Mette Flynt, 1 July 2017, Lake City; Ken Charles, "'Problem Identification' Explained in Long Range Planning," *Silver World*, January 1, 1984, 2.

32. Houston, interview.
33. Lowenthal, *The Past Is a Foreign Country—Revisited*, 438.
34. Ibid.
35. Frances Kranichfeld Myers, letter to the editor, *Silver World*, June 20, 1986, 3; Hazel Whitton, letter to the editor, *Silver World*, August 1, 1986, 2; Alicia Bailey, "School Board Hears Pros, Cons on Retaining School," *Silver World*, July 4, 1986, 14–15.
36. Grant Houston, "Sentimental Hogwash," *Silver World*, July 18, 1986, 2; Alicia Bailey, "School Board Hears Pros, Cons."
37. Houston, interview.
38. Downtown Improvement and Revitalization Team, *Annual Report*, 2014, on file, DIRT office; Hollingsworth, interview.
39. Ibid.; Kristie Borchers, interview by Mette Flynt, July 10, 2017, Lake City, CO; Downtown Improvement and Revitalization Team, *Annual Report*, 2012, on file, DIRT office.
40. Downtown Improvement and Revitalization Team, *Marketing Plan*, 2008, on file, DIRT office; Borchers, interview.
41. Hollingsworth, interview; Downtown Improvement and Revitalization Team, *Annual Report*, 2009, on file, DIRT office.
42. "CLG Money Funds Plaques, Brochures Featuring Lake City Historic District," *Silver World*, July 2, 2010, 12–13.
43. "DIRT Receives $20,000 Grant to Market Historic Lake City," *Silver World*, January 23, 2009, 3.
44. "Town Receives State CPI Honor Award for Historic Preservation Efforts," *Silver World*, June 22, 2012, 3; National Park Service, "National Register of Historic Places Registration Form: Lake City Historic District," by Cathleen Norman, 2005, 1–6.
45. "Outbuilding Preservation Focus of Town's Grant Application," *Silver World*, July 20, 2007, 1, 4; "Lake City Outbuildings Most Endangered Historic Structures List," *Silver World*, February 5, 2010, 1, 6.
46. "Lake City Outbuildings," 1, 6.
47. Ibid.
48. Houston, interview; Bureau of Land Management, *Alpine Triangle Final Recreation Area Management Plan*, 2006, 3.
49. "Historical Society, BLM Restore Snowden Cabin," *Silver World*, September 23, 1988, 1, 8; "Optimism High at Historical Society's Nov. 1 Meeting," *Silver World*, November 18, 1988, 8–9; Roger Alexander, "Volunteers Protect Historic Structures," *Bureau of Land Management Continental Crossroads* (October 1992), 6.
50. Bureau of Land Management, *Alpine Triangle*, 1–4.
51. Ibid., 14–15.
52. "Snowslide Demolishes Henson Creek Landmark," *Silver World*, May 16, 2008, 1, 10; "Hinsdale Museum Opens with New Displays Featuring

Empire Chief, Assaying, Immigrants," *Silver World*, June 20, 2008, 9, 13; "Old Timbers, New Uses," *Silver World*, August 19, 2011, 8.

53. Grant Houston, "Empire Chief Highlights Ongoing Preservation Challenges," *Silver World*, May 16, 2008, 2.
54. Jim Lovelace, interview by Mette Flynt, 11 July 2017, Lake City, CO.
55. Ibid.
56. "New Life at Old Golconda," *Silver World*, September 5, 2014, 7–9.
57. Jim Lovelace and Sally Thode, "Junior Explorer: Alpine Loop," Bureau of Land Management.
58. "Preservation Efforts Focus on Courthouse, Ute-Ulay Mine," *Silver World*, October 23, 2009, 1, 6; "County Designates Ute-Ulay as Resident Historic Site, *Silver World*, August 27, 2010, 1, 14; Hollingsworth, interview; Borchers, interview; "Commissioners Hear Upbeat Assessment of Environmental Study on Portion of Ute-Ulay Mine," *Silver World*, October 7, 2011, 1, 5–6.
59. Corkern, "Heritage Tourism," 15.
60. "County Designates Ute-Ulay as Resident Historic Site," *Silver World*, August 27, 2010, 1, 14.
61. Lovelace, interview.
62. Priest, interview.
63. "Mitigation, Stabilization Breathe New Life at Ute-Ulay," *Silver World*, November 9, 2012, 7; "Ute Ulay Mine and Mill EPA and BLM Removal Action," June 2013, *Environmental Protection Agency Region 8 Newsletter*, on file, DIRT office.
64. "Report to Hinsdale County Commissioners," October 2011, Hardrock Revision, on file, DIRT office.
65. Lowenthal, *The Past Is a Foreign Country—Revisited*, 482.
66. Nikolas Glover, "Co-produced Histories," 117–118.
67. RPI Consulting, *Hinsdale County, Colorado Business Plan Development for Ute Ulay Town/Mill Site*, February 2017, on file, DIRT office.
68. Bureau of Land Management and Hinsdale County, "Ute-Ulay Upper Town Site Self-Guided Walking Tour," 2017.
69. Borchers, interview; Hollingsworth, interview; Priest, interview.

CHAPTER 6

1. Levi Romero, "Following the Manito Trail: A Tale of Two Querencias," in *Querencia: Reflections on the New Mexico Homeland*, edited by Vanessa Fonseca-Chávez, Levi Romero, and Spencer R. Herrera (Albuquerque: University of New Mexico Press, 2020), 308–324.
2. Ibid.
3. https://www.manitotrail.com
4. Francisco E. Balderrama and Raymond Rodríguez, *Decade of Betrayal: Mexican Repatriation in the 1930s* (Albuquerque: University of New Mexico Press, 1995), 6.

5. William Hewitt, "Mexican Workers in Wyoming During World War II: Necessity Discrimination and Protest," *Annals of Wyoming* 54, no. 2 (1982):20–33, 21.
6. Ibid.
7. Zaragoza Vargas, *Crucible of Struggle: A History of Mexican Americans from the Colonial Period to the Present Era* (New York: Oxford University Press, 2011), 206.
8. Anselmo Arellano, *Los pobladores nuevomexicanos y su poesía, 1889–1950*. (Albuquerque: Pajarito Publications, 1976).
9. Sarah Bronwen Horton, "The Santa Fe Fiesta, Reinvented: Sacralizing Ties to a Disappearing Homeland," PhD diss., University of New Mexico, 2003, p. 236.
10. Sarah Deutsch, *No Separate Refuge: Culture, Class, and Gender on an Anglo-Hispanic Frontier in the American Southwest, 1880–1940* (New York: Oxford University Press, 1987), 10.
11. Juan Estevan Arellano, "La Cuenca y la Querencia," in *Thinking Like a Watershed: Voices from the West*, edited by Jack Loeffler and Celestia Loeffler. 120–150 (Albuquerque: University of New Mexico Press, 2012), 158.
12. Sylvia Rodríguez, "History, Memory, and Querencia." In *The Oxford Handbook of Southwest Archaeology*, edited by Barbara J. Mills and Severin Fowles, 193–205 (New York: Oxford University Press, 2017), 199.
13. Safran, William, "Diasporas in Modern Societies: Myths of Homeland and Return," *Diaspora: A Journal of Transnational Studies* 1, no. 1 (1991):83–99, 89.
14. *Following the Manito Trail*, interview with Avelinda Arguello Paskett by Vanessa Fonseca-Chávez and Levi Romero, 2015, Riverton, Wyoming.
15. Ibid.
16. Ibid.
17. Ibid.
18. *Following the Manito Trail*, interview with Ida La Febre by Vanessa Fonseca-Chávez and Adam Herrera, 2015, Laramie, Wyoming.
19. *Following the Manito Trail*, interview with David and Sibiliana Apodaca by Vanessa Fonseca-Chávez and Levi Romero, 2015, Riverton, Wyoming.
20. Vanessa Fonseca, "Donde mi amor se ha quedado": Narratives of Sheepherding and Querencia along the Wyoming Manito Trail, *Annals of Wyoming* 89, nos. 2–3 (2017):6–12.
21. Adam Herrera, "Following the Manito Trail: Los Nuevomexicanos en Guayomin (Wyoming)," *Annals of Wyoming* 89, nos. 2–3 (2017):13–15.
22. Troy Lovata, "Making Heritage and Place on the Trees: Arborglyphs by Latina/os in Wyoming," *Annals of Wyoming*, 89, nos. 2–3 (2017):113–122.
23. *South Park Paving Project*, directed by Levi Romero and Vanessa Fonseca-Chávez, produced by Adam Herrera, 2017, https://www.manitotrail.com/video.

24. Ibid.
25. Ibid.
26. This information comes from the Wyoming Institute for Humanities Research grant application. This section was compiled by Troy Lovata.
27. Fonseca 2017.
28. Herrera, Adam P., prod. 2017. "Deciphering the Past: The Arborglyphs of the Sierra Madres," directed by Levi Romero and Vanessa Fonseca Chávez. Following the Manito Trail Documentary.https://www.manitotrail.com/video.
29. https://www.uwyo.edu/artmuseum/exhibitions/archives/2017/following-the-manito-trail/index.html.
30. Mary Louise Sánchez, *The Wind Called My Name* (New York: Lee and Low Books, 2018).
31. Manitos Digital Resolana, https://www.manitos.net.

CHAPTER 7

1. Federal trust responsibility is the legally enforceable fiduciary obligation held by the United States to protect tribal treaty rights, lands, assets, and resources as well as the requirement that the United States must carry out the mandates of federal law when it comes to American Indian tribes. This obligation includes the legal duties, moral obligations, and the fulfillment of understanding and expectations between federally recognized tribes and the United States.
2. Mary Gaylord, BLM, Idaho, Burley Field Office, letter from the Shoshone-Bannock Tribes, May 23, 1995.
3. Martha Hahn, BLM, Idaho State Office, letter from the Shoshone-Bannock Tribes, January 14, 1999.
4. Emily Hone, "Tribal Members Tell Their Views Concerning Bureau of Reclamation Management Plan," *Sho-Ban News*, Fort Hall Idaho, vol. 17, issue 48, December 24, 1992.
5. Ibid.
6. American Falls Resource Management Plan, Bureau of Reclamation, Pacific Northwest Region, Snake River Area Office. Environmental Assessment and Finding of No Significant Impact, 1994.
7. Bureau of Land Management, Twin Falls District, Burley Field Office. Notice of Intent to Prepare a Resource Management Plan (RMP) Amendment and Associated Environmental Assessment for the Castle Rocks and Cedar Fields Areas, Burley Field Office, ID, Fed. Reg. 76, 163 (August 23, 2011).
8. The third was the Northwestern Band of the Shoshone Nation.
9. "The Protection of Indian Sacred Sites," Advisory Council on Historic Preservation, https://www.achp.gov/indian-tribes-and-native-hawaiians/protection-indian-sacred-sites.
10. "Taibo" is the Shoshone word for white man.

11. BLM-SBT Tribal meeting, meeting notes, August 14, 2014.
12. Ibid.
13. Dawn Stram Statham, "Camas and the Northern Shoshoni: A Biogeographic and Socioeconomic Analysis," Master's thesis, Dept. of Anthropology, Idaho State University, 1981. Statham's Master's thesis on camas roots provides another example of why non-Indians wanted information on the location of key subsistence resources. Conducting surveys in 1973 and 1975 of camas locations, Statham examined soil types and correlated historical gathering sites of the Shoshone and Bannock people. The soil type that produces high quality, good-sized camas bulbs is the Mollisol, which are among the most productive soils in the world (44). The Camas Prairie in the Fairfield, Idaho, area is now prime agricultural land. No Shoshone or Bannock Indians now live in the area.
14. BLM-SBT Tribal meeting, meeting notes, August 26, 2014.
15. Ibid.
16. Michel-Rolph Trouillot, *Silencing the Past: Power and the Production of History* (Boston: Beacon Press, 1995).

CHAPTER 8

1. Information in this section is drawn from the following works: E. Richard Hart, ed., *Zuni and the Courts: A Struggle for Sovereign Land Rights* (Lawrence: University Press of Kansas, 1995); E. Richard Hart, *Pedro Pino: Governor of Zuni Pueblo, 1830–1878* (Logan: Utah State University Press, 2003); and E. Richard Hart and T. J. Ferguson, *A Zuni Atlas* (Norman: University of Oklahoma Press, 1985).
2. *New Mexico v. Aamodt (Aamodt I),* 537 F2d 1102 (10th Cir. 1976); *New Mexico v. Aamodt (Aamodt II)*, 618 F. Supp. 993 (D. N. M. 1985). See also, for instance, Sarah Britton, "The Special Case of Pueblos," in *Tribal Water Rights: Essays in Contemporary Law, Policy, and Economics*, edited by Thorson, John E., Sarah Britton, and Bonnie G. Colby (Tucson: University of Arizona Press, 2006), 64–68. Jane Marx, telephone consultation, June 1, 2015.
3. Sarah Britton, "Groundwater, Tribal Rights, and Settlements," in *Tribal Water Rights: Essays in Contemporary Law, Policy, and Economics*, 93. For information on the acquisition of the land around Kolhu/wala:wa, see Hart, *Zuni and the Courts*, 199–221. Another lake sacred to the Zunis was also protected for the Tribe by Congress. See Hart, *Zuni and the Courts*, 97, 201, 224. Recently, efforts to construct a coal mine near the lake were prevented.
4. Leslie Spier, *Klamath Ethnography*, University of California Publications in American Archaeology and Ethnology, vol. 30 (Berkeley: University of California Press, 1930), 10–11.
5. Ibid.
6. George A. Dorsey, "Certain Gambling Games of the Klamath Indians," *American Anthropologist*, n.s. 3, no. 1 (1901):14–27; Dorsey was at Upper

Klamath Lake in June 1900, where he collected 250 specimens for the Field Columbian Museum. One game involved catching a fish vertebra "upon the point of a bodkin or needle." Also, Stewart Culin, *Games of the North American Indians*, Twenty-fourth Annual Report of the Bureau of American Ethnology for 1902–1903 (Washington, D.C.: Government Printing Office, 1907), 237, 293, 332, 528, 648, 659, 136–138, 247–248, 291–293, 327–332, 479–482, 550–551, 740–741, drawing heavily on Dorsey.

7. Gatschet to Commissioner of Indian Affairs, October 13, 1877, Letters Received at BIA, Oregon, Klamath, Modoc and Yahooskin, Docket 100 (Indian Claims Commission)/ National Archives, Bureau of Indian Affairs, microfilm, 5 reels (Microfilm E99.K7 K48 1960z), Assembled by firm of Wilkinson, Boyden, Cragun and Barker, University of Oregon Archives.
8. Albert S. Gatschet, "Oregonian Folk-Lore," *Journal of American Folk-Lore* 4, no. 13 (1891):139–143. Gatschet, "Songs of the Modoc Indians," *American Anthropologist*, o.s. 7, no. 1 (1894):26–31.
9. Albert S. Gatschet, "Mythologic Text in the Klamath Language of Southern Oregon," *American Antiquarian and Oriental Journal* 1, no. 3 (1879):161; Gatschet, *The Klamath Indians of Southwestern Oregon*, Contributions to North American Ethnology, vol. 2, part 1 (Washington, D.C.: Government Printing Office, 1890), lxxx; Patrick Mann Haynal, "From Termination through Restoration and Beyond: Modern Klamath Cultural Identity," PhD diss., Anthropology, University of Oregon, Eugene, 1994, 47, 50.
10. Roy L. Carlson, "Klamath Henwas and Other Stone Sculpture," *American Anthropologist* 6, no. 1 (1959):88. He also noted fetish-like stone objects associated with the Williamson River and the Klamath lakes.
11. Albert S. Gatschet, *Klamath Indians of Southwestern Oregon*, 2, parts 1 and 2 (Washington, D.C.: Government Printing Office, 1890).
12. Gatschet, *Klamath Indians of Southwestern Oregon*, 2, part 1, xi.
13. Vine Deloria Jr. and David E. Wilkins, *Tribes, Treaties, and Constitutional Tribulations* (Austin: University of Texas Press, 1999), 174n24; and Charles J. Kappler, *Indian Affairs, Laws and Treaties*, vol. 6 (*Laws*) (Washington, D. C.: Government Printing Office [reprint, n.d., 1971]), 614–615.
14. *United States v. Ben Adair, et al.* (723 F. 2d 1394). Some 15,000 acres (6,070 ha.) of land and water were purchased by the United States government in order to establish a bird refuge.
15. Ibid.
16. Thorson et al., "Introduction," *Tribal Water Rights*, 7; Lucy Moore and Steve Snyder, "Reassessing Klamath," in *Tribal Water Rights*, 142–154; Victoria Carchidi, review of *Water War in the Klamath Basin: Macho Law, Combat Biology, and Dirty Politics*, by Holly Doremus and A. Dan Tarlock, *Electronic Green Journal,* UCLA Library 31 (Spring 2011). This review was also republished in the University of Pennsylvania *Scholarly Commons.*

17. The material in this section is based on testimony presented in a case that went before the U.S. Supreme Court and that determined ownership of the southern one third of Lake Coeur d'Alene. E. Richard Hart, "A History of the Coeur d'Alene Tribe's Claim to Coeur d'Alene Lake," Expert Testimony Submitted to the United States Department of Justice, *United States v. Idaho*, April 28, 1994.

CHAPTER 9

1. Lucy Thompson, *To the American Indian: Reminiscences of a Yurok Woman*, Introduction by Julian Lang (Berkeley: Heyday Books, 1991), xxv.
2. Thompson, *To the American Indian*, xxvi.
3. Bureau of Reclamation, Klamath Basin Area Office, https://www.usbr.gov/mp/kbao/.
4. Ibid.
5. Leaf Hillman, interview by Brittani Orona, *Stories of the River, Stories of the People: Memory on the Klamath River Basin Oral History Project,* Orleans, California, January 2013.
6. Diana Hartel, "Doctor's Orders: Undam the Klamath-Settlement Could Restore Health to Rivers and Tribes," *High Country News*, May 16, 2011; http://www.klamathrenewal.org/.
7. Cutcha Risling Baldy, interview by Brittani Orona, *Stories of the River*, Davis, California, January 2013.
8. Hartel, "Doctor's Orders," 17.
9. Russ Rymer, "Reuniting a River," *National Geographic*, December 2008, http://ngm.nationalgeographic.com/2008/12/klamath-river/rymer-text/9.
10. Ibid.
11. Ibid., 3.
12. Leaf Hillman interview, January 2013.
13. Craig Tucker interview by Brittani Orona, *Stories of the River*, Orleans, California, January 2013.
14. Patrick Wolfe, "Settler colonialism and the elimination of the native," *Journal of Genocide Research* 8, no. 4 (2006):387–409, https://doi.org/10.1080/14623520601056240, 2.
15. Linda T. Smith, *Decolonizing Methodologies: Research and Indigenous Peoples* (London: Zed Books, 2013), 118.
16. Smith, *Decolonizing*, 120.
17. Linda T. Smith., Eve Tuck, and K. Wayne Yang, *Indigenous and Decolonizing Studies in Education: Mapping the Long Way* (Abington, UK: Routledge, 2018), 1.
18. Peter Burke, "History as Social Memory," in *The Collective Memory Reader*, edited by Jeffrey K. Olick (New York: Oxford University Press, 2011), 188–192.
19. Shaunna Oteka McCovey, "Religious Freedom?," *The Smokehouse Boys* (Berkeley: Heyday Books, 2005), 21.

20. Theresa May, *Salmon Is Everything: Community-Based Theatre in the Klamath Watershed* (Corvallis: Oregon State University Press, 2014).
21. Ibid., 85.
22. Amy Lonetree, *Decolonizing Museums: Representing Native America in National and Tribal Museums* (Chapel Hill: University of North Carolina Press, 2012), 1.
23. Ibid.
24. Ibid., 30.
25. Michelle Raheja, "Reading Nanook's Smile: Visual Sovereignty, Indigenous Revisions of Ethnography, and Atanarjuat (The Fast Runner)," *American Quarterly* 59, no. 4 (December 2007):1159–1185.
26. Vanessa Esquivido, "The Social Life of Basket Caps: Repatriation under the Native American Graves Protection and Repatriation Act, in Hopes of Cultural Revitalization," *McNair Scholars Journal* 11, 2013.
27. Eve Tuck and Rubén A. Gaztambide-Fernández, "Curriculum, Replacement, and Settler Futurity," *Journal of Curriculum Theorizing* 29, no. 1 (2013):76–77.
28. Burke, *History as Social Memory*, 191.
29. Lonetree, *Decolonizing Museums*, 22.
30. Jean M. O'Brien, "Historical Sources and Methods in Indigenous Studies: Touching on the Past, Looking to the Future," in *Sources and Methods in Indigenous Studies*, edited by Chris Andersen (London: Routledge, 2016), 15–22.

CHAPTER 10

The author received research support during completion of this project and offers thanks to the American Council of Learned Societies Fellowship, the Frederick W. Beinecke Senior Research Fellowship at the Beinecke Rare Book and Manuscript Library at Yale University, the Yale Center for the Study of Race, Ethnicity, and Transnational Migration, and Gonzaga University's sabbatical leave fund.

1. The use of "multivocal" in this context refers to multiple tribal and Native American voices representing distinct Plateau communities, not tribal and non-Indian voices. This distinction is important, particularly when we learn from Amy Lonetree's Mille Lacs experience in *Decolonizing Museums: Representing Native America in National and Tribal Museums* (Chapel Hill: University of North Carolina Press, 2012), 169.
2. Duane Champagne, "In Search of Theory and Method in American Indian Studies," *American Indian Quarterly* 31, no. 3 (Summer 2007):353.
3. La Donna Harris and Jacqueline Wasilewski, "Indigeneity, an Alternative Worldview: Four R's (Relationship, Responsibility, Reciprocity, Redistribution) vs. Two P's (Power and Profit). Sharing the Journey Towards Conscious Evolution," *Systems Research and Behavioral Science* 21, no. 5 (September/October 2004):4–5, https://doi.org/10.1002/sres.631.

4. "About Us," Native Project, http://nativeproject.org/about.
5. David Treuer, *Rez Life: An Indian's Journey through Reservation Life*, (New York: Atlantic Monthly Press, 2012), 21; Colin G. Calloway, *New Worlds for All: Indians, Europeans, and the Remaking of Early America*, (Baltimore: Johns Hopkins University Press, 1998); Susan Sleeper-Smith, Juliana Barr, Jean M. O'Brien, Nancy Shoemaker, and Scott Manning Stevens, eds., *Why You Can't Teach United States History without American Indians*, (Chapel Hill: University of North Carolina Press, 2015).
6. Spokane Historical, https://spokanehistorical.org/.
7. Gregory E. Smoak, "Beyond the Academy: Making the New Western History Matter in Local Communities," *The Public Historian* 31, no. 4 (Fall 2009):88, https://doi.org/10.1525/tph.2009.31.4.85.
8. Congressional Research Service, *Columbia River Treaty Review*, updated December 15, 2020, https://fas.org/sgp/crs/misc/R43287.pdf; https://ucut.org/.
9. Allan T. Scholz et al., *Fishes of Eastern Washington: A Natural* History, vol. 1 (Cheney, WA: Biology Faculty Publications, 2014), 86, https://dc.ewu.edu/biol_fac/12/.
10. Tara Justine, "The Ceremony of Tears," *Spokane Historical*, https://spokanehistorical.org/items/show/668.
11. Brook Swanson, "Native American Studies and Biology" (public talk, Gonzaga University, November 17, 2016).
12. Treuer, *Rez Life*, 304–305.
13. Lonetree, *Decolonizing Museums.*
14. Justus Caudell, "Mel Tonasket, Joel Boyd Testify on EWU Request for Lucy F. Covington Archive Funding," *Tribal Tribune* (Nespelem, WA), Feb 8, 2019, http://www.tribaltribune.com/news/article_4201420e-2bd8-11e9-888d-9310e743420e.html.
15. Katrine Barber, "Shared Authority in the Context of Tribal Sovereignty," *The Public Historian* 35, no. 4 (November 2013):23–24.
16. Katrine Barber and Donna Sinclair, "Decolonizing Sustainability: Students, Teachers, and Indigenous-University Partnerships," in *University-Community Partnerships*, edited by B. D. Wortman-Galvin, Jennifer H. Allen, and Jacob D. B. Sherman, (London: Routledge Greenleaf, 2016), 166–177.
17. Ibid., 167.
18. Ibid., 174.

CHAPTER 11

Although I own the ideas expressed in this piece, I wish to acknowledge coeditor Holly George for her brilliance, collegiality, and collaboration over the years.

1. Robert L. Dorman, *Hell of a Vision: Regionalism and the Modern American West* (Tucson: University of Arizona Press, 2012), xii, 4.
2. Previous texts of Utah history, written by respected historians, make no justification for a history of the state, since historians have taken for granted the

reasoning for state history. See, for example, Richard D. Poll, et al., *Utah's History* (Provo, UT: BYU Press, 1978); and Thomas G. Alexander, *Utah, The Right Place* (Salt Lake City: Gibbs Smith, 1996; 2nd rev. ed. 2007).

3. Anne W. Ackerson, "Local Historical Societies, Purpose of," in *Encyclopedia of Local History*, 2nd ed., edited by Carol Kammen and Amy H. Wilson (Lanham, MD: AltaMira Press, 2013), 320–321.
4. The editors of *Encyclopedia of Local History*, making the case for the study and practice of local history within the discipline of history, argue that the field "is much broader in historical scope . . . , more inclusive of source and type of question, more elusive of achieving a firm definition" (vii) than is often attributed to local and state history. The fact of the matter is that most local history is narrowly conceived and executed, as described above.
5. Peter Novick, *That Noble Dream: The "Objectivity Question" and the American Historical Profession* (New York: Cambridge University Press, 1988), 72–73.
6. Davis Bitton, "The Ritualization of Mormon History," *Utah Historical Quarterly* 43 (Winter 1975):68.
7. Wallace Stegner, *The Gathering of Zion: The Story of the Mormon Trail* (1964; Lincoln: University of Nebraska Press, 1992), 2.
8. Gary Topping, "One Hundred Years at the Utah State Historical Society," *Utah Historical Quarterly* 65 (Summer 1997):207–209.
9. For Utah monuments, see Gary L. Gregerson, *Utah Roadside History: A Compilation of Monuments, Markers, and Historic Sites* (Griffin Associates, 1995); Andy Weeks, *A History of Mormon Landmarks in Utah: Monuments of Faith* (Charleston, SC: History Press, 2015); and Matthew Kester, *Remembering Iosepa: History, Place, and Religion in the American West* (New York: Oxford University Press, 2013). More general studies include Françoise Choay, *The Invention of the Historic Monument* (New York: Cambridge University Press, 2001); Judith Dupré, *Monuments: America's History in Art and Memory* (New York: Random House, 2007).
10. Topping, "One Hundred Years," 209–210.
11. No published analysis of the publication exists, beyond general histories of the Utah State Historical Society by Topping and by Glen M. Leonard, "The Utah State Historical Society, 1897–1972," *Utah Historical Quarterly* 40 (Fall 1972):300–334.
12. "Salutatory," *Utah Historical Quarterly* 1 (January 1928):3–4.
13. William R. Palmer, ed., "Memoirs of Alice Parker Isom," *Utah Historical Quarterly* 10 (1942):54–83.
14. William J. Snow, "Robert Gardner: Typical Frontiersman and Early Utah Pioneer," *Utah Historical Quarterly* 9, nos. 1–4 (1941):179–183.
15. The best summary of Utah historiography before 1940 is Gary Topping, *Utah Historians and the Reconstruction of Western History* (Norman: University of Oklahoma Press, 2003), 12–42.
16. Charles Kelly, "Jedediah Smith on the Salt Desert Trail," *Utah Historical Quarterly* 3 (January 1930):27.

17. Juanita Brooks, "Indian Relations on the Mormon Frontier," *Utah Historical Quarterly* 12 (1944):1–48.
18. Marguerite Sinclair to Dale Morgan, April 13, 1945, box 49, fd. 2, reel 17, Dale Lowell Morgan Papers, 1877–1971, BANC MSS 71/161 c, Bancroft Library, University of California, Berkeley.
19. Ricks's traditional approach to Utah history led him to criticize Levi Edgar Young for inviting Father Robert Joseph Dwyer, also a member of the Board, who earned his doctorate in history at the Catholic University, to edit the centennial (1947) issue of *UHQ*. At the time of her departure and Ricks's promotion as chair of the Board, Sinclair complained of Ricks's "one-track mind" that emphasized "Escalante and Bolton"—a reference to the foot-dragging of Herbert Bolton to finish editing the Silvestre Escalante diaries—over other journal content; Marguerite Sinclair to Dale Morgan, August 10, 1949, box 49, fd. 4, reel 17, Morgan Papers.
20. Dale Morgan to "Gentlemen" of the Board of Control, May 27, 1945, box 25, fd. 5, reel 9, Morgan Papers.
21. See Topping, *Utah Historians*; Richard Saunders, "Placing Juanita Brooks among the Heroes (or Villains) of Mormon and Utah History," *Utah Historical Quarterly* 87 (Summer 2019):218–237. Morgan's voluminous papers are housed at the Bancroft Library in California, but his material is scattered through numerous other collections, including the Utah State Historical Society. His influence on Western American history and its historians cannot be overstated.
22. Marguerite Sinclair to Dale Morgan, July 9, 1946, box 49, fd. 2, reel 17, Morgan Papers.
23. Dale Morgan to Juanita Brooks, July 30, 1949, box 1, fd. 4; Dale Morgan to Juanita Brooks, November 15, 1949, box 1, fd. 4; Dale Morgan to Juanita Brooks, September 12, 1951, box 1, fd. 5; all in Juanita Brooks Papers, 1941–1993, MS 0486, Special Collections, University of Utah. Morgan confided to Brooks on the question of Utah or Washington, "I guess I would be a little unhappy either way, for as I have observed before now, I am something of a split personality, historically. Half of me belongs to the West, half to Washington, and each has opportunities essential to me which the other cannot provide"; Dale Morgan to Juanita Brooks, September 12, 1951, box 1, fd. 4, Brooks Papers.
24. Marguerite Sinclair to Dale Morgan, August 10, 1949, box 49, fd. 4, reel 17, Morgan Papers; Dale Morgan to Juanita Brooks, December 6, 1949, box 1, fd. 4, Brooks Papers. Here in full are Sinclair's comments to Morgan: "You were the only one to send me my obituary—the only one who cared enough about my work to send me a word of appreciation for the things I really strove to do for the society, though perhaps I did not always reach the mark. But with my failures, where the Society is concerned, no one can ever say I didn't give it the very best I had. Never having any children of my own, it was 'My baby.' I fought for it and loved it almost fiercely. I think

that is one of the reasons you mean so much to me is because you loved it too."

25. Dale Morgan to Marguerite Sinclair, June 27, 1949, box 1, fd. 5, Dale Lowell Morgan Papers, 1940–1969, Mss B 40, Utah State Historical Society, Salt Lake City (hereafter Morgan Papers, USHS).
26. Morgan to Sinclair, June 27, 1949, box 1, fd. 5, Morgan Papers, USHS.
27. Dale Morgan to Russell Mortensen, November 29, 1950, box 1, fd. 6, Morgan Papers, USHS.
28. Dale Morgan to Russell Mortensen, December 20, 1950, box 1, fd. 6, Morgan Papers, USHS.
29. See Dale Morgan to Juanita Brooks, August 12, 1941, box 1, fd. 5, Brooks Papers.
30. A. R. Mortensen, interview by Everett L. Cooley, August 16, 1980, p. 45, Everett L. Cooley Oral History Project, no. 12, ACC 814, J. Willard Marriott Library, University of Utah, Salt Lake City, Utah, https://collections.lib.utah.edu/ark:/87278/s69g783f.
31. Russell Mortensen to Dale Morgan, November 3, 1954, box 47, fd. 2, reel 16, Morgan Papers.
32. Russell Mortensen to Dale Morgan, October 20, 1958, box 47, fd. 6, reel 16, Morgan Papers; Mortensen interview, 45–51; Topping, "One Hundred Years," 255–256.
33. See Leonard, "Utah State Historical Society, 1897–1972," 309.
34. Mortensen to Morgan, November 3, 1954.
35. Saunders, "Juanita Brooks," 224. The Society's earliest directors and board members were Latter-day Saints, contributing to a particular ideological bent. Marguerite Sinclair had feared that Joel Ricks, then incoming president of the Board, would turn the society into a "church organization," while Russ Mortensen confided "a general feeling of being hemmed in by the orthodoxy of this community—all have made me feel at times as if I would be willing to go anywhere to get the hell out of it." Marguerite Sinclair to Dale Morgan, August 10, 1949, box 49, fd. 4, reel 17; Russell Mortensen to Dale Morgan, February 2, 1959, box 47, fd. 6, reel 16, all in Morgan Papers.
36. A 2014 review of all articles published since 1928 indicates that just over half are focused on the fifty years from Mormon entrance into the Great Basin until Utah statehood. Another quarter address the three decades from early statehood. The remaining quarter include a small offering of prehistory and pre-European Native American history, Euro exploration and migration prior to 1847, and the mid-twentieth through the twenty-first century. Geographically, the largest clusters of articles center on the Salt Lake Valley and the Colorado Plateau, two regions in Utah with a strong non-Mormon presence. My unempirical observation is that some in the history community regarded—and continue to regard—the journal as an outlet primarily for history beyond the Mormon or LDS scope.

37. Before the founding of the Mormon History Association's *Journal of Mormon History* in 1965 and the Western Historical Association's *Western Historical Quarterly* in 1969, regional and some national scholars writing on themes touching on Utah published in *UHQ*. Earl Pomeroy, W. Turrentine Jackson, Robert G. Athearn, and George Hammon contributed articles. The *UHQ* also published John D. Hicks's address at the first annual meeting of the Society, "The American Tradition of Democracy"—an essay that did not so much as touch on Utah or its history. Before his appointment as LDS Church Historian in 1972, Leonard Arrington had authored or coauthored twenty-seven articles in *UHQ*. Thereafter, in part due to the *Journal of Mormon History*, which Arrington helped found, and to *Dialogue: A Journal of Mormon Thought*, founded in 1966, manuscripts labeled as Mormon history only found their way to *UHQ* when these other options had been exhausted. For Arrington's publications, see "Works by Leonard J. Arrington," compiled by Jeffery Ogden Johnson, in *Confessions of a Mormon Historian: The Diaries of Leonard J. Arrington, 1971–1997* (Salt Lake City: Signature Books, 2018), 717–754.
38. See Utah Division of State History, "*Utah Historical Quarterly* Submission and Style Guide," https://history.utah.gov/wp-content/uploads/2018/08/UHQ_Submissions.pdf.
39. Utah State Historical Society Membership Survey, December 2019, in possession of the author. Current USHS membership is older—over 76 percent are fifty-five years or older—and 44 percent have been members for over ten years.
40. *Utah Historical Quarterly* White Paper, September 3, 2008, 3, in author's possession.
41. Kevin Fayles to Board of State History, April 22, 2020, email.
42. Alley to Kevin Fayles and Board of State History, April 24, 2020, email.
43. An editorial statement first published in the winter 2018 issue reads: "Even as *UHQ* continues its commitment to themes traditionally associated with Utah history, it challenges readers and authors to think across state lines to the forces of history, physiography, and culture that link Utah to a host of people, places, experiences, and trends beyond its geopolitical boundaries. *UHQ* seeks a regional approach, reflecting Utah's geographic and cultural position at the crossroads of the West."
44. Jared Farmer, *On Zion's Mount: Mormons, Indians, and the American Landscape* (Cambridge: Harvard University Press, 2008), 14.
45. Austin E. Fife, "Folklore and Local History," *Utah Historical Quarterly* 31 (Fall 1963):318.

CHAPTER 12

1. Quotations in "Undated Memo," Autry Museum Institutional Archives—Research Center/Institute, central files, box 1, department memos, 1989

and 1991; "Research Center—Past Efforts and Present Status," Autry Museum Institutional Archives—Research Center/Institute, central files, box 1, department memos, 1989 and 1991. See also John Langellier to Joanne Hale, September 6, 1990, Autry Institutional Archives, Research Center/Institute, director's files, John Langellier, box 1.

2. Quotations in Patricia Ward Biederman, "How the West Was Spun: A Symposium at the Autry Looks at the Shaping of Our Views of the American Frontier," *Los Angeles Times*, June 9, 1995.
3. Quotations in "Memo from Kevin Mulroy to Research Center Staff," February 16, 1994, Autry Museum Institutional Archives, Research Center/Institute, central files, box 1; Kevin Mulroy, "Strategic Plan for the Research Center, 1997," December 31, 1996, Autry Museum Institutional Archives, Research Center/Institute, central files, box 1, departmental goals, 1989–2000.
4. For examples of the "reductionist" press coverage of the merger, see Christopher Reynolds, "A Union of Cowboys and Indians," *Los Angeles Times*, December 11, 2002, http://articles.latimes.com/2002/dec/11/entertainment/et-reynolds11; Robert Greene, "Cowboys and Indians," *LA Weekly*, August 18, 2005, https://www.laweekly.com/cowboys-and-indians/; Edward Wyatt, "Gene Autry's Legacy and an Indian Museum Merge (and Collide)," *New York Times*, June 28, 2006, http://www.nytimes.com/2006/06/28/arts/design/28sout.html.
5. Stephen Aron, "Report to the Board of Trustees," September 12, 2002, Autry National Center Institutional Archives, Research Center/Institute, director's files, Stephen Aron, box 1.
6. Some of those workshop presentations were subsequently published in revised form in *Convergence*. See Malcolm Rohrbough, "The Grand Seduction," *Convergence* (Spring/Summer 2005):24–29; Ruth Ellen Gruber, "The View from Europe: The West in the World," *Convergence* (Spring/Summer 2005):30–37; Clyde Derrick, "The Breakout Gals: Iconic Female Rebels of the Western Film Musical," *Convergence* (Fall 2005):20–27; Louise Pubols, "All in the Family: The Global Business of a California Ranchero," *Convergence* (Spring/Summer 2006):14–19; Amy Scott, "Revisiting Yosemite," *Convergence* (Fall 2006):6–15; Carolyn Brucken and Virginia Scharff, "The Cosmopolitan World of Owl Woman and William Bent," *Convergence* (Fall 2007):24–31.
7. Virginia Scharff and Carolyn Brucken, eds., *Home Lands: How Women Made the West* (Berkeley: University of California Press, 2010); Virginia Scharff, ed., *Empire and Liberty: The Civil War and the West* (Berkeley: University of California Press, 2015).
8. "Report: Autry Museum Drops Expansion Plans," *Los Angeles Business Journal*, August 11, 2009, https://labusinessjournal.com/news/2009/aug/11/report-autry-museum-drops-expansion-plans/; "Daniel M. Finley to be

New Director of Autry National Center in Griffith Park," *Los Angeles Daily News*, August 13, 2010, https://www.dailynews.com/2010/08/13/daniel-m-finley-to-be-new-director-of-autry-national-center-in-griffith-park/.

9. David Burton, "The Autry Institute: A Vision for the Future," March 5, 2014, Autry National Center Institutional Archives, Research Center/Institute, director's files, David Burton, box 1.
10. Quotation in Edward Rothstein, "Museum with an American Indian Voice," *New York Times*, September 21, 2004, https://www.nytimes.com/2004/09/21/arts/design/museum-with-an-american-indian-voice.html; David Ng, "Autry President Dan Finley Abruptly Leaves; Rick West Taking Over," *Los Angeles Times*, June 21, 2012, https://articles.latimes.com/2012/jun/21/entertainment/la-et-cm-autry-national-center-rick-west-president-ceo-20120621.
11. Karen Wilson, ed., *Jews in the Los Angeles Mosaic* (Berkeley: University of California Press, 2013); Adam Arenson and Andrew Graybill, eds., *Civil War Wests: Testing the Limits of the United States* (Berkeley: University of California Press, 2015).
12. Anthony Grafton and James Grossman, "No More Plan B: A Very Modest Proposal for Graduate Programs in History," *Perspectives on History: The Newsletter of the American Historical Association* (October 1, 2011), https://www.historians.org/publications-and-directories/perspectives-on-history/october-2011/no-more-plan-b.
13. Ibid.
14. The best place to review the data that the AHA has assembled and to access articles about the project is on the section of the AHA's website devoted to Career Diversity. See https://www.historians.org/jobs-and-professional-development/career-diversity-for-historians.
15. For a fuller explication of the course's design and execution, see Karen Wilson and Stephen Aron, "Expanding Horizons and Diversifying Skills: Transforming Graduate Curriculm," in *The Reimagined PhD: Navigating 21st Century Humanities Education*, edited by Leanne M. Horinko, Jordan M. Reed, and James M. Van Wyck (New Brunswick, NJ: Rutgers University Press, 2021).

Contributors

Laurie Arnold is an enrolled member of the Sinixt Band of the Colville Confederated Tribes. She is Associate Professor of History and Director of Native American Studies at Gonzaga University. She has previously held positions at the D'Arcy McNickle Center for American Indian and Indigenous Studies at the Newberry Library in Chicago and at the University of Notre Dame. Her first book, *Bartering with the Bones of Their Dead: The Colville Confederated Tribes and Termination*, was published by the University of Washington Press (2012). Her publications have appeared in *Time Magazine* and scholarly journals including *Montana: The Magazine of Western History*, *Western Historical Quarterly*, and *Collection Management*. She holds a PhD in History from Arizona State University and a BA in History from Oregon State University.

Stephen Aron, who received his PhD from the University of California, Berkeley, is a past president of the Western History Association and is Professor of History at the University of California, Los Angeles. His books include *How the West Was Lost: The Transformation of Kentucky from Daniel Boone to Henry Clay*; *American Confluence: The Missouri Frontier from Borderland to Border State*; *The American West: A Very Short Introduction*; and *Worlds Together, Worlds Apart: A History of the World from the Beginnings of Humankind to the Present*. In 2021, he will become President and CEO of the Autry Museum of the American West in Los Angeles.

Leisl Carr Childers is Assistant Professor at Colorado State University. Her first book, *The Size of the Risk: Histories of Multiple Use in the Great Basin* (University of Oklahoma Press, 2015), won the Western Writers of

America 2016 Spur Award for Contemporary Nonfiction. Her research has been featured on KNPR's *State of Nevada*, "Bundyville," PBS *Frontline*, and in *High Country News*. She is a council member of the Public Lands History Center, a coprimary investigator with Michael Childers on a new administrative history of the U.S. Forest Service, and coeditor for the Environment in Modern North America series at the University of Oklahoma Press.

Michael Childers is Assistant Professor at Colorado State University, where he specializes in the history of tourism, the environment, and the American West. A graduate of the University of Nevada, Las Vegas, his first book, *Colorado Powder Keg: Ski Resorts and the Environmental Movement* tells the history of Colorado's ski industry and the environmental controversies surrounding its growth throughout the twentieth century. He is currently working on a history of visitors in Yosemite National Park, as well as coauthoring an administrative history of the U.S. Forest Service from 1960 to present.

Vanessa Fonseca-Chávez received her MA in Hispanic Southwest Studies from the University of New Mexico and her PhD in Spanish Cultural Studies from Arizona State University. She is Assistant Professor of English at Arizona State University, where she teaches courses in Chicana/o and Indigenous literature, Southwest literature and film, and graduate courses in Narrative Studies. She has published three books: *Spanish Perspectives on Chicano Literature: Literary and Cultural Essays* (Ohio State University Press, 2017), coedited with Jesús Rosales; *Querencia: Reflections on the New Mexico Homeland* (University of New Mexico Press, 2020), coedited with Levi Romero and Spencer R. Herrera; and *Colonial Legacies in Chicana/o Literature and Culture: Looking through the Kaleidoscope* (University of Arizona Press, 2020). She is the codirector of the Following the Manito Trail project with Levi Romero.

Mette Flynt is a historian at Historical Research Associates Inc. She has volunteered at the Hinsdale County Historical Society for twenty years. A specialist in environmental history, Flynt holds a PhD in history from the University of Oklahoma.

E. Richard Hart provides historical, ethnohistorical, and environmental historical services and expert testimony for North American tribes.

The former executive director of the Institute of the North American West, he has organized a number of influential conferences, authored or edited ten books, and published numerous articles and essays.

Trisha Venisa-Alicia Martínez is a postdoctoral fellow at the University of New Mexico, Taos, and Visiting Assistant Professor of Latina/o Studies at the University of Wyoming. She received her PhD in American Studies from the University of New Mexico in 2019. Her dissertation, "Living the Manito Trail: Maintaining Self, Culture, and Community," is an interdisciplinary ethnographic study that relies heavily on oral histories she collected from Manito communities that migrated from northern New Mexico to Wyoming. Martinez is passionate about engaging the various aspects of her sociocultural community and remains committed to mapping Manito migration.

Brittani R. Orona is an enrolled member of the Hoopa Valley Tribe. She is currently a PhD candidate at the University of California, Davis, in Native American Studies with a Designated Emphasis in Human Rights. She received her MA in Public History from California State University, Sacramento, and her BA in History from Humboldt State University. Orona is interested in repatriation, federal Indian law, cultural resources management, Indigenous environmental justice, and environmental history as they relate to California Indian tribes. Her dissertation research focuses on Hupa, Yurok, and Karuk perspectives of visual sovereignty, memory, and human and water rights on the Klamath River Basin. She was a 2019 Switzer Environmental Fellow through the Robert and Patricia Switzer Foundation.

Leighton M. Quarles is a historian with the U.S. Forest Service. A public lands scholar with expertise in oral history, the West, and the Circumpolar North, he served until recently as Assistant Director of the American West Center at the University of Utah. Quarles recently completed a PhD in Western American and Public History at the University of Utah and holds a master's degree in Northern Studies from the University of Alaska, Fairbanks, a graduate certificate in Historic Preservation from the University of Utah, and a bachelor's degree in History from Montana State University.

Jedediah Rogers is an environmental historian and coeditor of *Utah Historical Quarterly*. He is author of *Roads in the Wilderness: Conflict in*

Canyon Country (2013) and editor of *The Earth Will Appear as the Garden of Eden: Essays in Mormon Environmental History* (2019) and two volumes in Mormon history. With Jeff Nichols, he serves as coeditor of The Utah Series on Great Salt Lake and the Great Basin with the University of Utah Press.

Virginia Scharff is Emeritus Distinguished Professor of History at the University of New Mexico. She has published numerous books including *Taking the Wheel: Women and the Coming of the Motor Age* (1991); *Twenty Thousand Roads: Women, Movement, and the West* (2003); and *Home Lands: How Women Made the West* (coauthored with Carolyn Brucken, 2010). She edited *Empire and Liberty: The Civil War and the West* (2015). As Women of the West Chair at the Autry Museum, Scharff served as cocurator of *Home Lands: How Women Made the West*, an exhibit that opened in Los Angeles at the Autry in April, 2010, and traveled to the Missouri History Center, the Museum of New Mexico, and the Gilcrease Museum. She is currently at work on an exhibition and book about the Civil War and the West. She also cocurated *Empire and Liberty: The Civil War and the West* (2015). Scharff currently serves as Senior Scholar at the Autry.

Gregory E. Smoak is Director of the American West Center and Associate Professor of History at the University of Utah. He is the author of *Ghost Dances and Identity: Prophetic Religion and American Indian Ethnogenesis in the Nineteenth Century* (University of California Press, 2006) and a forthcoming environmental history of the Little Bighorn Battlefield National Monument. Smoak's association with American West Center began in 1988 and has included projects with the Shoshone-Bannock Tribes, the Ute Mountain Ute Tribe, the Big Sandy Rancheria of Western Mono Indians, the Navajo Nation, the Nevada Indian Commission, and the Utah State Division of Indian Affairs. He is currently President of the National Council on Public History.

Yvette Towersap Tuell is an enrolled member of the Shoshone-Bannock Tribes. She was born and raised on the Fort Hall Indian Reservation. She holds a BA in Anthropology with a minor in American Indian Studies from Idaho State University and an MS in Environmental Law from Vermont Law School. She earned an MA in History from the University of Utah in 2019, along with Certificates in Public History and Historic

Preservation. She is particularly interested in American Indian history and incorporating tribal history into federal land management and public history.

Richard White is Margaret Byrne Professor of American History, Emeritus, at Stanford University. His most recent book, coauthored with Jesse White, is *California Exposures: Envisioning Myth and History* (Norton, 2020).

Index

Ackerson, Anne W., 156
activism, and histories of marginalized groups, 126
administrative histories, of National Park Service, 43, 57–70
agriculture, and water rights litigation, 115–16, 122–23, 202n13
Albers, Patricia, 5, 14
Albright, Horace, 698
Alley, John, 5, 167
Alpine Explorer guide, 81
Alpine Loop Backcountry Byway (Colorado), 81–84
Alpine Triangle Recreation Area Management Plan (ATRAMP), 81–82
Alter, J. Cecil, 160
Amato, Joseph, 196n4
American Anthropologist (journal), 118
American Heritage Center (University of Wyoming), 98, 99
American Historical Association (AHA), 170, 171, 177, 212n14
American Indian History on Trial: Historical Expertise in Tribal Litigation (Hart 2018), 114
American Society for Environmental History (ASEH), 44–45
American West. *See* Western history
American West Center: fiftieth anniversary symposium and key address, ix, 1–2, 37–39; foundation and early history of, 2–3; Thompson's work at, *xii*, 5; Hart's work at, 114; legacy of, *ix–x*; and Native American Studies program at Gonzaga University, 141, 153–54; new direction of after retirement of O'Neil, 5–6; O'Neil and development of, 4–6; and practice of public history, 13–22; role of in teaching and mentorship of public historians, 6–12
American West magazine, 2
America's National Park Service: The Critical Documents (Dilsaver 2016), 192n3
Ancestry.com, 145
Anderson, Terry L., 27
Andrew W. Mellon Foundation, 171
Annals of Wyoming: The Wyoming History Journal, 97
Apodaca, David and Sibilia, 94
applied history: and management of public lands, 32–37; and roles of public intellectuals, 39
arborglyphs, and Manitos in Wyoming, 96

Archeological Resource Protection Act (ARPA), 102
archives: and difference between public and academic history, 16; research and creation of digital projects by Native American Studies program at Gonzaga University, 144–45
Arellano, Anselmo, 97
Arellano, Juan Estevan, 92
Arnold, Laurie, 11
Aron, Cindy, 51, 191n39
Aron, Stephen, 9, 12, 21, 170, 171, 172–73, 174, 175, 177, 180–81, 183, 212n15
Arrington, Leonard, 210n37
art: and Native American Studies program at Gonzaga University, 146; in *Stories of the River* and *River as Home* exhibits, 139
Assenheimer, Adolph, 74
Athearn, Robert G., 210n37
Atlas of the New West: Portrait of a Changing Region (Robb 1997), 51
Auerbach, Herbert S., 160
Autry National Center (California), 12, 21, 170–77, 183
Autry Western History Workshop, 173–74

BackStory with the American History Guys (radio), 33
Bailyn, Bernard, 20
Balderrama, Francisco, 89
Baldy, Cutcha Risling, 129
Bancroft Library (University of California, Berkeley), 124, 208n21
Bandelier National Monument (New Mexico), 42–43
Bangerter, Johnny, 61
Bannock Tribe. *See* Shoshone-Bannock Tribes
Barber, Katrine, 153
basketry, and *River as Home* exhibition, 135
Basso, Matthew, 5
Bayer, Laura, 5
Bears Ears National Monument (Utah), 58, 70
Beinecke Rare Books and Manuscript Library (Yale), 124
Benally, Clyde, 5
Berkshire Hathaway, 130
Between Ruin and Restoration: An Environmental History of Israel (Miller 2013), 55
Bill Lane Center for the American West (Stanford University), 6
bioregionalism, and environmental history, 45
Black, Joseph, 64
Blackfeet Tribe (Montana), 144
Blansett, Kent, 25
Blodgett, Peter, 196n2
boarding schools, and Native American Studies program at Gonzaga University, 145
Board of State History (Utah), 165, 167
Boat Dance (Hupa, Karuk, and Yurok), 127
Bokovoy, Melissa, 178–79, 182
Bolton, Herbert, 208n19
Boom (journal), 22
Borchers, Kristie, 79, 80
Boyd-Pates, Tyree, 177
Braun Research Library (California), 172
Britton, Brittany, 139
Britton, Sarah, 202n2
Brooks, Juanita, 160
Brown, William F., 61
Brucken, Carolyn, 172, 174, 176, 177
Bryce, Ebenezer, 64, 194n26
Bundy, Ammon, 26, 27, 29, 187n28
Bundy, Cliven, 23–24, 25–26, 27, 29–31, 70, 187n28
Bundy, Ryan, 26, 27, 187n28

Burcell, Suzanne, 133
Bureau of American Ethnology (BAE), 118
Bureau of Land Management (BLM), 81, 82, 101–13; Idaho BLM Burley Field Office (BFO), 101
Bureau of Reclamation (BOR), 104, 130
Burke, Bridget, 98, 136
Burke, Peter, 131
Burton, David, 175
By Hand Through Memory (exhibition), 151

California State Indian Museum, 136
California State University, Sacramento (CSUS), 136
Calloway, Colin, 143
Career diversity, for historians, 171, 177–82, 212n14
Carlisle Indian School (Pennsylvania), 145
Carlson, Roy L., 118, 205n10
Carrigan, Casey, 83
Cartwright, David, 176
Castle Rocks State Park (Idaho), 103
Cataldo, Joseph, 142
Cauvin, Thomas, 32, 35
Cedar Fields Archeological District (CFAD), 103, 104–7, 108
Center of the American West (University of Colorado), 6, 21
Center for Jewish Studies (CJS), 176
Center for Regional Studies (University of New Mexico), 99
Central New Mexico Community College (CNM), 182
ceremonies, of Hupa, Karuk, and Yurok Tribes, 127
Chiang, Connie, 191n39
Childers, Leisl Carr, 8–9, 11
Childers, Michael, 9, 11
Chinook Indian Nation, 153
Christensen, Jon, 22
City of Rocks/Castle Rocks TCP (Idaho), 103–13
Civil War, and historic mission of National Park Service, 60
Clark, Emily, 145
Clements Center for Southwest Studies Texas), 176
Coates, Ta-Nehisi, 27
Coeur d'alene Tribe (Idaho/Washington), 114–15, 120–23, 148, 204n17
Cohen, Michael, 46
collaborative, public history as, 17, 21, 39
colonialism: and creation of national parks, 62; ecological in northern California, 130–31; impact of on traditional life of Tribes of northwestern California, 126–27. *See also* decolonization
Colorado. *See* Lake City
Colorado Art Ranch, 84
Colorado Preservation's Most Endangered Places List, 80
Colorado State Historical Society, 77
Columbia Plateau, and Native American history, 142
Columbia River Treaty (CRT), 148–50
Columbia University (New York), 171, 177
Colville Confederated Tribe (Washington), 146, 149
community, and Manito trail, 91–92
Conard, Rebecca, 34
Confederated Tribes of the Colville Reservation (Washington), 148
Convergence (magazine), 174, 176, 211n6
cookbook project, and Hinsdale County Historical Society, 74–75
Cooperative Ecosystems Studies Units (CESUs), 59

Corkern, Wilton, 83, 196n5
Covington, Lucy, 151
Crampton, C. Gregory, ix, 2
Cronon, William, 46, 63
Crosby, Alfred, 42
Culver, Lawrence, 191n39
Curtis, Edward, 137–38

dams: and Columbia River, 149; and Klamath River Basin, 127–28, 130
Danborn, David B., 28
database, and Grand Traverse Ottawas, 16–17
Daughters of the Utah Pioneers, 158
Davis, Mike, 49, 52
deBuys, William, 53
Deciphering the Past: The Arborglyphs of the Sierra Madres (Herrera 2016), 97
decolonization: and museum presentations of Native American history and culture, 133–40; as social movement, 131. *See also* colonialism
Decolonizing Museums: Representing Native America in National and Tribal Museums (Lonetree 2012), 151
Deloria, Vine, Jr., 119
Deutsch, Sarah, 91
Devil's Bargains: Tourism in the Twentieth-Century American West (Rothman 1998), 50–52, 54
Dialogue: A Journal of Mormon Thought, 210n37
diaspora, and Manito migration, 92–93
digital humanities, and Native American Studies program at Gonzaga University, 144–48
Dilsaver, Lary M., 192n3
Donahue, Deborah, 27
Doris Duke American Indian Oral History Project, *ix–x*, 2
Dorman, Robert L., 155
Dorsey, George A., 202–3n6
Downtown Improvement and Revitalization Team (DIRT), 79, 80
Drake, Carol, 78
Duke, Doris, ix
Dunlap, Tom, 46
Dutton, Clarence, 63, 195n30
Dwyer, Robert Joseph, 208n19

Eastern Washington University (EWU), 151–52
Edison, Thomas, 14
Edmo, Genevieve, 105
Elkind, Sarah S., 33, 35
Ellis, Abby, 28, 29–31
Empire Chief Mill (Colorado), 82
Empire and Liberty: The Civil War and the West (exhibition 2015), 174
Endangered Species Act, 129
environmental history, and Rothman as public intellectual, 44, 47, 55
Environmental History (journal), 46, 54, 56
Environmental Protection Agency, 84
Environmental Review (journal), 44, 45–47
Espejo, Antonio de, 116
Esquivido, Vanessa, 135
exhibitions, on Klamath River dam removal efforts in northwestern California, 126–40. *See also By Hand Through Memory; Empire and Liberty; Home Lands*
Ewart, Helen, 75
Ewart, Mette, 75

Fall, Albert B., 27
Farmer, Jared, 168
Ferguson, Laura, 150–51
Ferguson, T. J., 202n1
Fife, Austin, 169
Finley, Dan, 175–76

Fish Dam Ceremony (Karuk and Yurok), 127
fishing and fishing rights, and Klamath Tribes, 117, 119. *See also* salmon
Fix the Earth Dance (Hupa, Karuk, and Yurok), 127
Flader, Susan, 46
Flores, Dan, 45
Flynt, Mette, 12
Foley Library (Gonzaga University), 144
Following the Manito Trail (FMT) project, 85–100
Fonseca-Chávez, Vanessa, 10, 86–87, 93, 94, 96–97, 99–100
Forest History Society, 46
Fox News, 24
Francisco, Liz, 82
Frazier, Ian, 35
Freedom of Information Act, 109
Frisch, Michael, 8
Frontline (television), 28, 29, 30–32, 187n21, 187n28

gardening project, and Hinsdale County Historical Society, 75
Gatschet, Albert S., 118
Gaztambide-Fernández, Rubén A., 136
genealogy, and database for Grand Traverse Ottawas, 17. *See also* Ancestry.com
Gene Autry Museum of Western Heritage. *See* Autry National Center
George, Holly, 206n1
ghost tour, in Lake City (Colorado), 75–76
Gilbert, Grove Karl, 195n30
Gilbert-Coleman, Annie, 191n39
Gitlin, Todd, 37
Glassberg, David, 9, 76
Glover, Nikolas, 196n5
Gold Butte National Monument (Wyoming), 70
Golden Gate National Recreation Area (California), 52
Gonzaga University (Washington), 141–54
Google Scholar, 166
Gottlieb, Robert, 45
Grafton, Anthony, 177–78, 180
Grand Canyon National Park (Arizona), 57–58, 66
Grand Coulee Dam (Oregon-Washington), 149
Grand Staircase-Escalante National Monument (Utah), 58
Grand Traverse Ottawas (Michigan), 16
Gray, John, 172, 175
Great Salt Lake (Utah), 168
Great Smoky Mountain National Park (North Carolina/Tennessee), 66
Greene, Robert, 211n4
Grinnell, Joseph, 193n9
The Grit Beneath the Glitter: Tales from the Real Las Vegas (Rothman and Davis 2002), 52
Grossman, James, 177–78, 180
Guadalupe Hidalgo, Treaty of (1848), 90, 91

Hall, Bob, 77
Hammon, George, 210n37
Handbook of North American Indians (Smithsonian Institution 1978), 124
Hannity, Sean, 23–24, 25
Harmon, David, 58
Harrison, Christian, 26
Hart, E. Richard, 4–5, 11, 14, 16, 202n1, 202n3, 204n17
Haskell, Thomas, 18
Hays, Samuel, 46
Hell of a Vision: Regionalism and the Modern American West (Dorman 2012), 155

Herbert, Gary, 33, 35, 36
Herrera, Adam, 88, 95, 96–97, 98
Hevewah, Hobby, 104
Hewitt, William, 89
Heyder, Robert, 69
Hicks, John D., 210n37
High Country News, 27, 41, 53
High Desert Museum, 153
Hillman, Annilea, 139
Hillman, Leaf, 128
Hinsdale County Historical Society (HCHS), 71–81, 84
Hinsdale County Museum (Colorado), 72–74
historical landmarks, and public history, 13. *See also* Interpretive plaques; National Register of Historic Places
HistoriCorps, 82
history: and career diversity initiatives, 171, 177–82, 212n14; key differences between public and academic forms of, 14, 22; and mission of National Park Service, 59. *See also* administrative history; applied history; environmental history; local history; oral history; popular history; public history; Southern history; Western history
History News Network, 27
A History of Southern Utah and Its National Parks (Woodbury 1944), 66
Holder, Don, 43
Holl, Jack, 37
Home Lands: How Women Made the West (exhibition 2010), 174
Homeland Standard, for water rights, 122, 123
Homestead National Monument (Nebraska), 61
Hoopa Valley Tribe. *See* Hupa
Houston, Grant, 72, 74, 78, 80, 82
Howe, Barbara J., 32
Hudson's Bay Company, 120
Huntington Library (California), 124, 172
Hupa (California), 126, 127, 128, 130, 137, 138, 139

Idaho Parks and Recreation, 103
Idaho State Historic Preservation Office, 103
Idle No More (Canadian Indigenous movement), 25
Ignatian Solidarity Network, 150
Imperiled Promise: History in the National Park Service (Whisnant et al. 2011), 66
Indigenous and Decolonizing Studies in Education: Mapping the Long Way (Smith, Tuck, and Yang 2018), 131
In Search of the Golden West (Pomeroy 1957), 51
International Water History Association, 114, 125
interpretation, and National Parks, 59–60
interpretive plaques, and Lake City (Colorado), 78, 79–80. *See also* historical landmarks
irrigation, and water rights, 115
Isom, Alice Parker, 159
Issett, John, 27, 28
"It's Your Misfortune and None of My Own": A New History of the American West (White 1991), 47

Jacinto, Irlanda, 98
Jackson, Duncan, 27, 28
Jackson, W. Turrentine, 210n37
Jesuit missionaries, and Coeur D'Alene Tribe, 120–21, 122
Jesuit Oregon Province Archives (JOPA), 144–48
Journal of Forest and Conservation, 46

Journal of Mormon History, 210n37
JSTOR (digital resource), 166–67
Junior Explorer program (BLM), 83

Kalispel Tribe of Indians (Montana/Washington), 148
Kannen, Carol, 74
Karuk (California), 126–27, 128, 130, 132, 137, 138, 139
Kelley, Robert, 8, 32
Kelly, Charles, 159–60
Kelman, Ari, 58
Kemp, Emory L., 32
Killen, Patricia, 142
King, Thomas, 5
Kirk, Andy, 49
Kittredge, William, 49
The Klamath Indians of Southwestern Oregon (Gatschet 1890), 118
Klamath Justice Coalition, 129–30, 131–32
Klamath Reclamation Project, 127–28, 129
Klamath Restoration Agreement, 130
Klamath River Basin, museum exhibitions on dam removal efforts, 126–40
Klamath Tribes (Oregon), 114–15, 117–20, 203n10
Kootenai Tribe (Idaho), 148
Kralick, Kolleen, 97–98
Kyvig, David, 196n5

labor, and Manito migration, 90, 91
La Febre, Ida, 93–94
Lake City (Colorado), revitalization of through tourism and public history, 71–84
Lang, Julian, 127, 139
Langston, Nancy, 26, 27
Las Vegas: growth and change of, 49–50; Rothman's work on, 52–53
Las Vegas Mercury, 53
Las Vegas Sun, 40, 53–54
Legacy of Conquest: The Unbroken Past of the American West (Limerick 1987), 47
Leise, Christopher, 150
Leopold Report (1963), 61
Limerick, Patricia, 6, 21, 27, 33, 34, 35, 36, 47, 58, 192n2
Little, Ann, 26
local history, study and practice of within academic history, 156, 207n4
Lonetree, Amy, 133, 134, 136, 137, 151, 205n1
Long, Patrick, 51, 191n39, 196n3
Los Angeles Times, 53
Lovata, Troy, 88, 96–97, 98
Lovelace, Jim, 82, 83–84
Lowenthal, David, 196n5
Lower Klamath River (California), 128–29
Lozano, Bob, 74
Lozano, Dana, 75
Lozano, Michael, 74
Luskin Center for History and Policy (UCLA), 182
Lyman, Will, 31

MacKay, Kathryn, 5
Main Street America program, 79
Malheur National Wildlife Refuge (Oregon), 26, 70
Manito(s), use of term, 85. *See also* Following the Manito Trail project
Manito Community Memory Project, 99, 100
Manzanar National Historic Site (California), 60
Maounis, John, 70
Markoff, Dena, 67–68
Marriott Library (University of Utah), x, 124
Martínez, Alice, 88

Martínez, Trisha Venisa-Alicia, 10, 88, 99–100
Masten, Kateri, 135
Mather, Stephen, 63
Matterhorn Motel (Lake City, Colorado), 77–78
Maucione, Jessica, 142, 150
May, Theresa, 132–33
Mayer, Vincent, 5
McCool, Daniel, 5, 14
McCovey, Shaunna Oteka, 132, 133
McMurtry, Larry, 48
McPherson, Jennifer, 178–179
Medina, Cleotilde, 93
Mejorado, Annie Vigil, 94, 95, 98
Mexican Americans, migration of within U.S., 90
Mi'kmaq (Canada/Maine), 25
Miles, Tiya, 76
Mille Lacs Museum (Minnesota), 134
Miller, Char, 42, 45, 55
Minnesota Historical Society, 134
Mississippi Valley Historical Association, 34
Modoc. *See* Klamath Tribes
monuments, and Utah State Historical Society, 158. *See also* historic landmarks
Mooney-Melvin, Patricia, 196n5
Morgan, Dale, 161–63, 167, 168, 208n21, 208n23
Morin, Jean-Pierre, 36–37
Mormon Church: and Church Historian's Office, 162; influence of on local history in Utah, 164, 168, 210n37
Morris Graves Museum (California), 134
Mortensen, A. Russell, 2, 163, 209n35
The Mountain Meadows Massacre (Brooks 1950), 160
Muir, John, 61, 194n19
Mulroy, Kevin, 172
museums: and concept of public history, 13; and exhibitions on Klamath River Basin, 126–40. *See also* Hinsdale County Museum; National Museum of the American Indian; Women of the West Museum
Myers, David, 176

Nash, Gerald D., 48
Nash, Roderick, 46, 63
National Archives (Washington, D.C.), 124
National Council on Public History (NCPH), 8
National Endowment for the Humanities (NEH), 150, 182
National Environmental Policy Act (NEPA), 102
National Finals Rodeo, 31
National Historic District, in Lake City (Colorado), 76, 77–81
National Historic Preservation Act (NHPA), 103
National Museum of the American Indian (NMAI), 136, 176
National Parks and National Park Service (NPS): and academic institutions, 193n9; administrative history and management decisions of, 43, 57–70; and ownership of public lands in West, 192n2. *See also* Olympic National Park
National Register of Historic Places, 77, 82, 103
Native American Graves Protection and Repatriation Act (NAGPRA), 147
Native Americans: American West Center and creation of tribal archives, 16; and creation of National Parks in West, 61–63; and federal trust responsibilities of

U.S. government, 201n1; and museum exhibitions on efforts to remove dams in Klamath River Basin, 126–40; and public land management, 101–13; as theme in Western public history, 10–11; treaties and need for public history, 15; tribal histories and adjudication of water rights, 114–25; use of term "multivocal" in context of, 205n1. *See also* Chinook; Coeur d'alene; Colville; Grand Traverse Ottawas; Hupa; Kalispel; Klamath; Kootenai; Mi'kmaq; Nisquallys; Ojibwe; Shoshone-Bannock; Shoshone-Paiute; Southern Paiute; Spokane; Tohono O'odham; Ute; Yurok; Zuni
Native American Studies (NTAS), 141–54
Native Voices Theater Company, 175
Nature's Economy: A History of Ecological Ideas (Worster 1977), 46
Nelson, Robert H., 27
Neon Metropolis: How Las Vegas Started the Twenty-First Century (Rothman 2003), 53
Nevada. *See* Las Vegas
New Mexico, and migration of Manitos to Wyoming, 85–100
New Mexico v. Aamodt (1976), 116
New Republic (magazine), 48
The New Urban Park: Golden Gate National Recreation Area and Civic Environmentalism (Rothman 2004), 52
New Western History: evolution of and debate on, 47–48; and public history initiatives in Lake County, Colorado, 74
New York Times, 26–27
Nisquallys (Washington), 19–20
Norkunas, Martha, 196n5
Northwest Museum of Arts and Culture (MAC), 147, 151, 153
Norton, Gale, 40, 129
Novick, Peter, 18, 157

OAH Newsletter, 37
O'Brien, Jean, 138
O'Donnell, Terence, 188n55
Off-Highway Vehicle (OHV) users, and public lands management, 104, 105
Ogsbury, James D., 33
Ojibwe Indians (Minnesota), 134
Old West, stereotypical notions of as theme in public history of American West, 12
Olympic National Park (Washington), 49
O'Neil, Floyd A., *ix*, *x*, 3–4, 13, 14–15, 20, 22, 114
On Rims and Ridges: The Los Alamos Area since 1880 (Rothman 1992), 44
"One River, Ethics Matter" (conference 2014), 149
Onuf,Peter, 33, 35
Opie, John, 44–45
oral history: development of American West Center as leader in field of, 2–3; on migration of Manitos from New Mexico to Wyoming, 85–100; and National Park Service, 68–69. *See also* Doris Duke American Indian Oral History Project
Oral History Association, 69
Oregon, and water rights of Klamath Tribes, 119–20, 127
Organization of American Historians (OAH), 37
Orona, Brittani R., 11
Ostendorf, Ann, 142, 150
Ouray (Colorado), 81
Overton, Russ, 16

Pacific Northwest American Studies Association, 150
PacifiCorp, 129, 130
Paiute. *See* Southern Paiute
Parker, John, 77
Paskett, Avelinda Arguello, 92–93
Pearce, Matthew A., 28
Philips, Albert, 159
Philpott, William, 54, 191n39, 196n2
photographs, and Native American Studies program at Gonzaga University, 145, 147
Pierce, Michelle, 79–80
Pinchot, Gifford, 45
Pitcaithley, Dwight, 60, 61
Pitney, Margaret Rawson, 74
place: literature on evolving sense of, 196n4; Rothman as public intellectual and understanding of, 41
policy: and federal policy of Termination for Indigenous peoples, 119; and federal trust responsibilities toward Native Americans, 201n1; influence of public history on, 17. *See also* public lands; water rights
Pomeroy, Earl, 51, 210n37
popular history, distinction between public history and, 38
Portland State University (Oregon), 153, 154
Powell, John Wesley, 61, 63
Practicably Irrigable Acreage (PIA), and water rights, 117, 122, 123
Preserving Different Pasts: The American National Monuments (Rothman 1989), 43
Preserving Nature in the National Parks: A History (Sellars 1997), 193n9
Priest, Steve, 76
Prior, David, 179
Prusch, Robert, 142
Public Employees for Environmental Responsibility (PEER), 63
The Public Historian (journal), 8
public history: and Autry National Center, 170–77; and career diversity initiatives, 177–82; Childers on work as public historian, 28–32; definition of, 7–8, 22, 38–39; difference between academic history and, 14, 22; and Indian water rights adjudications, 123–25; and local history, 155–56, 169; and museum exhibitions on dam removal efforts in Klamath River Basin, 126–40; and Native American Studies program at Gonzaga University, 143–48, 152–54; and regional history, 9–10; role of American West Center in development and practice of, 13–22; shared authority and nature of practice, 8–9; themes of in American West, 10–12; tourism and revitalization of Lake City, Colorado, 71–84
public intellectuals: applied history and role of, 39; and definition of public history, 7–8, 38; and public service in American West, 23–28; Rotham as example of, 41–56
public lands: and applied history, 32–37; Native American history and management of, 101–13; and patterns of management, 24–25; and special issue of *Utah Historical Quarterly*, 168; as theme of public history in American West, 11. *See also* Bundy, Cliven; Sagebrush Rebellion

Quarles, Leighton M., 11
querencia, and Manito identity within diaspora, 92–93
Quintasket, Christine, 147

race, centrality of in Southern public history, 10
Rael-Galvez, Estevan, 99–100

Raheja, Michelle, 134
Raritan (journal), 37
Rassenfos, Joe, 33
Rebmann, James, 142
regions and regionalism: American West Center and regional studies centers, 2, 6; intersection of with public history, 9–10. *See also* Southern history; subregions; Western history
Reid, Harry
Resource Advisory Council (RAC), 102
Reynolds, Christopher, 211n4
Ricks, Joel, 160, 208n19, 209n35
Ridge, Martin, 172
Riebsame, William, 51
Righter, Robert, 44
Risling, Lyn, 139
river(s). *See* dams; fishing and fishing rights; water rights
River as Home (museum exhibition), 126, 134–40
Robb, James, 51
Roberts, Mimi, 99–100
rock climbing, and public lands management, 111
Rodríguez, Raymond, 89
Rodrique, Charlotte, 27
Rogers, Jedediah, 10
Romero, Jeana Rodarte, 85
Romero, Levi, 85, 87–88, 93, 94, 99–100
Rosenstock, Fred, 171
Rothman, Hal K., 9, 17, 39–40, 41–56, 196n3
Rothstein, Edward, 176
Routt National Forest (Colorado), *86*
Runnels, Chay Rees, 72
Runte, Alfred, 193n13

Safran, William, 92
Sagebrush Rebellion (late 1970s), 25–26, 28, 70
St. Louis University (Missouri), 144
salmon: and Columbia Plateau tribes, 149; and Klamath River Basin, 128–29. *See also* fishing and fishing rights
Salmon is Everything: Community-Based Theatre in the Klamath Watershed (May 2004), 132–33
Sánchez, José Victor, 88
Sánchez, Mary Louise, 98–99
Sand Creek Massacre National Historic Site (Colorado), 60
Saunders, Richard, 164
Savage, William, 48
Scenic and Historic Byways, 81
Scharff, Virginia, 9, 12, 21, 170, 171, 174, 175, 176, 177, 183
Schneider, Christie, 98
scientific management, of National Parks, 66
Scottish Power (corporation), 129–30
Sears, John, 51, 191n39
Seeing and Being Seen: Tourism in the American West (Long 2001), 51
Sellars, Richard West, 61, 193n9, 193n13
"Serial Set," and state libraries, 124
settler-colonialism. *See* colonialism
Shaffer, Marguerite, 51, 191n39
Shambaugh, Benjamin, 34, 36
shared authority, and definition of public history, 8
sheepherding, and migration of Manitos to Wyoming, 96–97, 98
Shellenbarger, Melanie, 196n2
Sherwood, Morgan, 63
Shoshone-Bannock Tribes (Idaho), 16, 101–13, 202n13
Shoshone-Paiute Tribes (Idaho/Nevada), 101–13
Sierra Club, 24
Sierra Madre Mountains (Wyoming), 96
Silverton (Colorado), 81

Sinclair, Donna, 153
Sinclair, Marguerite, 160, 208n19, 208–9n24, 209n35
The Size of the Risk: Histories of Multiple Use in the Great Basin (Childers 2005), 24
slavery, legacy of in Southern public history, 9–10
Smith, Jedediah, 160
Smith, Linda T., 131
Smithsonian Institution (Washington D.C.), 124
Smoak, Gregory E., 6–7, 14, 16, 148
Snow, Leo A., 64, 195n30
Snow, William J., 159
social justice, and mission of Gonzaga University, 149–50
social movements, and decolonization, 131
Sottile, Leah, 28, 186n17
Southern history, and legacy of slavery, 9–10
Southern Nevada Public Land Management Act, 40
Southern Paiute (Arizona/Utah), 62
Southern Utah Wilderness Alliance, 63
Southern Ute (Colorado), 16. *See also* Ute
Southwestern Energy Company, 25
Southwest Hispanic Research Institute (SHRI), 99
Southwest Museum of the American Indian (California), 172, 175
Southwest Youth Conservation Corps, 83
Sowards, Adam, 27–28
Spatial History Project (Stanford University), 21
Spence, Mark David, 62
Spier, Leslie, 117
Spokane River (Washington), 149
Spokane Tribe (Washington), 142, 148
Sproul, David, 43, 54
Stanford University (California), 21, 22, 192n2
Statham, Dawn Stram, 202n13
Steen, Harold, 46
Stegner, Wallace, 64, 157
Steiner, Erik, 17
Stigall, Mary, 74
Stories of the River, Stories of the People: Memory on the Klamath River Basin (museum exhibition), 126, 136–40
storytelling, and museums, 134–35
subregions, and local history, 155
Swanson, Brook, 149

Tarr, Joel, 34–35
Taylor, Alan, 47
Taylor, Joseph E., 26, 29, 31, 192n2
Termination, and U.S. policy on Indigenous peoples, 119
That Noble Dream: The Objectivity Question and the American History Profession (Novick 1988), 18
Thompson, Gregory C., 5
Thompson, Lucy, 127
Time (magazine), 48
Tohono O'odham (Arizona), 16
Tolowa (California), 126, 132
Topping, Gary, 157–58, 159, 207n15
tourism: and public history initiatives in Lake City, Colorado, 71–84, 197n12; and Rothman on understanding of American West, 42, 51–52
traditional cultural properties (TCP), 102, 103. *See also* City of Rocks/Castle Rocks TCP
trails, and Manito landscape, 91
Treuer, David, 143, 149
Tuan, Yi-Fu, 196n4
Tuck, Eve, 131, 135
Tucker, Craig, 130

Tuell, Yvette Towersap, 11
Turner, Frederick Jackson, 47, 61, 63

Uintah-Ouray Reservation (Utah), 16
United States v. Ben Adair, et al. (1985), 119
U. S. Forest Service, 68
University of California, Berkeley, 193n9
University of California, Los Angeles, 171, 173, 177, 180–82
University of Chicago, 171, 177
University of Illinois Press, 166
University of Montana, 22
University of Nevada, Las Vegas, 50
University of New Mexico, 22, 97, 99, 124, 171, 177–82
University of Utah, ix, x, 124
University of Washington, 22
University of Wyoming, 22, 95, 98, 99
Upper Columbia United Tribes (UCUT), 148–50
urbanism: and Rothman on character of modern West, 42; and transformation of Modern West, 48–50
Utah, and local or regional history, 155–69, 206–7n2, 208n19, 210n43
Utah American Indian Digital Archive (UAIDA), 5
Utah Historians and the Reconstruction of Western History (Topping 2003), 207n15
Utah Historical Quarterly, 10, 156–69, 209n36, 210n37, 210n43
Utah History to Go, 167
Utah Indian Curriculum Project, 5
Utah Navajo Development Council, 16
Utah Pioneers Trails and Landmark Association, 158
Utah State Historical Society, 156–69, 208n21, 210n39
Utah Studies, 168–69
Ute, 3–4, 16. *See also* Southern Ute
Ute-Ulay Mine (Colorado), 81, 83–84
Utley, Robert M., 59

Valdez, Antonio, 88
Vargas, Zaragosa, 90
Veneman, Ann, 129
Vigil, Emilio, *87*, 94–95
Vigil, Susana, 95
visual sovereignty, and reframing of histories of Indigenous peoples, 134

walking tours, and public history initiatives of Hinsdale County Historical Society, 75
Wallace, Mike, 196n5
Warren, Brooke, 186n16
Warren, Louis, 27
Washington (state): and history of Coeur d'Alene Tribe, 121; role of public history in litigation with Nisquallys, 19–20
Washington State University (WSU), 151, 152
water rights: and agriculture of Shoshone and Bannock Tribes, 202n13; and management of public lands, 30; tribal histories and adjudication of, 114–25
Watt, James G., 27
Webb, Melody, 42
websites: and career diversity for historians, 212n14; and digital humanities project at Gonzaga University, 145; online bibliographies on water rights adjudication of Zuni, Coeur d'Alene, and Klamath tribes, 125; and public lands, 192n2; and *Utah Historical Quarterly*, 166–67
West: geographic definition of, 192n2; stereotypical concepts of in public

West (*continued*)
history, 12; tourism and Rothman on understanding of, 42, 51–52; urbanism and transformation of modern, 48–50. *See also* Western history
West, W. Richard, Jr., 136, 176
Western Governors' Association (WGA), 32–34
Western Heritage Partners, 67
Western Historical Quarterly, 43–44
Western history: and administrative histories of National Parks, 57–70; Morgan's influence on, 208n21; and Rothman as public intellectual, 41–56. *See also* New Western history; Old West; West
Western History Association, 2
Western Humanities Review, 163–64
"Western Lands, Western Voices: The American West Center at Fifty" (symposium 2014), *ix*, 1–2, 37–39
Whisnant, Anne Mitchell, 66
White, Richard, 6, 8, 37–39, 47, 192n2
Whitman College (Washington), 150, 151
Whitman Mission National Historic Site (Washington), 58, 61
Whitton, Hazel, 78
Wichita State University (Kansas), 43
Wilderness in the American Mind (Nash 1967), 46
Wiles, Tay, 28, 186n16
Wilkins, David E., 119
Wilkinson, Charles, 6
Williamson, Harry, 51
Wilson, Karen, 181, 212n15
The Wind Called My Name (Sánchez 2018), 98–99
Wineburg, Sam, 18
Winter Park Manifest (newspaper), 51
Women of the West Museum (Colorado), 172
Woodbury, Angus, 66
World Renewal ceremonies (Hupa, Karuk, and Yurok), 127
Worster, Donald, 46
Wright, George Melendez, 121, 193n9
Wrobel, David, 51, 191n39, 196n3
Wyart, Edward, 211n4
Wyoming, migration of Manitos to from New Mexico, 85–100
Wyoming Institute for Humanities Research, 96
Wyoming State Historic Preservation Office, 96

Yang, K. Wayne, 131
Yellowstone National Park (Wyoming), 57–58, 66
Yosemite National Park (California), 57–58, 66
Yosemite News, 67–68
You Can't Teach United States History without American Indians (Sleeper-Smith et al. 2015), 143
Young, Levi Edgar, 208n19
Young, Rick, 30
YouthCorps, 79
Yurok (California), 126–27, 128, 130, 132, 137, 138, 139

Zenzen, Joan, 65
Zinke, Ryan, 27, 28
Zion National Park (Utah), 57, 61, 62–65, 66, 67, 69
Zuni (New Mexico), 16, 114–17, 125